Citizenship
and the
European Community

Elizabeth Meehan

First published 1993
Reprinted 1994

SAGE Publications Ltd
6 Bonhill Street
London EC2A 4PU

SAGE Publications Inc
2455 Teller Road
Thousand Oaks, California 91320

SAGE Publications India Pvt Ltd
32, M-Block Market
Greater Kailash – I
New Delhi 110 048

British Library Cataloguing in Publication Data

Meehan, Elizabeth M.
 Citizenship and the European Community
 I. Title
 323.6

 ISBN 0–8039–8428–6
 ISBN 0–8039–8429–4 (pbk)

Library of Congress catalog card number 93–083042

Typeset by Mayhew Typesetting, Rhayader, Powys
Printed and bound in Great Britain by
Biddles Ltd, Guildford and King's Lynn

Contents

This book is dedicated to
the Department of Government
of Manchester University
in gratitude for a happy year as a
Hallsworth Fellow

Preface

Sometimes when people ask me what my work is about, I can almost hear them thinking that I have jumped on to two band-wagons of interest – in citizenship and in the European Community. But in 1984 when I began to look systematically at rulings of the European Court of Justice and reports from other Community institutions which referred to the rights of Community citizens, few political scientists were talking about citizenship at all and, when they talked about the European Community, they usually presented it as an intergovernmental organization whose primary purpose was economic – the liberalization of production and markets from the constraints of national boundaries. It was not seen as something that might much affect the national relationship between citizens and rulers, let alone as an innovatory framework for the exercise of those rights and duties we customarily associate with citizenship of a nation-state. Unlike Members of the European Parliament, few people in the United Kingdom thought of the European Community as an embryonic polity in which a different understanding of citizenship might play a part. In 1986, I was alone in 'reading' an invitation to contribute to a European Consortium for Political Research (ECPR) workshop on the European Welfare State as meaning the European Community Welfare State. The academic and political lacunae had parallels in the mass media. News about the European Community was often trivialized in the popular press and allocated to the foreign or international pages of the serious newspapers.

The failings of my discipline to help me make sense of what I was discovering about the legal, political and social evolution of the European Community are symptomatic of general problems of epistemology. Körner (1991) has reminded us of the preoccupying questions of whether a distinction can properly be drawn between empirical facts and how we arrange them, or whether our language and systems of categorization influence what we think we observe. This is connected to competing views about what counts as an explanation – a description of causes, which must be universally true or false, or a description of the meaning of concepts and actions and their consistency with general systems of thought, all of which will vary in different social or cultural contexts. The inability of much political science to discern what I was seeing in the Community stems from a combination of the Community's

being a phenomenon to which we are unaccustomed, because of
the unusualness of its innovatory features, and systems of thought
that inhibit the possibility of seeing anything new in the unfamiliar.

It has become commonplace now to admit the innovatory
features of the Community: that it is neither wholly intergovernmental nor wholly supranational, yet also both; that it is a legal
federation, yet not a political federation; that it is not a state but
has some state-like features. But it is rare for writers to move from
conceding that governments acting in concert have caused new
things to exist to exploring the alternative meanings their actions
might bring about in how we all understand our world. And, if
they do, they generally restrict themselves to immediate phenomena
instead of the longer-term dynamics of consequences that governments might not have intended to cause.

The silence of modern political science – at least, Anglo-
American political science – on the meaning of citizenship lies in
the dominance during the past forty years or so of two general
systems of thought within the discipline. These have displaced
consideration of the ethical foundations of the state, the normative
elements of citizenship and the role of law and constitutions in
determining the powers and limits of government – all of which
once formed the core of the discipline. Recently, several writers
(Dearlove, 1989; Smith, 1986, 1991; Vincent and Plant, 1984) have
identified the two systems as radicalism and behaviourism.

In radical approaches, influenced by Marxist sociology, citizenship is of interest only in so far as the rights attached to it succeed
in creating a fiction of equality between economic classes or elites
and masses. This does have some bearing on the growth of
Community rights but, as at the national level, it is not the whole
story. Behaviourists, whose analyses often have conservative
implications, try to make the discipline more scientific by
elucidating laws of political action. Thus, they deal only with the
observable manifestations of citizenship – for example, actual
contacts between citizens and their representatives and voting
behaviour. Behaviourists cannot adequately explain the European
Community, if they conform to the view that states determine the
international order and employ their usual assumption that the
behaviour of states, like that of individuals, can be explained by
reference to the rational pursuit of self-interest. What I have
found, and try to explain in this book, is that the Community's
evolution reflects an interplay of forces; governmental conceptions
of national interests, histories that governments do not determine
but which provide the context that shapes how they decide to act,
and the life of its own that the Community has, which stems from

those histories and is carried forward by the new movements and interests that follow the creation of new institutions.

In line with the predominant approach to the Community, most general accounts of the Community have treated social policy as an instrument of economic policy, in the sphere of 'low politics'. This had two consequences for how social policy was construed – at least until this decade. It was an area in which agreement could be reached more easily than in the realms of the 'high politics' of foreign policy and security. And national governments could retain control over the line between national and Community regulation, avoiding unwanted 'spill-overs'. But this did not fit with what I had been discovering for a long time about the entrenchment of particular social policies as rights and the implications of this for common legal, and now, political rights. Thus, in trying to understand the driving forces and consequences of an outgrowth of Community social rights from economic cooperation among governments, I had to turn elsewhere – to the history of political ideas and the kind of political sociology written more often by sociologists than political scientists. Both bodies of knowledge often concentrate on the physical and cultural development of the nation-state. As a new kind of polity, the Community, though not a state, has some state-like features which are illuminated by accounts of national modernization and democratization; that is, transformations from feudalism to national citizenship in states as we have known them, under the twin forces of economic liberalization and political liberalism, have some analogies at the Community level.

In addition to being a new form of political system, the European Community may also provide a means through which sub-nation-state identities may be expressed in new ways – a re-expression that is already taking the form of transnational relations that are not channelled vertically through nation-state governments. Since it is unique in its capacity to combine supranationalism, intergovernmentalism, the re-articulation of subgovernmental regionalism and transnational regional relations, and in the absence of an appropriately cohesive language with which to explain it, I have had to draw on a very wide range of literature.

Most theories of integration come from international relations and the internationalization of domestic economies. The insights of these schools of thought are touched upon where necessary in this book but, since this book is about the common regulation of civil and political life within a set of territorial boundaries, it draws also on the literature about developments within nation-states or comparisons of such matters in different nation-states. In addition to the general reasons for this, noted above, such works have a practical significance because the Community, sometimes quite self-consciously, adopts policies and institutional features precisely because they are familiar in at least one of its constituent Member States. Although my eclecticism is necessary, in my view, to understand and explain something that is unique, it also carries several, fundamental risks.

First, the worries in Abram de Swaan's introduction (1988) are also mine. In the eight years of preparation of my subject, I have become more aware every day of how much more I ought to have read. I cannot pretend that my bibliography is exhaustive. To have covered the complete collections of books on international relations, international political economy, political philosophy, comparative and single country studies of jurisprudence, political sociology and policy-making, as well as descriptions of the Community itself, would have turned the project into a life-time's work without necessarily adding proportionately or in timely fashion to matters that are of intrinsic interest to us now. On the other hand, selectivity means that my accounts of political ideas and policies are very likely too obvious and oversimplified for philosophers and social policy experts. I hope that my mistakes will inspire others to do a better job. Secondly, and more fundamentally, there is the view that citizenship is an essentially contested concept (van Gunsteren, 1978) and an idea imbued with ideological and polemical value (Leca, 1990). Thus, I enter disputed territory. But as Leca points out, the concept has no objective meaning and we must deconstruct and explain how 'real historical participants' use it in historical contexts. Since it seems to me that those commentators who have considered the idea of European citizenship have done so with a preconception, I have begun by trying to summarize the meanings of citizenship over time, the different emphases in its content and the categories of people included in it. I think that it is precisely because there is no single, unvarying, objective definition that it is not meaningless to speak of European citizenship or, at least, the coexistence of national and European citizenship.

There are many people to whom I am indebted. My first debt is to Desmond King who encouraged me to start and to carry on. For similar reasons, I am grateful to someone whom I have never met – Eric Gorham, who has corresponded with me about our overlapping interests. I have had a good deal of help over sources from officials at the European Commission, European Parliament and European Court of Justice. I should like especially to thank the Gray family in Brussels, and Tom and Liv-Ellen Kennedy in Luxembourg for introductions, access to information and warm hospitality and friendship. Similarly, I am very grateful to Dermot Scott and Nancy Mullins of the Dublin office of the European Parliament. The Nuffield Foundation was kind enough to provide the money that enabled my project to begin and the British Academy assisted me to present findings at ECPR Workshops. I am grateful to the ECPR for funding Research Sessions and to participants at them for their help with my project, especially Percy Lehning, Albert Weale, Jean Leca and all those at Forli in 1991. I should also like to thank Ghita Ionescu for his meeting of the International Political Science Association (IPSA) Research Committee on European Unification at the European Parliament, Ray Pahl for the Economic and Social Research Council (ESRC) seminars on citizenship and Kevin Boyle and Stuart Weir and our colleagues on the Democratic Audit of the UK project.

The first draft of the book was written while I was a Hallsworth Fellow in the Department of Government at Manchester University. I am deeply indebted to the University for enabling me to be replaced by my then employer, Bath University, and to the whole department for their welcome and help. It is because of this that I dedicate this book to the Department of Government but I should like to pay special thanks to Ursula Vogel, Martin Burch, Karen Hall, Marilyn Dunn, Simon Bulmer, Stephen Gill, Martin Rhodes and, in the Social Policy Department, Martin Baldwin-Edwards. The Fellowship could not have been taken up without the cooperation of Bath University and I am grateful to my colleagues there for enabling my absence. I should also like to thank Eileen Maguire and Eileen McNeill who helped me, on my move to The Queen's University of Belfast, through the traumas of having to use three different systems of information technology in order to produce a final version from drafts done in different places.

After my move to Belfast, I discovered a greater consciousness of the significance of the European Community for everyday civil and political life than I had found in England. What I learned from, for example, the Cultural Traditions Group, public servants in other agencies, voluntary organizations and university colleagues gave me new insights into what I was doing. I should like to thank them all through Paul Arthur, Evelyn Collins, Mourna Crozier, Bernard Cullen, Jennifer FitzGerald, Richard Jay, Dennis Kennedy, Patricia-Anne Moore, Edward Moxon-Browne, Fionnuala Jay O'Boyle, Margaret O'Callaghan, Paul Teague, Rick Wilford, Robin Wilson and Tom Wilson.

I am eternally grateful to those among the above who read and commented on conference papers, draft chapters and the penultimate version of the book. The care of loved ones in the private sphere nurtures one's ability to participate in civil or public society; as ever, I especially appreciate the care given to me by Mary Turnbull, Margaret Saunders and Edward Horesh. Also as ever, all mistakes in this book are of my own making and not of those who have been so generous to me.

Elizabeth Meehan
The Queen's Unversity of Belfast
December 1992

1
National or European Citizenship?

'There are no such animals as "European citizens". There are only French, German, or Italian citizens.' This was the view of Raymond Aron (1974) when he was asked to consider whether multi-national or European citizenship were possible. Seventeen years later Lord Jenkins, despite his own Europeanism, told an audience at The Queen's University of Belfast that he could not foresee the day when citizens of Member States of the European Community (EC) would say in Japan that they were European instead of French, German or Italian – unlike the Texan who would say that he or she was American. These views contrast with the territorially more inclusive language of Community institutions which speaks of 'a People's Europe' (note the position of the apostrophe), sometimes of 'industrial citizens' and now 'Citizens of the Union'. The argument of this book is that the language of the European Community is justifiable.

My thesis is not that Aron's concept of national citizenship is being relocated to a new level. It is that a new kind of citizenship is emerging that is neither national nor cosmopolitan but that is multiple in the sense that the identities, rights and obligations, associated by Heater (1990) with citizenship, are expressed through an increasingly complex configuration of common Community institutions, states, national and transnational voluntary associations, regions and alliances of regions. This is not to say that the emergence of a new 'public space' for citizens (Tassin, 1992) is inevitable in a form that is precisely identifiable now. But, if unpredictable, the form will not be accidental. The new order comprises states and peoples which have some common experiences and intellectual traditions and some differences. Sometimes, different national traditions are deliberately welded in new institutions. Sometimes, they seem to appear in their new form by default. Conversely, Community institutions and policies are sometimes the subject of difficult disputes about the proper concepts to use and the proper way to go about things. Then, the outcome will depend upon what concessions may or may not be made when a plurality of different interests confront one another in the common 'public space' that exists because of the creation of the Community. What is certain is that the European Community now provides a framework that coexists with those of its Member States, through which nationals of those Member States can claim certain rights. These are economic and social rights which will be extended in these fields and into the political sphere if the Maastricht Treaty is ratified. Even if it is not, the forces referred to in my Preface are likely to mean that the issues will remain on the agenda and that some kind of recognizably similar provisions will come about. The nature of European citizenship may continue to have a national focus, enriched with a European dimension (Leca, 1990); or, it may become more like, as I believe it is now, citizenship of the Roman Empire[1] in which citizens were able to appeal to more than one set of enforceable standards when claiming their rights.

My belief that something like the neo-imperial model exists now has to depend on the view that social rights, together with civil and political rights, form a triad, which must be regarded as interlocked if we are to be able to speak of the existence of equal citizenship. This is a disputed position. As noted in my Preface, the meaning of citizenship is bound to the historical, sociological and cultural contexts which provide the reasons for particular understandings. But, if my understanding is one of various positions that could reasonably be held, it follows that Aron's cannot be the only truth about the European Community. Indeed, both of us are obliged to explore what citizenship has meant to participants in the European Community and how these meanings affect the outlooks of governments and what might be the expectations of those whose lives are regulated by national and common institutions. The plan of how I try to do this follows shortly but, since a sharp contrast between Aron and Heater has helped me to formulate my thinking, I introduce the book by comparing the two approaches.

Raymond Aron's Case for National Citizenship

Aron distinguishes between the rights of man and the rights of the citizen in the 1789 French Declaration on the Rights of Man and in the 1948 United Nations Universal Declaration of Human Rights, which also declares the rights of woman. Though a single belief – in the natural equality of human beings – justifies natural or human rights and citizenship rights, the two sets are not the same. To show this, Aron draws upon the Hegelian distinction, also used in a transformed way by Marx, between burghers and citizens. The first are participants (subjects, for Marx) in the economic life of civil society. Their roles may be associated with natural property rights, as in the eighteenth century, or with the right to have socio-economic needs met, as in the twentieth century. Citizens are recognizable by the status conferred upon them in rules about the administration of justice and political participation. Human or burghers' rights may be recognized or denied, irrespective of political status. Citizenship rights may also be denied but they cannot be guaranteed except in the context of nationality and the state – often a nation-state, sometimes a state of several nations which are culturally distinct but share the same legal nationality. Together, Aron's distinctions inform his separation of regulation by the EC of the lives of its economic participants from the civil and political rights guaranteed by their different (nation-)states.

There are four main elements to Aron's case that European citizenship is logically impossible and politically unlikely. First, as indicated, national and Community authorities provide sets of rights of a different order from one another. Secondly, European citizenship would have to involve a transfer of legal and political powers from the national to the EC level (similar to the transfer of Scottish and English citizenship to a single set of British entitlements). Thirdly, Aron argues that citizens can insist that a nation-state respect their rights because the state can demand that citizens fulfil their duties to defend the state, whereas there is no inter- or multi-national polity which has such authority.[2] Usually, this has meant military service and makes men citizens, while women have been said to have a duty to be mothers, a duty traditionally without corresponding rights. The fourth element in Aron's case is that there was, in 1974, no popular demand for a European federation which would be simultaneously responsible for legal-political rights and economic regulation and which could command duties of citizens. Moreover, there was every sign then, perhaps unlike the 1940s, that national leaders intended the Community to remain a regime in which burghers or economic subjects cooperated in the absence of a political federation. In so far as people criticized nation-states and the association of citizenship with legal nationality, they did so because of the treatment of nationalities submerged within contemporary boundaries. Aron observed cynicism about the idea that domestic problems could be resolved by regulation at a still more remote level and was sceptical, himself, of views that burghers and economic subjects could be made more equal through changes closer to home – such as workers' control, which is one component of Community aspirations.

Aron's thesis can be criticized for three reasons. First, it is based on only one conception of citizenship, although there are others.

Secondly, he links his conception of citizenship to an understanding of international relations that emphasizes the significance of states as the determinants of the world order, while others contain elements that are compatible with alternative ideas about citizenship. Thirdly, his evidential judgement about lack of support for the transformation that would be necessary to be able to speak of European citizenship has not stood the test of time – a claim I make despite controversy at the time of writing over the Maastricht Treaty of Union.

Alternative Conceptions of Citizenship

Though both Aron and Leca (1990) emphasize connections between nationality and citizenship, the link is mainly logical for the former and sociological for the latter. In building the logical case, Aron does what Leca says we must not. That is, though he refers to historical ideas and practice in order to elucidate *a* conception of citizenship, this conception is based on a specific historical experience and, once elucidated, has the status of making others incorrect. A broader sweep is taken by Heater (1990), who provides grounds for being persuaded by Gunsteren's view (1978) that citizenship is a contestable concept and Leca's that its meanings are socially contextual, both of which mean that different meanings must be explored. Heater reminds us that:

> from very early in its history the term [citizenship] already contained a cluster of meanings related to a defined legal or social status, a means of political identity, a focus of loyalty, a requirement of duties, an expectation of rights and a yardstick of good social behaviour. . . . No subsequent discussion of the topic has required any more components nor would have been complete with any fewer. (1990: 163)

Moreover:

> the early history of citizenship may also lead us to question the *modern* assumption that the status necessarily adheres to the sovereign nation-state. [It] can be associated with any geographical unit from a small town to the whole globe itself. (1990: 163, emphasis added)

The 'cluster of meanings' as to the content of rights and duties, the question of who inside a regime has entitlements and the territorial basis of inclusion have been defined and redefined in five distinct contexts: the Greek city-state, the Roman Republic and Empire, the medieval and Renaissance city, the nation-state (from the late eighteenth century) and in the long-lived Stoic ideal of the cosmopolis (1990: 161, 167). Where direct engagement in the process of ruling, not merely the 'crude indicator' of suffrage (1990: 65) is emphasized,

> the intimacy of the Greek or medieval city seemed essential. If loyalty [is] to a moral code, then the whole of humanity must be embraced. If legal status is the essence, the Romans revealed the flexibility of dual city and imperial citizenship. Only if the nation-state is sovereign, commands the complete loyalty of its inhabitants and is the sole source of rights and duties must citizenship necessarily be exercised in that particular geographical context. (1990: 164)

Though the link between citizenship and nationality is strong for strategic (Zolberg, 1991) and ideological (Leca, 1990) reasons, Heater's account shows that it is neither inevitable nor the defining feature of being a citizen. His discussion of Roman Imperial citizenship, where nationality and legal rights were not coterminous, will recur. For the moment, I concentrate on how his perspective modifies Aron's claims that workers' and welfare rights are not part of citizenship rights.

Heater draws attention to a remarkable continuity in the belief that citizenship includes what Aron counts as human rights – a collective memory which transcends the rise of the nation-state. One example is his discussion of John Stuart Mill's idea that workers' rights could be a substitute in large societies for the direct democracy of the Greek city-state – as a means of fulfilling the human need for participation and of developing civic virtues (1990: 73–4) and not merely for the purposes of pursuing self-interest (see also chapter 2). The move towards common standards of workers' rights in the European Community certainly embodies the idea that individual self-interest lies in avoiding disadvantages arising from migration and that this should be dealt with. But Community language also often refers to the need to construct a common moral order if not, I grant, as an end in itself but as a way of inspiring loyalty to a new and wider regime (see chapter 4). If belittled by Aron in their *social* promise and defined out of the search for *political* equality, Heater's approach means that we must at least consider the possibility that workers' rights might be part of an emergent notion of European citizenship.

Another area in which a historical approach provides a different way of viewing current European developments stems from ideas about rights to welfare (see chapters 2, 3 and 5). Even if people in the eighteenth century *did* distinguish, as Aron suggests, between natural rights and citizenship in abstract thought, practical political arrangements linked human circumstances and political status. The ideas that only those who are rational ought to participate in politics and that rationality was demonstrated by the accumulation of property together justified the denial of rights for the poor and women, the latter also being debarred for other reasons (see chapters 2 and 6). In the twentieth century it has seemed obvious that there can be a different conclusion. That is, not to exclude, but to provide the deprived with the material basis for rationality and, hence, to enable their political participation (King and Waldron, 1988) – a conclusion that can also be accepted by those whose primary concern is not with entitlements but the maintenance of order.

Modern advocates of social citizenship are shown by Jordan (1989) to be of two types. One sort inherits a version of human nature that radicals see in individualism and capitalism; that is, the individual as private and instrumental, albeit, in the new formulation, with welfare needs.[3] This justification for social rights undermines the nineteenth-century view that meeting need was an obligation of *charity* towards those who, because of economic deprivation, had ceased to be citizens (Heater on T. H. Marshall, 1990, 286). But, though it posits rights instead of charity, it is not a fundamental challenge to individualism because these rights are thought of as enabling people to function effectively as persons[3] or relatively equally in civil society. For the other type of social rights advocate, the concepts of the individual and interests are Aristotelian and/or Idealist; that is – expanding on my earlier references – individuals are human beings only when they belong to a community and, being essentially political, their humanity is expressed when they take part in constructing and maintaining their community. The good society is not only the same as participatory society but is also a moral order of well-being and conviviality. Private interests (of the self-interested type[3]) and public interests cannot exist distinctly from one another since they converge on the common human need for the good society in all its dimensions. Political rights to discharge public duties entail trying to find a fair distribution of social justice. In the modern version of this approach, social rights are *not* an instrument for the pursuit of personal ends but are both the cause and reflection of a solidaristic moral order – which, unlike its Greek predecessors, claims not to include male property rights over slaves and women.[4]

Though the origins of a nation-state concept of citizenship coincided with a period in which the 'cluster of meanings' emphasized legal and political rights, the creation and development of the EC took place at a time when it was accepted in a substantial body of political theory, by citizens and even by governments (see chapters 2 and 4), that there was a connection – natural, logical, instrumental or expedient – amongst civil, political and social rights. Community regulation of social security, social assistance and sex equality in income maintenance (from paid work and social security) embodies bits of both the individualistic and collectivist understandings referred to above. On the one hand, its legal rights and 'permissive' measures are designed to reduce national and sex discrimination in the exercise of economic and social opportunities in a transnational order. But, as in the case of workers' rights, traces of the idea of a common moral order can be found in many references to common standards of living, social cohesion and harmonious regional development to facilitate the exercise of economic and social roles in a transnational regime. Even if not self-consciously intended by Member State governments as a step towards a common citizenship, these policies cannot be discounted, in the life of their own that they have acquired, as a dimension of European citizenship.

Nor should it be overlooked that Community instruments confer a legally defined status on citizens as 'Community nationals' or, in the words of the Maastricht Treaty, 'Citizens of the Union'. The consolidation of this process, which is discussed in most of this book, means Community policies *do* contribute to Aron's political transformation as a result of 'spill-overs' from social regulation into the legal and political competences of Member States (see below and chapters 3–8).

However, Aron is, of course, right that the governments of nation-states remain the primary actors and that the Member States of the EC vary in their traditions and practices of nationality and citizenship (see also Moxon-Browne, 1992). This is acknowledged in the regulation of a common order through twelve, diverse national orders. But, as Heater's historical account shows, this need not necessarily rule out the possibility of common citizenship rights. While the Stoic ideal of cosmopolitan citizenship has remained largely, though not entirely, abstract (the Nuremburg trials assumed there were 'higher duties' than loyalty to temporal authority wrongly exercised), the Romans developed 'a form of citizenship which was both pragmatic and extensible in application' (1990: 16). They extended the status of Roman citizenship to residents of parts of the Empire taken by conquest. Thus, St Paul, declaring himself a citizen of Tarsus when arrested in Jerusalem, was able to claim also his Roman citizenship and to demand a trial under the Roman, not local, system of justice (1990: 17–18).

This early practice of dual citizenship, continuing intellectual interest in it and in the Stoic ideal, as well as the modern practice of popular participation in the work of international organizations, inspire Heater to think that propositions about dual and multi-national citizenship are not unrealistic (1990: 320–45). His final reference is to the European Community. But the Community is not an expression of Stoic universalism, given its distinction between Community migrants and those from outside ('third country migrants'). Nor, obviously, is it an empire; sovereign states voluntarily founded it and agree to its developments. But, as noted before, there is more than one set of standards that can be appealed to by claimants of rights. In this neo-imperial regime of rights, as in any other, certain issues need to be addressed which include: identities, loyalties, obligations and institutional frameworks for participation and the exercise of rights and duties (Heater, 1990: 322).

International Relations and the 'Globalization' of Citizenship

Aron's understanding of Community developments up to 1974 coincides with the emphasis on state sovereignty in the Realist and Positivist schools of international relations, whereas other approaches pay attention to the relationship between societies and the international order (Hall and Ikenberry, 1989; Wight, 1991). The influence of different understandings of international relations is discussed in chapter 4. Here, I deal only with the idea that civil society in the world order may be facilitating an unravelling of the association of citizenship with nation-states and nationality. This is plainest in conceptions of international relations that are informed by both liberal and socialist ideas about human relations. For liberals, the more that cultural and economic transactions take place on a global scale, the more states and competition between them become redundant. Turner (1986, 1992) is more structural. When he refers to the 'globalization of citizenship', he argues that, on the one hand, international economic trends have diminished the capacities of nation-states to respond to the demands of their citizens. On the other hand, modern global communications facilitate widespread knowledge of what is possible elsewhere, thereby informing domestic conceptions of the rights of citizenship, raising demands or dampening them according to knowledge of successes and failures in other systems. Both of these understandings are part of, but neither is the same as, the argument of this book. The argument here is not only that national lessons are learned through the transactions and dissemination of ideas that take place in the networks of European civil society, but also that a reconceptualization is taking place in which, as noted before, the citizen's legal status and the content of his or her rights are not determined by nationality alone. There are four dimensions to this.

The first stems from an argument by Dahrendorf (1988). This is that, in national modernizations, the interests of the burghers or creators of wealth from industry lay in the freeing of land, capital and labour from feudal entailments. This coincided, or could be made to coincide, with the interests of the *citoyens* and their advocacy of equal citizenship (see chapter 2). A similar coincidence can be seen at the European level between the freeing of factors of production from national restrictions on their deployment and the way in which policies to promote freedom of movement – of goods, services, capital and labour – have been reformulated as rights instead of economic instruments; albeit that, for reasons mentioned earlier, the order in which civil, political and social rights have come on to the agenda differs in the two arenas.

Secondly, it is the tracing of this coincidence of interests that makes it possible to dispute the view that Community social policy is immune from so-called 'spill-overs' into areas over which national governments had wished to retain sovereignty. Though many writers assert, or have done until their most recent works, that there are no significant 'spill-overs' in social policy, there *have* been extensions over many years, strongly contested by governments, of the kinds of benefit brought under the aegis of Community regulation and claimable by workers defined in an ever-wider category. It is the same criteria that were employed by the Court of Justice in these expansions that are now used by others to support the development, for persons rather than workers, of political rights (see chapter 8), reserved by Aron to distinguish citizens from burghers.

Thirdly, there is the same debate about the meaning of Community rights for the real lives of citizens that has occurred in the national context; that is, do they serve the interests of the burghers but constrain economic subjects and women through fictions about equality; or do they empower people, enabling all to act more autonomously (Turner, 1986, 1990, 1992 on class; Pateman, 1985, 1988b, 1989 on women; see also chapters 2, 5 and 6)? Moreover, the question of exclusions from citizenship is also contested at the European level (see chapters 7 and 8).

Fourthly, and going beyond the national analogies, new administrative arrangements are taking shape which, like Community social rights, are showing political implications. These are a little reminiscent of much older conceptions of, for example, Proudhon and Saint-Simon (Tassin, 1992), of a Europe of the regions and must modify Aron's assumption that reasserting submerged national identities is incompatible with remoter sources of regulation. Keane (1989) and Jessop (1992) tell us that global economic transactions and the demands of 'new social movements' are encouraging industrial and political elites to reform their institutions, including those at the subnational level. In the context of the regions of the European Community, changes are also taking place, more often perhaps than elsewhere, as a result of initiatives from lower and higher levels of authority instead of national governments (see chapter 8). As a result of this, as well as ease of communications, there is popular support for closer links in Europe – notwithstanding opposition in recent referendums. Growing numbers of people say they feel European as well as national, approve of the idea of integration, want more common standards of social protection and call for stronger democracy in the common institutions (Commission, 1991a; *Women of Europe*, Supplement 35, 1991; and see chapter 8) – though, as political science warns, we must temper extensiveness with salience when we interpret public opinions. These topics recur at various points in the book in ways that I now outline.

Outline of the Book

Since the ordering of civil, political and social rights is different in the Community compared to its Member States, the main part of this book is about EC legal entitlements in the social sphere. I do not deal with the whole range of Community policies that have given rise to the 'People's Europe' but only with those that have formed the principle basis of general claims that social rights are part of a triad of citizenship rights; that is, social security and assistance, participation by workers in the undertakings in which they are employed and the equal treatment of men and women.

Chapter 2 discusses what citizenship has meant in its national context – its formal aspects and its practical significance for different members of national communities. The content of this chapter will be self-evident to some readers but I feel it is necessary for those who are interested in the Community but have not yet considered it in the light of analogous features in the development of national polities. It outlines arguments about the civil, political and social rights of national citizenship that are relevant to debates about the meaning of the EC for citizens of its Member States; for example, disagreements about whether civil and political rights were revolutionary or were inspired by elites to facilitate the transition from feudalism to capitalism and the development of industrial society, their universalism disguising, or making more palatable, economic and social inequalities. This has its parallels in the identification by political leaders of a need for a 'human face' for the Community and the critical response by the 'new social movements' that the basis of Community rights is a stunted one. The chapter also expands upon what has been said already about the conditions which have given rise to an environment in which it is possible to speak of a European civil society in which such movements can play a part.

Other disagreements – about whether social rights can or cannot enjoy the same status as political rights because of competing views about the propriety of specific public interventions – are dealt with in later chapters on class and sex. Before dealing with these, the book sets the legal and political context. Chapter 3 on the constitutional framework is necessary because certain basic information has to be provided for readers to make sense of the powers of Community institutions and the role of the Court of Justice of the European Communities (ECJ) that are to be discussed subsequently. Most importantly, the chapter emphasizes the significance of the Community's being a legal federation when it is not a political one. The chapter refers to the 'four freedoms' (of movement of goods, capital, services and labour) that are the objectives of the Treaties of Rome and Paris and that provide the basis of Community rights. In the context of the legal and state traditions of Member States that have influenced the shape of the Community, the chapter draws attention to the powers that the Treaties grant to Community institutions to implement Treaty provisions and to develop further policies that may be considered necessary to advance common objectives. It outlines the relationships among the Commission, Council of Ministers, the European Parliament and the ECJ. It explains the relationship between Community law and national laws and, in particular, the quasi-constitutional role of the ECJ and the significance of Regulations and Directives in national courts. These are the main instruments of Community social policy and they give citizens rights, or may do so, irrespective of the content of national legislation.

Chapter 4 draws upon two bodies of literature – on the welfare state and ideas about integration – as a context for a discussion of how European policies on social security, workers' rights and sex equality came to be as they are. This involves a difference of economic interests among the original six and a consequent disagreement over whether social security objectives should be achieved through 'harmonization' – that is, the bringing about of common standards of material and legal protection through the 'approximation' of national legislation – or through the coordination of different national schemes. This is connected to conflicts between the Commission and Council of Ministers, and within the intentions of the politicians, about the relative status of economic and social policy. The chapter explains that, in addition to the economic motives behind the equal pay provision in the Treaty of Rome, it was in an effort to resolve disputes about economic and social integration that Directives on workers' rights and sex equality were issued in the 1970s, the latter becoming that part of social policy that was at the forefront of social action in the 1980s. It is argued here that, despite opinions in the European Parliament, neither the Council of Ministers nor the Commission arrived at their first Social Action Programme because of convictions that European citizens had rights, over and above those provided nationally, but because they thought economic cooperation was in danger as a result of a feeling among ordinary people that they had no stake in it. This contrasts markedly with the views of the ECJ which are outlined in the next three chapters.

References in chapter 1 to the meaning of citizenship for the working class are elaborated in chapter 5 on class and citizenship. In particular, this chapter discusses the idea that negative freedoms cannot be exercised without the positive provision of minimum standards and that the formal universalism of freedoms in liberal democracies coexists with class bias in participation in political and civil society. These matters have two dimensions: the question of enabling private citizens to operate more effectively in their own interests and the question of the creation of a solidaristic moral order. As noted earlier, both kinds of ideas are present in the language of Community policy. This discussion provides the framework within which to outline the rulings of the ECJ on Regulations about the coordination of national social security and assistance schemes and Directives (and Social Charter provisions) on workers' rights to participate in decision-making in the enterprises in which they work. Here, it is argued that the Court's insistence that social security, in particular, is a fundamental human right means that the protection of migrant workers goes beyond what was originally intended by Member States. The financial and political implications of this are taken up again in chapter 7.

Chapter 5 expands on references in chapter 2 to disputes about whether the notion of citizenship could encompass women. In particular, the chapter takes up the critiques of liberalism and 'liberal-feminist' thinking; that is, that female autonomy cannot be achieved when inadequate attention is paid to gender and sexual differences and to motherhood. The chapter also considers arguments about whether social rights of the type proposed by Marshallians succeed in addressing this and the idea that they, too, are flawed, either because they do not 'individualize' assessments of income and need or because both liberal and welfare social contracts are fundamentally patriarchal. These ideas provide a framework for examining existing EC laws and those policies which might have taken account of women's 'dual role' but which have been diluted or vetoed. The chapter examines the rulings of the ECJ which establish sex equality as a 'fundamental human right' and argues that it has expanded the meaning of equal treatment beyond what was intended by Member States, placing the costs of compliance more directly on governments themselves. It also examines those rulings which reveal the limitations of Community policy in addressing the general condition of equality between men and women, especially in view of sexual difference. The chapter also points out that, so far, the Social Charter makes only a modest reference to the reconciliation of occupational and family roles and, according to some writers, solutions to immediate problems may institutionalize sexism. An alternative argument that women can capture meanings is referred to here and taken up again in chapter 7.

From the more abstract point of view, one of the issues usually taken up in the debate about social rights is the question of whether they are a special case of, or can be approximated to, the legal rights of citizenship. This argument is particularly relevant to the transformation into rights by the ECJ of what politicians saw as instruments of or adjuncts to economic goals and is discussed in chapter 7 on the civil right of the equal protection of the laws. Here, the book draws attention to the different conceptions of social security for migrant workers, on the one hand, and workers' participation and sex equality, on the other, in terms of the equal protection of the laws *within* states and the equal protection of the laws *across* states. Social security rules are intended to eliminate discrimination based on nationality for workers who move across the Community, while entitlements to participation and equality provide rights for workers who do not move. Nevertheless, the latter are also intended to promote common standards of legal and material protection on a Community basis. Some of the Court's rulings seem to demand harmonization of methods of assessing income and need – a minimalist step towards the social integration that was originally rejected by the Council of Ministers. This emerges in the implications of rulings for equity within states, between individual migrants and either their compatriots or new neighbours. And rulings on workers' participation and sex equality within states are bringing about some convergence in what is or is not unlawful, and in the consequences of unlawful practice. It is argued, however, that the equal protection of the laws is only imperfectly realized because of Treaty limitations, inconsistencies in different sets of regulations and by cases where the ECJ has left things to piecemeal solution. These imperfections particularly affect young people, different categories of the unemployed, foreign members of EC families and women. It is also the case that Community rules are not systematic in the protection they offer, or not, to 'third country migrants'. Their position is referred to here and in chapter 8. However, there are arguments that the meaning of rights can be made to bring tangible benefits to supposed beneficiaries and chapter 7 also deals with the informal means through which such redefinitions can take place. This involves the exercise of secondary political rights – such as the right to lobby in association with others.

Chapter 8 deals with the transition from legal and social rights to primary political rights. In so doing, it discusses competing views about whether a sense of citizenship or solidarity can arise only from national identity or might arise from the many social identities we all possess that often cross national boundaries. It outlines the growth of the Community concept of 'Citizen of the Union' from the early 1980s to the proposals in the Maastricht Treaty. This is tempered by reference to the negative aspects of Community citizenship which exist because of governmental conceptions of national interests. This raises Leca's question of whether the emergent, new notion of citizenship might be a 'neo-national' instead of a 'neo-imperial' one (1990). In one sense, the upshot might depend upon the admission of new Member States, the choice of 'widening' the Community instead of 'deepening' it being seen by some governments as a means of ensuring that Community rights are relatively vacuous. However, the chapter, and the book, conclude by introducing a new 'claim of right'[5] – that is, a new version of the right to self-determination – which challenges the authority of states from below, on the basis of 'subsidiarity', which governments thought protected them from above and which is a major factor in the growth of an extraordinarily complex framework for the exercise of Heater's good social behaviour, loyalties, rights and duties (1990).

Notes

1 It should be emphasized that no reference to the Holy Roman Empire is intended. Suspicions of links between Catholicism and politics or the church in general and the polity lingered on in the separation, only recently ended, between independent conservatives and Christian democrats in the European Parliament.

2 The second and third points also rule out the possibility of using 'multi-national citizenship' to circumvent the problems of conceptualizing 'European citizenship'. If the two transformations did take place, the 'multi' element would by definition disappear into a new citizenry legally defined by a single label. It would remain only as an indicator of the multiplicity of ethnic groups subsumed in the overarching, common legal nationality.

3 Kymlicka (1991: 251–6) points out that 'private' does not always mean a-social or anti-social, which many critics of liberalism like to believe, but has been used to distinguish collective life that is regulated or guaranteed by public authorities from that which arises from society and is free from surveillance. In this sense, the private realm is the same as the civil arena in which people engage in Mill's 'social suasion'. In another strand of liberalism, the idea of the 'private' is related to the notion of self-development, which can be valued as part of the route to civic consciousness but which may be construed by critics of liberalism as personal or self-interested.

4 Kymlicka (1991: 251–6) also points out that all male political theory, liberal or not, excludes consideration of the family even from reference to the private realm. The criteria of justice applied to the public sphere and the private realm, in its social meaning, are never applied to relations between men and women in the family.

5 The Claim of Right was first used by the Estates in Scotland in 1689 as the title of their offer of the crown to William and Mary, an offer with more radical conditions than those proposed by their English counterparts (Mackie, 1978: 244–5). It is now the title of the 1989 declaration of the Scottish Constitutional Convention on the need for a Scottish Parliament in a reconstituted United Kingdom (Scottish Constitutional Convention, 1990).

2
National Citizenship to European Civil Society

Introduction

Chapter 1 referred to the ideas of the People's Europe, industrial citizenship and Citizens of the Union. In the light of Aron's distinctions (1974) between sets of rights and their respective guarantors, they seem inconsistent signifiers of the status of nationals of the Member States of the European Community (EC). But it is possible to expand on some of Heater's themes (1990) about the meaning of citizenship to suggest otherwise.

A people, according to Edmund Burke, cannot exist except when individuals inhabiting 'rude nature' have entered into common agreement to form a civil society and to create a state (Gough, 1956 [1936]: 194). Leca (1990, trans. 1991) cites Kelsen's view (1989 [1929]) that 'the people is an artifact, the unity of which is nothing more than submission of its members to the same State-imposed order'. Even though no trace can be found of an actual agreement – made willingly or under coercion – people behave, it is argued, as though they had contracted to regulate civil life and to distribute rights and duties to rulers and associates. The citizenship rights of the associates, once confined to freemen or male property-owners, are now claimable by all native or naturalized members of a political community. Clearly, the EC is not a national community, though more obviously than the nation-state it is based on a compact, which is both voluntary and an agreement to submit to a new regulator of certain spheres of life. Its founders and developers, however, are not individuals but states. Political leaders of the twelve Member States can claim to represent the interests of their peoples in all their capacities, be they best articulated through common or distinctively national policies. But the idea of industrial citizenship does not include, by definition, all those peoples in all their capacities. On the other hand, since property or economic independence has almost always been a criterion of eligibility for citizenship, it may be possible to argue that the Community's approach to citizenship, originating in the rights of migrant *workers*, is a more honest indicator of status than the normal and normative connotations of universalism – instead of denying the possibility of European citizenship, on the ground that Community regulation is restricted to the social and economic spheres.

The purpose of this chapter is to explain what citizenship has meant in its national context. This involves its formal aspects, for example expressed in constitutions, and its normative dimensions. The latter requires some discussion of exclusions, participation and social rights. The chapter then deals with those aspects of the universalization of rights within nation-states which, as suggested in chapter 1, may be analogous to EC developments and, finally, with the growth of European civil society.

The Characteristics of National Citizenship

Chapter 1 introduced the view that the meaning of citizenship is neither fixed in time nor the same in different societies. The citizen, literally the inhabitant of a citadel and then a city, was originally a person who enjoyed the full rights of membership of a city-state. The original citadel is the source of the ideas that citizenship is characterized by military, as well as civic, virtues; that citizens are warriors and have a duty to defend the political community. In the Greek city-state, economic transactions were associated with the private or social sphere (see notes 2 and 3 in chapter 1 on the social meaning of 'private'); the public realm was where free men acted as citizens, contributing to the elucidation of justice and collective self-government. Associated in Greece with equal liberty, at least for those who qualified, medieval European rights of citizenship were linked to a more aristocratic conception of freedom – the enjoyment of privileges rather than commonly shared rights (Aron, 1974 on de Tocqueville). The Magna Carta, like most continental social contract theories of the same period, was about the rights of barons *vis-à-vis* kings or about the distribution of powers as between different units of authority. The idea that citizenship was about equal or common rights for all – men, in particular – did not re-emerge until the seventeenth and eighteenth centuries. It was the Enlightenment idea about the natural equality of (male) human beings that informed the political theories of, for example, John Locke, Tom Paine and Jean Jacques Rousseau, movements for democracy and the ethical bases of the French Declaration of the Rights of Man and the Constitution of the United States of America. The growth of these ideas coincided with the consolidation of the nation-state (Heater, 1990) which brought about the need to control borders. This was the source of the dependence of rights on the inheritance of the appropriate nationality or the acquisition of it (Zolberg, 1991).

The legal and political entitlements of citizenship might be illuminated by contrasting the citizen with a denizen, metic or subject. A denizen is a lawfully resident alien with the same primary rights of political participation as native or naturalized citizens. A metic is also a resident alien with legal status but enjoying only some of the rights of citizenship; for example, not the primary right to vote but with secondary rights such as the capacity to belong to political parties (Leca, 1990). The extent of rights granted to metics depends on the attitudes of the political authority and these values stem from particular conceptions of the relationship between citizenship and nationality (see below). A subject may be of the same nationality as a citizen and the lives of the two are regulated by laws passed by the same political authority; but, unlike the citizen, the subject has no rights to participate in law-making. The position of Irish citizens in Great Britain (i.e., not the United Kingdom, as different rules about the right to vote sometimes apply in Northern Ireland) is denizen-like, whereas 'guest-workers' are or have been like subjects. Despite sharing nationality with men, women may have rights that are more like those of metics (Vogel, 1991); that is, a legal status without political equality.

The content of citizens' rights is often written down in constitutions, constitutional-type statutes or Bills of Rights. Before the eighteenth century these rights were usually rules governing the extent of monarchical power. The Magna Carta has been mentioned; other examples are to be found in coronation oaths and investiture agreements in most European countries. Although kings might claim to be accountable only to God, their barons (particularly like the Scottish ones of King James II of Great Britain, see Mackie, 1978: 244–5) were convinced that they were contracted through their oaths to govern within agreed limits and impeachable if they did not. The need to control executive power remained a feature of enlightened constitutions but the emphasis on the institutional or contractual limits of rule has been overlaid by the idea that abuses of power are best prevented by the existence of universal individual rights. Continuing mechanisms for the control of public power can be found in arrangements for the separation of powers. For example, the United States Constitution allocates different responsibilities to President, Congress, the Supreme Court, and Federal and State governments. In France, the Constitutional Council and the Council of State advise respectively on the constitutionality of procedures and the content of legislation, the latter acting also as a court of appeal if laws are subsequently thought to be invalid. In the German Basic Law, these functions are combined in the Constitutional Court.

Declarations of the legal rights of individuals include 'due process' and 'equal protection' clauses in all constitutions, requiring that no person be prosecuted and detained except for a breach of a specified law, that detention follow a fair trial, that punishment be reasonable, not cruel or degrading, and that all citizens be equally protected by and subject to the known laws. Political rights are those constitutional provisions that guarantee popular sovereignty, including procedures for amending constitutions, the right to stand for public office, universal suffrage, rules about voting age and the conduct of elections. Political rights are also present in provisions allowing for freedom of speech and rights of assembly. As in the case of the United Nations Declaration and related conventions, most European constitutions specify the equal rights of men and women. In line with modern conceptions of citizenship, these also apply to equal treatment in socio-economic matters. Only the Irish Constitution declares that women may be protected from the need to find paid employment.

The United Kingdom is alone among its European partners in not having a formally written constitution and Bill of Rights. This is not to say that there are no rights or limitations on public power. For example, the Treaty (or Act) of Union between England and Scotland stipulates that no tax be raised in one part of the Kingdom that is not raised in the other, a matter recently considered in the Court of Session in connection with the introduction of the Community Charge or 'poll tax' a year earlier in Scotland than in England (Neal Ascherson, writing in *The Independent on Sunday*, 27 May 1990). And, though the aims of legislation cannot be challenged in the courts, having been passed by a 'sovereign' Parliament, executive action to implement them can be reviewed (Zellick, 1985). The common law (see chapter 3) is said to serve the protection of individual legal rights in the way that constitutions do elsewhere and political rights are generally specified in statutes. Both the means of controlling public power and the protection of individual rights in the United Kingdom are often regarded as inadequate (e.g., Harden and Lewis, 1986; Johnson, 1977; Lester, 1984; Scarman, 1979). But practices in the United Kingdom, like those elsewhere, are subject to scrutiny by international bodies such as the United Nations and the European Commission on Human Rights. Membership of the European Community brings about some elements of judicial review of legislation in areas where there is a Community competence.

In analytical philosophy, discussions of rights often refer to correlative duties. In the history of political ideas, it is not always so clear that there are duties of citizenship and, if so, what they might be. There is general agreement that citizens have a duty to one another to obey lawful rules. Defence of the country, in order to protect the compact, is often taken to be a prime, collective duty of citizenship and it was the charge that women could have no part in this that was the main justification for opposition to female suffrage. Nowadays, the payment of taxes (the obverse of 'no taxation without representation') and willingness to work are sometimes considered to be duties of citizenship. But all of these are controversial because of the continuing Stoic belief that human beings have duties to a 'higher law', as well as to their own communities and authorities. Actual rules might contravene human rights (and international laws about them, as at Nuremberg) and those of minorities; taxes might be used for what are regarded as immoral purposes; and, if it is being human, not a particular economic status, that is now alleged as the justification for political rights, it is hard to see how the paying of taxes and willingness to work can logically be demanded as duties. Sometimes, the right and duty inhere in the same action. We speak of a right, as well as a duty, to work; voting can be, and often is, seen as a public duty. And individual recourse to the law may be not only a right to resolve a private problem but also the discharge of a duty to promote a public purpose or good order – as in the case of the European Community (see chapter 3).

In chapter 1 it was noted that the connection between citizenship and the nation-state is mainly logical in Aron (1974) and sociological in Leca (1990, 1991). Leca argues that there is a powerful social construct in which the terms 'national', 'citizen' and 'ruler' overlap. However, rules about the right to hold political office and the right to vote are not necessarily coterminous with shared nationality. Chapter 1 referred to the example of St Paul. American women in the nineteenth century were defined as citizens if they held American nationality but were denied the franchise, since, according to the Supreme Court, citizenship did not necessarily carry the right to vote. In the United Kingdom, 'persons-without-legal-disability' were entitled to vote but women were 'persons-*with*-legal-disability' who could not (Sachs and Hoff Wilson, 1978, discuss both of these). There is still controversy about women's voting rights in Switzerland, although they have the same nationality as men. Rules about immigration and naturalization vary from country to country, some migrants being able to acquire legal and political rights without a new nationality, some having to go through procedures of varying degrees of difficulty to become naturalized before being treated as citizens. Migrants within the Eu̇ ꞌpean Community have been, hitherto, like metics, their economic and social activities protected by common regulation, with secondary political rights but, until the ratification of the Maastricht Treaty, without primary political rights in their new places of abode except in those countries which already have specific arrangements. In this sense Aron is right – there are no 'European citizens'. But, since it is possible to argue that social rights *are* part of citizenship, it is also possible to suggest that what is happening is simply a different ordering in national and Community histories of the acquisition of a triad of citizenship rights. As indicated in chapter 1, this might be connected to the existence of a different emphasis in Heater's 'cluster of meanings' (1990) during the development of the Community from that which was present in nation-states in the eighteenth and nineteenth centuries. This requires some discussion of the normative aspects of citizenship.

Normative Aspects of Citizenship

Conceptions of human nature and community influence ideas about who should be included and excluded from citizenship ('closures', Leca, 1990, 1991), the nature of the relationship between citizens and rulers and the status of social rights.

'Closures' between and within Political Communities

As noted in chapter 1, Aristotle believed that men were not self-sufficient and the Stoics believed their interdependence could be recognized as global, not confined to the close neighbours of a city-state. But Leca (1990, 1991) argues that an essential feature of citizenship, as experienced, has been a sense of being able to distinguish between 'ourselves' and 'others' from outside our community, whatever the territorial dimension of that community. With the need for emergent nation-states to control borders, the distinguishing characteristic became nationality. Leca (drawing upon Bosanquet, 1925 and Walzer, 1983) appears to corroborate Aron by suggesting that in most European countries nationality, *imparted by the nation-state*, 'constitutes a barrier to full citizenship' and that legal security cannot exist when 'one is not in a position to guarantee one's rights by participating in political functions'. But, nationality, like citizenship, has different social constructions. In one of Leca's schemas, 'individual as well as collective identities are contractually founded' which means that the 'political community is potentially inclusive of all those remaining on the outside, legally, socially and physically'. In the second, 'identities are founded morally and pre-contractually' which means that the political community is 'a community of character, historically stable, an association of men and women especially committed the ones to the others, and endowed with a specific sense of their common life'. As a result, 'the community is intrinsically entitled to exclude, or at least deny admittance to outsiders just as a club would'. In the first of these constructions, nationality and, hence, citizenship rights can be legally *acquired* through *ius solis*, as in France and Italy; the second resembles the emphasis on nationality by descent, *ius sanguinis*, in Germany and the United Kingdom. If the modern association of citizenship with nationality rests on a legal or contractual view of communities, then it would not be too difficult to envisage a new form of it at the European level. If it is based on a communitarian or *gemeinschaft* outlook, it would be more difficult to do so. This issue recurs later in this chapter and in the conclusion.

The exclusiveness of citizenship is not only national and/or territorial but can occur within communities. Slaves and women were not citizens of Athenian democracy. Ethnic differences and religious affiliation, even among those with the same legal nationality, have often been barriers to citizenship. Subsistence workers were debarred in Locke's ideas from influencing the social contract. It was not until the twentieth century that working-class men became full citizens in the political sense. For similar reasons, stemming from connections made between property and rationality (discussed more fully in the following sections), and for additional, special reasons, women were excluded for even longer. Aristotle, unlike Plato (Bluestone, 1987), believed that the dispositions of women rendered them incapable of rational thought about the public interest; their place was in the family where they were to create havens for men during retreats from public life. An association of femaleness with nature, partly to be subdued, partly the source of emotional sustenance, continued throughout the middle ages. It contrasted with an association of maleness with both military and civic virtue, the civilization of nature and with the fostering of an antithesis between rationality and emotion (Lloyd, 1984). Maleness was constitutive of citizenship; women could not be citizens because they were not men (Vogel, 1991) and the 'generality of the public realm', epitomized by 'manly virtue', could be sustained only by insisting on its separateness from the 'particularity' of women and domestic concerns (Kymlicka, 1991: 256; Young, 1989: 253–4).

At the beginning of the French Revolution, there was, briefly, to be a woman's revolution as well as a class one. Despite the influence of Rousseau, whose views on women were hardly different from the medievalists',[1] women's civil and political status were to be transformed through the secularization of laws about marriage, divorce and the family and through the granting of equal suffrage (Zweigert and Kotz, 1987: ch. 7). But, in the period that followed, the feminism of the revolutionaries became attenuated and, under Napoleon, pre-révolutionary patriarchal powers over women were re-established (Vogel, 1991). In the century after the French Revolution, John Stuart Mill was one of the few male advocates of women's rights. He and his collaborator, friend and wife, Harriet Taylor, argued that we could not know that women were by nature different from men; if they seemed different, it might be because of artificial, man-made constrictions on their development. In any case, if men might differ naturally from one another and still be equal citizens, it was illogical to withold civil and political rights from women on the ground that they were naturally different.

The impact of ideas about women's nature on their political rights was compounded by their limited right to property, itself a general qualification for political participation. Married women were not allowed to own property or to enter into contracts in their own right. In many places, such rules lasted into the twentieth century. In some political thought, property is a natural right, brought into civil and political society from the natural equality of men in pre-civil society; for others, property is a conventional right established with the foundation of civil society and protected under the political compact. The debarrment of women from property rights cannot fully be explained as a matter of the nature of women or of a natural right naturally inhering in males. For example, during long periods of Roman law, its underlying concept of humanity enabled married women to hold property and, sometimes, in the Empire, political rights (Schulz, 1936: ch. X). By convention, later Europeans considered single or widowed women as adequate administrators of property and, in some of the early American townships, property-holding women were sometimes allowed to vote. But women's political participation was limited by the general idea that the ability to accumulate property was an indication of the possession of the rationality necessary for disinterested judgement. Slaves would have no time to ponder upon questions of justice, even though they might have an inherent ability to do so. Workers would be stunted by the sheer need to find the means of assistance. And married women, who might have brought property to their marriage, were assumed to be adequately represented by the husbands who controlled their property. Indeed, opponents of female suffrage tried to argue that women would have 'two' votes if they were allowed to vote themselves while being able, informally, to persuade their husbands to vote in their interests (Vogel, 1991).

Even though the property qualification has gone for both men and women, ancient assumptions about women's nature, their economic status and the division of labour in the private and public spheres still influence policy and affect women's capacities to act as citizens. This means that the foundation of Community rights on working status has asymmetrical implications for men and women. Discussion of these issues will recur. Before that, it is necessary to say something about how ideas have changed in respect to the democratization of participation and the need for social rights.

Participation: Self-government and Citizens' Control of Rulers

Aristotle's conception of human nature included an identity between the good society and participatory society and men's equal potential to be able to discern the just from the unjust (Jordan, 1989, 67–8). Some medieval and Enlightenment thinkers shared his views about the human need for participation and the naturalness of a degree of self-regulation. The very idea of moving from a state of nature into an ordered one of reciprocal rights and forbearance was inconceivable without pre-existing ideas that rules were needed to protect the liberties of all. Law, or at least informal rules – embryonic civil rights – must be anterior to the development of state institutions.

The need for political institutions arises from the fallibility of human beings. Though intrinsically law-abiding, they can make mistakes about what is and is not just or in the common interest. But government, too, must be conducted according to the natural laws and the terms of the compact that gave rise to government. This implies political rights in order to influence rulers and to make judgements about their activities. The idea that holders of state office occupied a position of trust and could be resisted if the trust were broken reached its height in the work of John Locke and contrasts with the earlier ideas of Thomas Hobbes, which rested on a different conception of human nature. For the latter, men were essentially competitive and life in the state of nature was 'nasty, brutish and short'. To bring about a stable order, he argued, virtually all rights had to be ceded to a powerful sovereign (single monarch or republican body). Hobbes's citizens had no rights except the ultimate right of self-defence, possibly even against the sovereign.

Jean Jacques Rousseau's ideas also embodied the idea of a strong state but with a difference. He believed that the social contract was corruptible by the powerful and could be used for the 'institutionalization of rule by the rich over the poor' (Lesnoff, 1986: 79), ostensibly in the name of all. With similar ideas to Aristotle's about the common interest, participation and the good society and to Locke's about the corrigibility of man, however, he believed it possible to redesign the social contract so that the General Will genuinely expressed the common good and not the particular wills of powerful individuals. Though his ideas have been argued to have totalitarian implications (Berlin, 1958), they, and those of John Stuart Mill, have inspired twentieth-century advocates of more participatory forms of citizenship.

The proponents of participatory democracy challenge the so-called Revisionist school by arguing that they have turned Aristotle's conception of democracy on its head, defining the good society as one that minimizes participation and restricting it again to a skilled political class (Pateman, 1970). Like Locke, Schumpeter (1952, [1943]) argues that those who have to be concerned primarily with their day-to-day needs and immediate personal interests are not in a position to make disinterested judgements and are susceptible to demagoguery. Since this is so, it is best to limit participation to the periodic choice of competing teams of leaders who have had experience in pursuing the public interest. There are two main counter-arguments. One is that, if mass political attitudes are, indeed, irrational, the answer is not to make people more like subjects but to provide self-governing institutions through which they may become better participants. This is inspired by John Stuart Mill's proposals, introduced in chapter 1, for worker participation in decisions about their industries – a practice which is part of Community policy ambitions. There are at least three aspects to the ideas of Mill and his followers. On the one hand, the workplace is an arena close to home where participants could be expected to have some knowledge. Secondly, the experience of participating in organizations close to home is educative, helping people to develop a wider civic consciousness and sense of justice. And thirdly, since the political features of Athenian democracy cannot be replicated in large and complex societies, workplace democracies could be a substitute outlet for the human capacities fulfilled by other means in the city-state (Heater, 1990; Pateman, 1970). The other counter to the Revisionists is to suggest that, if the possession of property is, indeed, a condition for the free intellectual development that enables disinterested judgement, it is not necessary to deprive the naturally equal, but property-less, of political rights; the problem can be resolved equally by providing them with the conditions under which they can become rational; for example, health and guaranteed incomes (King and Waldron, 1988). This leads to the third dimension of this section: the arguments for including social rights as part of citizenship.

Social Rights and Citizenship

In Aristotle's self-governing community, citizenship meant membership of a community where assets were distributed so that all had an interest in contributing to as well as benefiting from the goods of association, which were not just money but things like conviviality and communality (Jordan, 1989: 67–8). But, though subsequent thinkers have continued to share his view of the political nature of human beings, we have also seen, since the eighteenth century, the consolidation of a concept of individualism, related to economic rights, which destroys the coincidence of personal and common interests (Jordan, 1989). Under the influence of a particular interpretation of Adam Smith (distorted, according to Sen, 1990, by Friedrich von Hayek and Milton Friedman), a dominant way of thinking is that citizens are essentially economic, not political creatures. Their rights lie in being free to do what is lawful and in being protected from enforced transfers to other members of society. The interests of the poor are not in a strong, redistributive state dedicated to egalitarianism but are best served by one that minimizes impediments to individual prosperity, the benefits of which will 'trickle down' from the rich to others. Such a way of thinking is compatible with the restriction of citizenship rights to abstract legal and political equality. But consistency does not necessarily mean correctness. Earlier, it was noted that Heater discerned a 'cluster of meanings' in the history of citizenship and that Leca construed it as a social construct fraught with ideological dispute about its meanings. The issues that have been referred to above – the status of women, constraints on power and the material basis of rational participation – have all contributed to several versions of the view that citizenship is not only about civil and political rights but implies social entitlements and even means an indivisible triad of civil, political and social rights. This, and disputes about it, are discussed more fully in later chapters and briefly in the next section.

The Universalization of Citizenship: Political Revolution
or Economic Transformation?

According to classic accounts of thinking about the social contract
(Barker, 1947; Gough, 1956 [1936]; Lesnoff, 1986), versions of the
theory sometimes upheld established orders, like feudalism, and
sometimes justified revolutionary claims for religious freedom and
the overthrow of political tyrannies.[2] The central promise of the
idea of the social contract for the Ancients, and for medieval and
eighteenth-century revolutionaries (and even early socialists, despite
the association with bourgeois property rights) was that, by
providing an ethical foundation for government by consent, it
imposed duties upon temporal and spiritual rulers to govern
according to law and gave citizens rights against rulers.

The triumph of the social contract way of thinking in political
liberalism is commonly seen as a revolution against patriarchal rule
as theorized by Robert Filmer; that is, against political power being
associated with the headship of families superimposed by the
'highest' family, the royal family. Though, as we shall see in
chapter 6, it is now argued that the revolution against patriarchy
must be understood as one of brothers against fathers, women,
too, claimed the right of resistance – not only to unjust laws but
to laws made unjustly. Abigail Adams wrote to her husband, John,
when he was helping to frame the United States Constitution, that
women would not hold themselves bound by laws in the making of
which they had no part. She declared that the 'ladies . . . [were]
determined to foment a rebellion' (Cary and Peratis, 1977: 1–2).
Civil disobedience on a large scale was undertaken, especially in the
United Kingdom, in the fight for votes for women.

It has been proposed that the flowering of social contract
theories in Britain in the seventeenth and eighteenth centuries was
connected to the beginnings of new forms of economic organization (Macpherson, 1962; Polanyi, 1944). The argument is that the
industrial order which emerged in the nineteenth century could not
have developed unless land and labour could be bought and sold
freely; that is, unless feudal entailments and status relationships
were transformed. The individualism upon which the Enlightenment form of the social contract rested encouraged this, political
liberalism providing a rationale and a motor for economic
liberalization. Although feudal relationships among a hierarchy of
families were susceptible to description in contractual terms, now
all individual men could be equally free to enter contracts with
whomsoever they chose, thus freeing capital and labour necessary
for the new economic order. Although many people dispute

Macpherson's contextualization of the abstract ideas of Hobbes and Locke in his own interpretation of the material conditions of society, many also accept the kinds of ideas in the work of Dahrendorf (1988); that is, that for a moment in history in Britain, and at different times elsewhere, the economic interests of the new wealth-creators coincided with the advocates of equal citizenship. This connection is sometimes seen in positive ways, sometimes negatively.

For example, it is often argued that manifest socio-economic inequalities in industrial society could be more readily lived with under the legitimating features of formal legal and political equality. A sense of political obligation could be made more widespread if the franchise were extended beyond property-owners, to rate-payers and eventually to all adults. Others suggest that the coincidence of the needs of those who oversaw the means of economic growth and the aims of those who wanted more universal, real liberties continued. It can be argued that the growth of welfare states was a consequence of an increasingly organized working class using its political rights (see chapters 4 and 5). Yet it can also be argued that political obligation could be more deeply entrenched through the existence of a state that took responsibility for basic matters of health and welfare; and, moreover, it was convenient for employers, needing literate and healthy workers, to have services provided collectively. If general social policy could reduce costs for employers of male labour, comparable arguments exist about later legislation for women's equal rights at work. Politicians in the 1960s were being advised that the rationalization of labour forces was desirable. Such advice coincided with perceptions that it was increasingly necessary to make special appeals to women voters (for example, Ellickson on the United States, discussed in Meehan, 1985; Mazur on France, 1991). And it was notable that advocates of women's rights in the United Kingdom, who thought in terms of justice, often couched their appeals in the more readily heard language of economic rationality (for example, Seear, in Meehan, 1985).

Arguments about class and equal citizenship are similar in some ways to accounts of the process of nation-building. Though some of the former assume that class conflict is inevitable while the latter do not, both are about the fostering of national, social cohesion. In Britain, there was the additional feature of the empire. Bendix (1964) argues a sense of nationhood was established early in Britain compared to other countries but that the maintenance of colonial power depended upon the continued availability of a healthy and loyal people willing to defend it. That a lack of cohesion persisted in the United Kingdom until the time of the foundation of other nation-states is vividly illustrated in *Sybil: A Tale of Two Nations*, the novel by Benjamin Disraeli, who, recognizing the need to create a sense of loyalty, persuaded his Conservative Party to extend the franchise and recognize the right of combination. The unification of Italy was completed in 1870 and of Germany in 1871. In Germany, it was not only paternalism (Rimlinger, 1971) that encouraged the fostering of cohesion through appeals to nationhood. Other motivations included an awareness of the potential of an increasingly well-organized working class and a sense that building a nation, after war and conquest, under the sway of Prussia had to be legitimated (Leca, 1990; Roberts and Lovecy, 1984). All these influenced Count von Bismarck's foundation of the Social Rights State. The first extensions of rights to women often took place after wars. If citizenship rights are regarded as the obverse of the duty of defence, this timing can be seen as an acknowledgement of the war-time tasks undertaken by women as nurses and ambulance drivers. But it is also possible to interpret the coincidence in the light of the nation-building thesis as a belated recognition by governments that women could contribute to social cohesion in public as well as family roles.

The welfare provisions initiated between the late nineteenth century and the 1930s and expanded after 1945 came to be regarded as entitlements, perhaps even rights – during the same period as the first moves towards European integration took place. Though they are not reducible to nationality because they may be available to non-nationals (Leca, 1990) and regulated supranationally (Aron, 1974), it has been argued by T.H. Marshall (mainly 1963 but also in many other works), his followers and even his critics that they have become part and parcel of national citizenship. Whether they function as a means of enabling individuals to be more fulfilled in their personal lives and more effective in social relations or as a means of promoting a solidaristic moral order is a topic that recurs. So, too, is an argument that they are not separate from civil rights but are a special category of civil right. Whatever the philosophical puzzles, governments have acknowledged that social rights have a place in citizenship. They have ratified a range of international declarations and conventions that include them along with civil and political rights.[3] National constitutional provisions about sex equality often embrace socioeconomic as well as civil and political status. Though social rights have been criticized and undermined in many national communities, they are still an important feature in the growth of European civil society.

Towards a European Civil and Political Society

Several contradictory things seem to be happening at once in domestic political systems, to different extents in different countries and perhaps most of all in the United Kingdom. First, influential political ideologies prescribe the deregulation of economies and the dismantling of social rights guaranteed by the state, for reasons that are discussed in chapter 5.[4] Yet, it can also be shown that there are contradictions between theory and practice. For example, the actual reduction in welfare provision is slighter than might have been expected. Secondly, economic liberalization also seems to require *more* public intervention. King (1987b) suggests that this can be explained by distinguishing between the state and government; a more minimal state requires a strong government to bring it about. Ensuring good order in the absence of a strong state is sometimes thought to be achievable by re-creating the controls that are believed once to have been provided in families and schools. The new public philosophy is also introducing another element into 'the cluster of meanings' of citizenship. 'Active citizenship' can invoke the sentiments of Aristotle's good society in which all citizens participate but many of its components are similar to the American idea of citizenship as duty (King, 1991). Nowadays, 'active citizenship' means taking part in neighbourhood watch schemes, caring for dependants, running schools and housing estates, exercising consumer rights and, in (east) Germany, citizen initiatives for 'fixing things'. While there is a social democratic, as well as New Right, case that welfare states have been too intrusive, harming human autonomy, restoring responsibilities to 'active' or 'dutiful' citizens can also be coercive. Taking an interest in neighbours could be construed as spying and, in the name of extending choice, 'community care' can be thrust upon people, particularly women, with few resources (the latter being particularly pertinent to some of the topics of chapter 6). If this were not paradoxical enough, the governments of the Member States of the European Community are consolidating an order where regional economic liberalization is accompanied by a regulatory order of legal, social and, soon, political rights.

The origins of this are economic and political. The underlying economic dynamics are reminiscent of the transition from feudal to industrial society. The 'four freedoms' of the 1957 Treaty of Rome which set up the Common Market are the removal of the restrictions of national boundaries on the movement of capital, labour, goods and services. These are analogous to the needs identified by Macpherson in respect of national development and met through the abolition of feudal entailments. The political dimension is that relatively autonomous governments were willing to enter into agreement with one another, though there are disputes now about the distribution of powers between common and respective national institutions (see below) which echo controversies during the consolidation of the United States. The sociological arguments about class, nation-building and the universalization of rights also have a parallel at the Community level.

Chapter 1 referred to the internationalization of capital. Though expected by their peoples to control national economies, national governments, it is argued, can do little to regulate transfers by multi-national corporations of capital and production across borders in search of lower costs and higher profits. It is not necessarily the case that such corporations explicitly determine what national governments do but their freedom reduces the range of possibilities in economic planning open to governments; for example, in respect of regional policy, taxation, public investment, employment conditions and public expenditure. Counter-inflation policies are also affected by the interdependence of the fiscal, as well as economic, instruments of state intervention; exchange and interest rates depend on situations in other countries. Recognition of economic and fiscal interdependence and a common interest in making the EC a competitive bloc in the international order both lie behind moves towards Economic and Monetary Union (EMU). But domestic instruments of economic management can still be significant and the implications of losing control of them are reflected in recent crises in the EC. When the United Kingdom found itself unable to remain in the Exchange Rate Mechanism (ERM) in 1992, the Chancellor of the Exchequer said that there were renewed domestic opportunities for encouraging economic recovery. Conversely, the Italian government is finding it difficult to meet simultaneously the conditions of remaining in the ERM and the socio-economic demands of Italian citizens. Whereas some politicians and analysts would prefer to resolve the contradiction between interdependence and what may still be effective among domestic controls by appealing to national sovereignty, others suggest that the circle can be squared only by going for fuller integration in which economic management, including a full-scale regional policy, would be carried out at the common level.

The period during which the processes of European integration have come to their current difficulties is one in which apocalyptic versions of the interdependence theory have held that 'the nation-state has had its day' and is giving way to 'world government'. But more dispassionate observers also note that nation-states are re-arranging domestic institutions in acknowledgement of their interdependence and that there is a trend towards the inter-nationalization of civil society (Jessop, 1992; Keane, 1989). A European example of such rethinking can be seen in the strategy of the then British Prime Minister Edward Heath for the moder-nization of the British economy in the early 1970s. His plan for domestic modernization hinged upon a determination to enter the European Economic Community. Competition in the wider, common market was expected to force the pace of change in the physical condition of plants and in management and production methods (Gamble, 1974). There is, however, no direct, causal chain between economic forces and willingness to rearrange institutions and law that is the same for all countries.

Though welfare theories tend to predict convergent outcomes among industrialized societies (see chapter 4), *different* political and economic interests motivated the various Member States of the European Community to take a hand in encouraging common standards. For example, Nugent (1989, 1991) and George (1985, 1991) argue that France was concerned about its small enterprises and farmers. Preventing a renewed German dominance was part of France's political hopes in 1951 and this kind of motive continues in connection with unification and the inclusion of the former German Democratic Republic in the Community. The Common Agricultural Policy was not a German interest in the 1950s but both Germany and Italy needed the Community as a means of regaining respectability after the defeat of national socialism and fascism. According to George, the concept of 'packages' is central to the development of Community policy; that is, sets of proposals that are inseparable and contain costs and benefits in a mix that will command support for different reasons in different countries. This is a feature of Community life which, it is claimed, is less acceptable to the British while being necessary to their continental partners. It is the existence of historical 'particularities' in philosophical and political traditions and in interests that leads Tassin (1992: 188) to suggest that the European Community cannot be communitarian but can be a public space in which 'the plurality of political initiatives stand face to face'.

Aron's emphasis on the continuing autonomy of states is, of course, borne out by the existence of other intergovernmental organizations and intergovernmental processes in the Community. The Community was preceded by and/or coexists with institutions of economic cooperation such as the European Free Trade Associa-tion (EFTA), the Organization for Economic Cooperation and Development (OECD) and the General Agreement on Tariffs and

Trade (GATT), and with fora for social and political cooperation such as the United Nations (UN), the Western European Union (WEU), the International Labour Organization (ILO) and the Council of Europe. Some organizations, like the Nordic Council and the European Convention on Human Rights, have elements of supranationalism but the Community is the most ambitious experiment in ceding or 'pooling' national sovereignties. The Community is a new legal federation which regulates not only the economic transactions of civil society but also some of its social dimensions. As such, it reflects the two elements of endeavour noted by Dahrendorf (1988); the pursuit of growth by burghers or wealth-creators and the pursuit of justice or freedoms by the *citoyens*. This is not to say that all its founders or joiners saw it in both senses but it does provide another arena that can be shared by Dahrendorf's two sets of actors.

Tassin (1992: 189) suggests that for the European Community to be a political community it is necessary for there to be a 'public space of fellow-citizenship', breaking the association of citizenship and nationality without imposing a false sense of common identity and will. The connections between European civil and political society (be they 'pulled' into existence by economic forces or 'pushed' by the politics of its more visionary leaders and its new transnational social and administrative networks) are discussed in later chapters. Some of the indications are as follows. In contrast to perceptions that national economies need fewer or weaker social guarantees, the Community is thought by many to be at a stage where further economic liberalization – the Single European Market – needs *more* common social policies to bring about equal conditions of competition and to encourage mobility. To generate social cohesion and popular support for the Community in the context of dislocations caused by liberalization (similar motivations to those in the class and nation-building accounts of national citizenship), these policies are described in popular terms – a 'People's Europe' with a 'Social Charter' for the 'Citizens of the Union'. In giving effect to measures to mitigate the disruptive transition to a full, internal market, states are having to cede, not always willingly, more sovereignty in the social field, possibly both upwards to common institutions and downwards to regional governments and social actors.

The prohibition of national discrimination in matters of social freedoms and entitlements is now extending into the political sphere with plans for individual rights as well as the control of public powers in a 'European Union'. Debates about the respective powers of common and national institutions (the issue of 'subsidiarity') are not unlike those once heard in the United States (Gough, 1956 [1936]). Then, one side of the argument stemmed from the radical contract theory. It was that states, like individuals, had compacted to form a federal government that was obliged to act only as far as the articles of the compact allowed; the compact was dissolved when the government exceeded its powers. The other was the Hobbesian contention that the agreement left no rights with the states to decide that the actions of the government had dissolved the compact, because they had agreed to set up a fully sovereign body. In particular, no single state could break up the union by disobeying a law it judged *ultra vires*. Although protagonists of the Social Charter and European political union deny that they are moving towards a fully fledged federal system, the present debate in the Community is again, as it was in 1965 (see chapter 4), exactly about what will be the legitimate distribution of powers between common and national institutions.

A second element of the debate in America was about whether it was legitimate to use a social contract theory to determine the respective powers of two levels of government when the key element of the theory was about the rights of individual persons. The argument was proposed that it was not states but the people of the United States who had contracted to form a federal government. Clearly, the peoples of Europe did not contract to form the Community, except in so far as they elected governments who acted on their behalf. But the legal order of the Community works on the assumption that the Community confers rights and imposes duties, not only on governments, but also on individuals (see chapter 3); and these rights and duties transcend the 'dogma of nation-states' that insists on 'an amalgamation of nationality and citizenship' (Tassin, 1992: 189).

A third element to note is the nature of European civil society. It is often suggested that the League of Nations embodied Locke's conception of human nature, applied to states; that is, that states were naturally law-abiding and corrigible, without the need, therefore, of a coercive international regime. The United Nations, in contrast, is said to be based on the Hobbesian assumption that states, like individuals, would always strive against one another for dominance and that an international body of force was necessary (Wight et al., 1991). The European Community is Lockean in that its very foundations include the motivation that cooperation would help to stop European countries from again going to war with one another. Its assumptions about social rights embody both an individualistic view of human nature and an Aristotelian one. Dominant, perhaps, is the idea that individuals have the right to pursue their own, lawful interests throughout the Community. Perhaps this is only to be expected in view of Leca's belief (1990) that peoples' *gemeinschaft* aspirations continue to lie with smaller communities, albeit that their local lives might be affected by policies emanating from the European public space. But it is likely that their outlooks would be modified by the experience of interacting with others in that space and it is the case that the Community policies provide such opportunities (see chapters 4 and 8). Common social policies invariably refer to the ambition to harmonize living standards and to create a more solidaristic moral order. Moreover, as mentioned in chapter 1, a consequence of these policies is a set of networks of transnational groups which might have an impact on the development of Heater's multiple loyalties (1991) and which might play the same heuristic role that Richard Titmuss saw in working-class organizations in Britain – that is, modifying immediate, common interests with a wider sense of collectivity and, one should add, pluralism. As noted in chapter 1 and to be discussed later, this must involve a more complex set of loyalties and a more complicated set of institutions than have existed in national systems.

Notes

1 Unlike Hobbes, who was one of the few thinkers who did not believe that women were different from men in the state of nature though he did not carry this over into his theory of politics (Pateman, 1988b).
2 Too often, perhaps, the dissenting theological systems of thought which led to liberal political systems have turned into practices of religion which try to impose conformity and stifle free-thinking.
3 For example, United Nations Declarations and Conventions, the European Convention on Human Rights, International Labour Organization Conventions; though, of course, the content of the UN Declaration owes a lot to the need to include the kinds of rights that enabled the former USSR to become a signatory.
4 Leruez (1978) and Jobert (1978), for example, discuss disillusionment with planning and uncertainty about the social aspects of it in France; Plant (1988, 1991) discusses the rise of a New Right philosophy in the United Kingdom and desires to dismantle social rights.

3
The Constitutional Framework
of Community Rights

Introduction

The European Community (EC) is a new political and legal order which both affects and draws upon the constitutions and laws of the states that constitute it. Although not a federal state, it has some state-like features that are recognizable from accounts of the three, broad state traditions in Western Europe discussed by Dyson (1980). Though Community institutions and law incorporate elements of those traditions, the fact that there are different ways of thinking about the state affects conceptions of the proper nature of public powers in the Community, the roles of its executive and legislative institutions, the relationship between law and politics and that between the common interest and the rights of individual states and individual citizens. European cooperation is also affected by perceptions of national economic interests and particular circumstances in international relations between Member States and in the world at large (George, 1985). Some of these issues have been referred to already and will recur more extensively in chapters 4 and 8.

This chapter concentrates on state and legal matters. It begins by referring to those features of the major state and legal traditions in Western Europe that are relevant to the constitution of the EC and criticisms of it. Then the chapter describes the Community institutions established by the Treaty of Paris and the two Treaties of Rome. This is not exhaustive, there being many other books about them. My purpose is to refer to those features that need to be understood in order to make sense of later chapters. In this section, it is noted that ideas about European integration have veered between supranational and intergovernmental approaches so as to influence the *de facto* distribution of powers among the institutions. Since the ambitions of the founders and the early Commission have been attenuated by the intergovernmentalism of Member States, the principal supranational or federative force in the European order is, or has been, its Court of Justice (ECJ). The Court's development of Community and national law has been particularly significant, compared to that of other institutions, to the idea that there are rights in the Community that exist independently of the state of national legislation. Consequently, this chapter also explains, in its last two sections, the sources and instruments of EC rules through which the Court has developed, with the cooperation of national courts, the doctrine of the primacy of Community law over national law.

Traditions of the State

Dyson's three intellectual and political state traditions (1980) have their representatives in the twelve Member States of the EC; for example, France, Germany and Italy are part of the continental tradition, while Denmark and the United Kingdom are examples of the Scandinavian and Anglo-American traditions, respectively. The basic elements in such categorizations (see also Page, 1990 on Otto Hinze) are patterns of feudal arrangements and receptivity to Roman law. The thesis about the state (for law, see the next section) is that different power relationships between sovereigns and barons in the central and peripheral regions of Europe had an impact on post-feudal institutions of public authority and administration; more centralized and unified power in the continental heartlands, more dispersed and diffuse in the English periphery, as witnessed in the Magna Carta, and something of a hybrid in Scandinavia. This is not to say that broad categories are static or that the traditions within each are alike in all respects. For example, it is sometimes argued that decentralized power in the United Kingdom is more of a myth than a reality, especially in the past decade or more (Ashford, 1978; Harden and Lewis, 1986; Johnson, 1977). And France and Germany, though in the same broad category, have reconciled state power and the advent of mass democracy in different ways. Nevertheless the broad division of types of tradition, particularly the continental and Anglo-American, do represent different modes of thinking about public power and the law and politics that are recognizable in the form of Community institutions and attitudes towards them.

In the continental tradition, the state is both the sum of its parts and more than the sum. To talk of the state is not to list its institutions; the state represents the spirit of the community and is the site of all legitimate power. This is summarized in the German and French cases as the 'social rights' state and the 'policy' or 'public utilities' state, respectively (Dyson, 1980). In the Anglo-American tradition, it is hardly possible to talk of the state in the same way. Here, the state can only be thought of as a list of all the components of institutional authority, legitimate power being dispersed among the centre, regional bodies and groups. Though the trial of Clive Ponting under the Official Secrets Act brought about some sense that it was proper and possible to think of the state as an abstraction that was different from the government of the day, Harden and Lewis (1986) suggest that the nearest equivalent in the United Kingdom to the idea of the state is the Crown-in-Parliament but that this does not capture the inclusiveness of the idea of the state in France and Germany – and other countries in the Community which have similar influences.

This is not to say that absolute power resides in the continental state while the power of the Anglo-American state is limited by the rights or claims of its citizens in the American constitution and the English common law. It may be so in popular conception because of the origins, ideas and innovations of the American revolutionaries and the sovereignty of the representative British parliament on the one hand and because, on the other, the French 'policy' state can be construed, and often is by critics, as the 'police' state (Dyson, 1980) and, moreover, a state in which parliament is weak (Roberts and Lovecy, 1984). On the contrary, the power of the continental state, though great and unified, is defined and delimited according to legal codes which grant powers to, for example, the German constitutional court to declare state actions invalid. In France, such powers are weaker and divided between two bodies. In the UK, the Crown-in-Parliament is said to mean the British are subjects rather than citizens and it is often argued that the executive, even if not really monarchical any more, has considerable freedom from the alleged supremacy of Parliament because of the electoral system and party discipline. In some ways, it is possible to speak of the *de facto* supremacy of the government – as the majority party in Parliament.

Traditions in protecting rights vary considerably. In the UK, rights are secured, at least in theory, through the representation of interests in a democratic parliament, elected by universal suffrage. Although control of the Assembly was a triumph of democracy for the French revolutionaries, its powers were overshadowed by the executive under Napoleon and, according to Dyson (1980), the French have continued to find it difficult to graft the characteristics of mass democracy on to a strong state system. In contrast, the Germans have been able to reconcile the two by integrating party functions into state functions, the Belgians and Dutch by analogous means that pay particular attention to national identities and in Scandinavia interests are reflected in corporate as well as representative institutions. All these forms of representation have their counterparts in the European Community, though it might also be said that it is a regime in which executive policy-making, even in the field of social rights, has tended to prevail over parliamentary representation.

Legal Traditions

As Zweigert and Kotz (1987) point out, the relationship between state traditions and legal approaches is not straightforward. Although political influence may have been dispersed in England, a common or uniform law was developed centrally by the king – so there was no early need to import legal systems in order to bring about uniformity. Scots law was continental, influenced by the French before the Treaty of Union. When the kingdoms of England and Scotland contracted to form Great Britain, it was agreed that two systems that were uniform in each part but differed from one another should coexist. In continental states which were amalgamations of different regions, or principalities, early in France and later in Germany and Italy, it was necessary to consolidate new territories by making different local legal systems uniform with one another. A version of Roman law – in form rather than content – appeared first in France in the codification of various customary laws. The French Code influenced directly and indirectly most other continental legal systems whereas the German Basic Law also owes its existence to the work of legal scholars directly on Roman law. Zweigert and Kotz also explain that, in one sense, legal codes are the same as English common law, with which they are usually contrasted; that is, they are both systems of unified law applying uniformly throughout a given territory. But the English common law also means something different; that is, the principles of equity, developed by judges in the Court of Chancery. This 'judge-made law' forms the basis of the rights held at common law today, rights expressed elsewhere in written constitutions. Statutes emanating from a sovereign parliament have had supremacy since the seventeenth century but are expected to have incorporated the principles of common or equity law.

Whereas civil codes embody separate bodies of law governing private individuals and public authorities, the English common law is the same for all kinds of disputes. Dicey's disapproval of the French system of *droit administratif* as a licence for arbitrariness and his corresponding approval of the absence of a separate body of law to control public powers in the United Kingdom (1959 [1885]) still resonates in political discourse. So, too, does the absence of codified individual rights – though this is changing – on the ground that common law allows new interests to be accommodated flexibly. This is not the place for an account of the extent of quasi-public law overlooked by Dicey and his followers or of defects in it and in the protection of individual rights. The point is simply to contrast the two ways of thinking, though they are converging. That one is about the application of deductive and rationalist principles to particular cases and the other is judge-made law through inductive reasoning in cases and precedents to general principles has been modified by the need to adapt older codes to modern constitutional realities. Like Dyson, Zweigert and Kotz ask whether the end of distinctive national traditions is coming about not only because of domestic circumstances and the cross-fertilization of ideas, but also because of the EC. As noted in connection with state traditions and EC political institutions, it is possible to see embodiments of both legal traditions in the work of the ECJ. The main features of state and legal traditions that need to be remembered as a background to the rest of this chapter are as follows.

First, there is the idea of a state, unified in its institutions and authority, as the source of legislative and executive power compared to the idea of a state as a collection of competing loci of power, regulated but not completely subordinate to the highest political institutions. This pair of ideas helps us to understand, on the one hand, the *dirigiste* and interventionist conceptions of the European communities held by the founding fathers and early Commissioners and, on the other, the fear, associated perhaps most with the British, that the Commission may exercise too much initiative in and control over common affairs. Conversely, it also illuminates the French concern that the existence of Community intervention increasingly rules out the possibility of state intervention (Dutheil de la Rochère and Vandamme, 1988).

Secondly, there is the idea that a state, re-creating the spirit of a community, be it through social rights or public utilities, must do so within a legal framework which sets out first principles of law and the public interest and under which actions may be reviewed in a deductive rationalist manner. This contrasts with the idea of a state, virtually unconstrained by judicial review, which acts by responding to problems from which principles may later be inferred. These two approaches characterize intergovernmental debates about how business is conducted in Community institutions such as the Parliament and the Court of Justice and about the meaning of political union.

Thirdly, there is the continental problem of reconciling state power and mass democracy compared with the Anglo-American facility of adapting the representation of élite interests to accommodate the universal franchise. This is compounded by the difficulty of institutionalizing representation at the common level in ways that are consistent with democracy at home. This is discussed in chapter 8. For the purposes of this chapter, it should be noted that both the continental problem, and the Scandinavian sectoral solution, are reflected in EC consultative procedures. And competing ideas about parliamentary representation are evident in the changing role of the European Parliament.

The Treaties of Paris and Rome: Community Institutions

The initial stage of the EC was the creation of the European Coal and Steel Community (ECSC) in the Treaty of Paris in 1951, followed by a common atomic energy community (Euratom) and the common market, the European Economic Community (EEC) in the Treaties of Rome in 1957. The three communities are now known as the European Community. The treaties have been changed and augmented by subsequent acts and agreements: for example, in 1965 a treaty which established a Single Council and a Single Commission of the European Communities (the 'Merger Treaty') merged institutions but left legal powers as they were laid down in the founding treaties; various Treaties of Accession increased the Member States from six to twelve; and the Single European Act (SEA), agreed in 1985 and effective in 1987, legalized European Political Cooperation and initiated a programme for the completion of the internal market (Single European Market or SEM) by 1992.

The 1991 Maastricht Treaty proposes measures for full economic and monetary union and steps towards political union, the latter including provisions about the powers of institutions and the rights of citizens. Although the Treaty contains many 'opt-outs' for different Member States, the most significant departures from the idea of union being those negotiated by the United Kingdom, ratification of the Treaty is in disarray. A Danish referendum rejected it by a narrow margin; an Irish referendum supported ratification but the legal and political confusion resulting from the Danish vote has unleashed uncertainty in other Member States. The next referendum – in France – resulted in a small majority for the Treaty. In the United Kingdom, complicated calculations of the domestic balance of political forces caused the Labour Party to vote against the government's 'paving bill', ostensibly designed to authorize the continuation of parliamentary scrutiny of the Treaty, though official Labour policy is to support the Treaty and 'opt-in' to the Social Chapter when the Party is re-elected to office. The Conservative Prime Minister, John Major, was obliged to assure dissidents in his own Party that parliamentary procedures would mean that the final decision on UK ratification would not take place until after the outcome of a second referendum in Denmark – to the dismay of his continental partners who believed that he, as President of the European Council, should not imply that the UK position hinged upon that of the most reluctant ratifier. The German Bundestag gave Chancellor Kohl a resounding majority vote for the Treaty in December 1992 but on condition that, like the UK Parliament, the Bundestag could discuss whether convergence criteria for monetary union had been adequately fulfilled and vote upon entry into its final stages. The Bundestag, unlike the UK, also sought and obtained an assurance that provincial organs of government – the Länder – would have co-decision-making powers, through the Bundesrat, over future developments.

It would be a mistake to equate all opposition to specific Maastricht proposals with opposition to integration. This is discussed further in the last chapter. Here, it is necessary to deal with the constitutional uncertainties. A conundrum now exists that is similar to that described in chapter 2 in connection with the United States. The Treaty of Rome – the constitution, as it were, of the EC – requires unanimity in decisions to amend it. Even before the Danish referendum, this requirement, according to some viewpoints, cast doubt on the legality of the 'opt-out' protocols. Since then, it has been argued that the Danish decision has wholly invalidated further union as it is proposed in the Maastricht Treaty. This legal position undermines political solutions proposed by those who wish to push ahead. An early idea was that, as in the case of the Social Protocol of the Treaty where the British were allowed to exclude themselves (see chapter 4), eleven Member States might have an agreement to implement the Maastricht proposals, 'borrowing' Community institutions to do so, while the twelve would continue to operate according to the Treaty of Rome as amended on previous occasions. But, since Maastricht amends the original Treaty so comprehensively, it would have been impossible for eleven to act under the aegis of one and twelve under the other. Except nominally, there would be no Treaty of Rome and the Danes would effectively be excluded from an arrangement of supposedly equal partners. What is hoped to be a legal and political solution was brought by John Major to the final summit of the UK Presidency in December 1992. This is a series of protocols which make exceptions of Denmark on monetary union, foreign policy, citizenship and judicial cooperation – which, it should be noted, are the main 'pillars' of the Treaty. It is hoped that these might be acceptable in a second referendum during an extended ratification period. It had been thought that, from a strictly legal point of view, fundamental amendments would require a re-run of the pre-Maastricht preparations and another summit in which all Member States signed what would be a different Treaty. Even now, some doubt remains, despite assurances from the Community's legal adviser, as to whether the 'decision' or 'declaration' to adopt these changes is legally binding. Though on the eve of the summit the continental partners appeared to be using the legal uncertainty and the Pandora's box of a re-run of the ratification process to cast doubt upon the validity of such a solution, they have accepted the new situation. This is true even of Spain, whose negotiators were among the most vocal of the doubters but who successfully linked the constitutional crisis with a bargain on the cohesion fund for regions; that is, that the richer countries should not insist upon cutting the budget as drastically as they had wanted to, from the level proposed by the Commission. But the Community is not 'out of the woods'; it is not yet clear that what was an extremely contradictory set of Danish objections can possibly be accommodated by this or *any* proposed solution. Whatever the upshot, something like the Maastricht proposals will stay on the agenda. This is discussed in chapter 8. In the meantime, this chapter continues with the institutions which give effect to the 'four freedoms' – the free movement of goods, capital, services and labour. The following account draws primarily on Nugent (1989, 1991).

The European Commission

The powers of the European Commission stem from the ECSC and Euratom treaties and from Articles 155–63 of the EEC Treaty. In each case, the Commission's duty is 'to ensure that the objectives set out in this Treaty are attained in accordance with the provisions thereof'.

The present Commission, responsible for all three treaties, has seventeen Commissioners, two each from France, Germany, Italy and the United Kingdom and one each from other Member States – whose mandates run for four years or, subject to the Maastricht Treaty, five years. This change is proposed so that the Commission and its President may become subject to approval by the European Parliament. This would have an effect on the current difference between theory and practice. Current Treaty rules require national nominees to act as guardians of the common interest; that is, independently of their national governments. The Commissioners are supposed to choose a President from among themselves. In practice, national interests play a part. Presidents are chosen after consultation (and this would continue after Maastricht) which takes place before each new set of Commissioners is known and informal connections between Commissioners and their nominating governments are maintained. Sometimes, this facilitates the reaching of agreement on common policies; sometimes, as in the case of Lord Cockfield, national governments will not renew appointments if 'their' Commissioners stray too far from a national to a Community viewpoint. Commissioners are assisted by *cabinets* and the Commission bureaucracy. Most Commission staff are recruited to career posts on a competitive basis, though attention is paid to the national distribution of staff. The Commission is organized into twenty-three Directorates General of which DG V on Employment, Industrial Relations and Social Affairs (formerly Employment, Social Affairs and Education) is responsible for the policies discussed in this book.

According to Article 155 of the EEC Treaty, the Commission 'shall formulate recommendations or deliver opinions on matters dealt with in this Treaty, if it expressly so provides or if the Commission considers it necessary'. Nugent (1989: 67) points out that this means that the legislative capacity of the Council of Ministers 'is heavily dependent on the ability of the Commission to put proposals before it'. He therefore suggests that the formal powers, combined with the absence of Community equivalents of prime ministers and cabinet ministers, give the Commission a 'major policy initiating role'. It is also responsible for financial management and many executive and regulatory functions, the last two involving monitoring which may lead to infringement proceedings in the Court of Justice against Member States. They also allow delegated rule-making by the Commission which may go beyond 'technical' or 'administrative' and verge on 'policy' law-making (Nugent, 1989: 71–2). In many of these respects, the Maastricht Treaty would give greater powers to the European Parliament (see below).

The Single European Act requires the Commission to exercise its powers and carry out its duties through advisory, management and regulatory committees. Among those that are relevant to this book are committees overseeing equal treatment. There are fourteen, covering not only existing enforceable provisions, but also more 'permissive' policies such as childcare and women's vocational training. The Commission also has to consult the Economic and Social Committee set up under the original Treaties. At the time of the ECSC, such a consultative body was thought necessary because similar consultative arrangements existed in Member States (Germany, for example; neither the UK nor Denmark was a member then) and because it was thought that the Assembly then proposed would not be able to represent effectively the sectoral or sectional interests that would be affected by the new supranational arrangements. Similar concerns lay behind the creation of a common consultative body for Euratom and the EEC. The Economic and Social Committee is composed of national nominees representing three groups; employers, workers and a mixture of small businesses, agriculture, professionals in the private and public sectors, consumers and environmental protection organizations. Generally regarded by most writers as weak despite the constitutional duty of the Commission to consult it, the Committee now has a rival in a European Parliament that is more powerful than it once was.

Nugent (1989: 55) describes the Commission as being rather more and rather less than a civil service of the Community. This is because the Treaties give it greater policy initiation powers than is the case in national civil services, while much routine administration and implementation of EC policies is the responsibility of Member States (problems stemming from this are discussed in chapter 7). The original tone was set in the powers granted to the High Authority of the ECSC conceived of by its founding father, Jean Monnet, as a *dirigiste*, supranational body to articulate and defend the common interest (George, 1985: 4-6). As a planner in the French state, his conception of a European 'public utility' state, as it were, is not surprising. However, George also explains that Jean Monnet's preference for planning and supranational direction was forced to cede to national preferences for the free market, albeit one that crossed national boundaries. The first appointees to the High Authority were chosen from among those whose beliefs would make them unlikely to use the independent powers of the High Authority and, indeed, they did defer to the Council of Ministers. Resigning from the presidency in 1955, Monnet began to focus upon the idea of Euratom which became linked with proposals for a common market. George (1985: 7) points out that dislike of *dirigisme* was carried into these two sets of ideas and this was reflected in the proposed institutions. He points out that, although the basic ECSC High Authority pattern was adopted, the relationship between the Commission and the Council of Ministers was changed so that the Commission was obliged to submit its proposals to the Council of Ministers and, only if they agreed to them, could they become law. Nevertheless, the Commission continued to be led by people like Walter Hallstein

(President) and Sicco Mansholt (Commissioner responsible for agriculture) whose outlooks were similar to Monnet's. But their authority was undermined because, even with an emphasis on the Council of Ministers, the Community with an influential Commission was too much of a rival to the authority of the French state for President de Gaulle who precipitated a crisis in 1965 and boycotted its institutions. Another factor which may have contributed to a decline in the supranational leadership of the Community was a weakening of a sense of European purpose among the Commission's staff. George (1985: 13) argues that it was not until Roy Jenkins became President in 1975 that the Commission began to reassert some independence. Now, of course, President Jacques Delors is well known for his commitment to European Union and for the difference between his outlook and that of recent governments in the United Kingdom on the need for common policies instead of national ones. His period of office has coincided with the development of the idea of 'subsidiarity', a concept whose origins and meanings are full of contradictions (Harden, 1991a; Spicker, 1991). In the Maastricht Treaty, it means that 'the Community will act only if and in so far as the objectives of the proposed action cannot be sufficiently achieved by national governments. Any action by the Community shall not go beyond what is necessary to achieve the objectives of the Treaty' (Commission, 1991d; see also chapters 3 and 8).

Even though many writers agree that there was a shift from supranational to intergovernmental decision-making between 1965 and 1975, and – despite the presidency of Roy Jenkins – even beyond, policy continued to be very dependent on initiatives by the Commission. Moreover, Commission agreement is needed by the Council, unless there is a unanimous vote, before the Treaties can be amended (Article 149). And it is necessary for there to be a body that can respond on a regular basis to changing circumstances (Nugent, 1989: 70, 87). It is important to note that Article 155 refers not only to specific Treaty objectives but also to other actions that the Commission considers necessary, in the light of circumstances, for the realization of Community goals. It is on this basis, for example, that the Commission has been able to issue Directives on equal pay for work of equal value and equal treatment in recruitment, training and social security when the Treaty of Rome itself refers only to equal pay for the same work (Article 119). In the general field of social policy, both Commissioners and staff do take the lead over national governments in circumstances that are explained in later chapters of this book. This is not to say that their scope is unreined; the Commission is subject to scrutiny by the Court of Auditors and has to cooperate with the other institutions discussed below.

The Council of Ministers

Articles 145–154 of the EEC Treaty make the Council of Ministers the final decision-making body of the Community. But its legislative capacities are restricted by its relationship to other Community institutions. Its legislation must be based on proposals submitted by the Commission and it must seek advice from the Economic and Social Committee and the European Parliament (rather more than advice from the latter, if the Maastricht Treaty is ratified, see below). However, it can contribute to policy initiation under Article 152 which enables it to 'request the Commission to undertake any studies the Council considers desirable for the attainment of the common objectives, and to submit to it any appropriate proposals' (Nugent, 1989: 89).

Under the formal terms of the Merger Treaty, there is only one Council of Ministers composed of one Minister from each Member State. In practice, there are several 'sectoral' Councils as different Ministers attend for different kinds of meetings, of which there are about eighty a year. The General Council is attended by Foreign Ministers and 'Technical' Councils by appropriate other Ministers, such as Agriculture. The Social Affairs and Employment Council meets about twice a year. The Presidency of the Council rotates amongst the Member States and the duties of the office give considerable control over agenda-setting and progress (Nugent, 1989: 92–3, 107–8). As in the case of the Commission, incumbents of the Council presidency have had an impact on social affairs (see chapter 4). Both President and Council are assisted by the General Secretariat, a Community service, and by national delegations and various committees and working groups.

The heads of national delegations (embassies, as it were, to the European Community) and their deputies meet in the Committee of Permanent Representatives (COREPER). There was no constitutional provision for COREPER in the Treaty of Paris but the Treaties of Rome acknowledged what had been happening informally and Article 4 of the Merger Treaty gives it the responsibility of preparing the work of the Council. This means that it receives Commission proposals, first seen in committees described below, and considers the areas of agreement and disagreement likely to be encountered at ministerial level (Nugent, 1989: 84, 99). The matters considered in this book are dealt with mainly by a less senior COREPER composed of deputy permanent representatives.

COREPER can have a significant effect on the content of proposals during this 'filtering' stage and has had on Directives on women's rights (Hoskyns, 1985, 1986; Hoskyns and Luckhaus, 1989).

Of the network of committees and working groups, the one that deals with employment (the Standing Committee on Employment) is unusual in being composed not of national officials but of sectional interests (Nugent, 1989: 95). Its meetings, where Commission proposals are first considered, are also attended by the relevant Commissioner and the President of the Council of Ministers who generally prepares a paper for the subsequent Council meeting.

Decision-making conventions at the apex of this structure, that is, the Council of Ministers, are of three types: unanimity, qualified majority voting and simple majority voting. The first is required over matters that involve new policies or developments of existing ones that are not explicitly in the treaties (i.e., most sex equality policies) and when the Council wants to amend Commission proposals against the wishes of the Commission. The others are used in decisions to implement or clarify existing policy. As a result of the Single European Act, qualified majority voting is used in many measures (but not workers' rights) designed to bring about the Single European Market. Under the qualified system, France, Germany, Italy and the United Kingdom have ten votes, Spain has eight, Belgium, Greece, the Netherlands and Portugal have five, Denmark and Ireland have three and Luxembourg has two. No one large state (or coalition of them) can outvote the smaller states because a majority of fifty-four is required. Nugent (1989: 102–4) suggests that decisions are rarely pushed to a vote and that the popularly termed 'veto' on issues requiring unanimity is applied sparingly, decisions being postponed until some kind of consensus can be reached. In the social field, however, the use or threat of the veto has *not* been sparing (see chapters 4 and 6). The possibility of vetoing was precipitated by President de Gaulle's boycott of Community institutions in 1965 because of what he considered to be too supranational an approach in agriculture. His return was the occasion of the Luxembourg Compromise in 1966 when it was agreed that, when a government considered a vital interest to be at stake, it could insist that discussion continue until there were revised proposals which could command unanimous support; in effect, a veto. Although better implementation is likely to follow agreements willingly reached, a state may abuse its power to define an issue as a vital interest (Nugent, 1989: 182–3). Even majority voting can mean that general progress is tempered by that of the slowest (1989: 105) – as President Delors has found in respect of the social dimension of the Single European Market.

According to most writers, it was once expected that the Council of Ministers would develop supranational characteristics. In one sense, it might be argued to have taken over such a role from the Commission through its increasing use of powers granted by Article 152 of the EEC Treaty. But, in practice, it uses this power to behave like an intergovernmental body in which perceptions of national interest play a significant part. The intergovernmental character of the Council of Ministers has been evident in its inability to achieve cohesion where there are national disagreements over common policy areas. Ministers are often not able to reach agreement without referring back to national cabinets. Moreover, there has been a tendency for agreements over areas not in the treaties to be reached on an intergovernmental basis, outside the Community's regulatory framework. Both these features are relevant to the development of the European Council.

The European Council

The European Council (not to be confused with the Council of Europe) is the one principal institution that has no foundation in the original treaties. The occasional meetings of heads of government that took place in the 1960s and early 1970s became authorized in 1974 but, even then, the communiqué from the Paris summit did not make such meetings part of the legal-institutional framework nor was the European Council incorporated into the treaties by the Single European Act in 1986. Nevertheless, both documents refer briefly to its membership and role. Associated most publicly with European Political Cooperation (the Community's common foreign policy), its origins lie in the features mentioned above: the weakening of the Commission by the intergovernmental approach symbolized in the Luxembourg Compromise; the inability of the Council of Ministers to provide authoritative leadership; the 'sectoralization' of the Council; and the convention of proceeding by unanimity. For the sake of effectiveness within the Community and abroad, a new source of cohesion was necessary.

Composed of heads of governments, (usually) foreign ministers, the President of the Commission and one Commissioner, all accompanied by a few officials, the European Council meets at least twice a year. Intended to give strategic direction and to deal with deadlocks and without any treaty rules about its responsibilities, it is free to determine its own activities but, if it intends

Community action to follow from its agreements, this has to go through normal procedures (Nugent, 1989: 171–5). In matters related to this book, the European Council has inspired action on the direct election of Members of the European Parliament, and contributed, through the Single European Act, to a more federal and integrated Community (majority voting and the internal market programme), and, in summits in 1989, 1990 and 1991, to European Union. Notwithstanding its agreements on integrative steps, it has been argued that the development of the European Council also represents a shift away from supranationalism to intergovernmental relations. For example, the European Monetary System exists because of intergovernmental agreement and cooperation outside, for the time being, the formal auspices of the Community. Similarly, the Schengen Agreement on the abolition of internal frontiers and subsequent intergovernmental conventions about the control of external borders are multilateral policies, not common policies subject to scrutiny and review by Community institutions. Strictly speaking, the way the eleven propose to proceed with the Social Chapter of the Maastricht Treaty in the absence of the United Kingdom is intergovernmental or multi-lateral, though the protocol allows them to 'borrow' Community institutions. On the other hand, the Commission, unlike the Parliament, has acquired a reasonably significant role in the deliberations of the European Council; indeed, the views of Vasso Papandreou (Commissioner in charge of DG V) and President Delors have been prominent in intergovernmental discussion of the Social Charter[1] and European Union.

The European Parliament (Assembly)

The Treaty of Paris set up an Assembly for the ECSC which, in 1962, called itself the European Parliament. Its first members were nominated by national parliaments and often held a dual mandate. Plans for direct elections were called for under Article 138 of the EEC Treaty of Rome. This contributed to the crisis of 1965, noted above. For President de Gaulle, direct elections were another unwelcome step away from the unity of the French Republic, and Denmark and the United Kingdom, despite stronger attachments to parliamentary representation, came to share his view (Nugent, 1989: 120–1). Nor could the Council agree upon a common elec-toral system. It was not until 1979 that the first elections were held and, although agreement was reached that they should be held every five years, they are carried out by different means in different countries (this will end if the Maastricht Treaty is ratified). As well as becoming more legitimate by being elected, the Parliament has also acquired more formal powers through amendments to budgetary and consultative processes in the 1970s and through the Single European Act. Further powers to supervise the Commission and to legislate with the Council of Ministers are proposed in the Maastricht Treaty (see chapter 8).

The 518 MEPs are mostly elected on proportional representation systems which bring about a correspondence of votes cast and seats gained but, in order for smaller countries not to be swamped, the size of constituencies varies enormously with, for example, one MEP per 750,000 inhabitants in Germany and one per 66,000 in Luxembourg. In the election of June 1989, ninety-five women (18.3%) were returned. Once elected, MEPs organize themselves into transnational groupings that reflect 'families' of national parties and ideologies. The business that they carry out is arranged by the President of the Parliament, elected for a two-and-a-half-year term, vice-presidents and the leaders of the political groupings. Much of the work that the Parliament does is done in eighteen permanent committees and *ad hoc* ones set up for special purposes. Those most relevant to the issues in this book are the committees on Legal Affairs and Citizens' Rights, Social Affairs and Employment and Women's Rights. In addition to developing parliamentary initiatives which MEPs hope the Commission may take up, these committees are the first place in which Commission proposals for Council legislation are considered; it is required by treaty and case law that Opinions from the Parliament are known before final decisions are taken by Council. Parliament as a whole not only considers reports on proposals from committees but may also make budget allocations for policy items that have not been proposed in the hope or expectation that the Commission and Council will then try to provide a legal basis. Although, on the whole, the Council need not take account of parliamentary Opinions, the Single European Act requires that those provisions relating to the completion of the internal market over which the Council is obliged to develop a common position must be referred back to the Parliament for a second reading. Nugent argues (1989: 112, 116–20) that these new cooperation procedures and amendments to the budgetary processes (all of which would be strengthened by the Maastricht Treaty – see chapter 8) provide more opportunities for the Parliament to have its views taken seriously by the Council and Commission. While, in his view, the Commission is likely to be more sympathetic than the Council to the Parliament's ideas, neither body is firmly susceptible to parliamentary control and supervision; the former because matters of detail are often for national implementation, the latter, not only because it may choose not to attend to parliamentary amendments, but also because it is an intergovernmental body of ministers who are accountable to national parliaments.

Just as there is a view that there were 'democracy deficits' in the strong continental states, sometimes only more-or-less rectified, many people argue that the European Parliament is similarly defective. Low turn-outs in the European elections are explained by reference to its having less power than national parliaments, making it more of an advisory body than a legislature. However, the practical powers of many parliaments are less than constitutions sometimes indicate and, combined with changes in the role of the European Parliament over the past twenty years, this means that the distinction is less significant than is often supposed (Nugent, 1989: 141). Moreover, the European Parliament is becoming as much a focus of lobbyists as the Commission, a factor which suggests that it must have some influence. This is likely to increase if and when it is empowered to supervise the Commission more closely. Vallance and Davies (1986) argue that it played a significant role in the promotion of women's equality policies, although social policy suffers from the fact that its committees do not always speak with the same voice (Interview). It can be argued, however, that the Parliament's promotion of sex equality appeared to be effective because the Commission found it convenient, for reasons of legitimacy, to be seen to be responding to a popular institution – at least, up to a point (see chapters 4 and 6). The Parliament felt obliged to pass motions condemning the Council of Ministers' rejection of further steps on sex equality and threatened to disapprove the budget if the Commission were to go on diluting the Social Charter – which it was doing in order to try to keep the UK on board.

The Court of Justice of the European Communities (ECJ) and the Court of the First Instance

If the Commission is the guardian of the Community, this is a role that it shares with the ECJ, and Parliament's imperfect capacity to control the Community's governing institutions is buttressed by the Court. Its duties are contained in Articles 164–170 of the EEC Treaty, Article 136 of Euratom and Article 31 of the ECSC; that is, 'to ensure that in the interpretation and application of this Treaty the law is observed'. Under the Single European Act, it has been supplemented by a Court of the First Instance which began its duties at the end of 1989.

Situated in Luxembourg (it is the European Court of Human Rights that is at Strasbourg), the Court of Justice is composed of thirteen judges and six Advocates General who analyse and prepare cases for consideration by the judges. The new Court of the First Instance has twelve judges. According to treaty provision, judges and Advocates General are supposed to be appointed for six-year terms, as the result of 'common accord' among the Member States; in practice, only one is, since twelve of the thirteen senior judges in the main Court are nominated by governments and automatically accepted (Nugent, 1989: 160–1). The judges elect one of themselves to be President of the Court for three years.

In carrying out its duties, the ECJ provides a means of controlling Community institutions and fostering common policies by influencing national laws. It does so through hearing three types of cases; those brought to it in its capacity as an administrative staff tribunal, direct actions and references for preliminary rulings.

As an administrative staff tribunal, the Court controls Community institutions, not in their capacity as regional organs of government, as it were, but as employers. It is perhaps ironic that these institutions have been brought before the Court almost as many times as the United Kingdom for breaches of those sex equality principles that the Commission itself devised as common European standards.

Direct actions are disputes heard and settled directly in the ECJ. The main forms of direct action are specified in Articles 169–70, 173 and 175 of the EEC Treaty. They may be brought against a Member State by the Commission or, less usually, by another Member State, alleging failure to fulfil obligations under or arising from the treaties; against the Commission by the Council or a Member State and against the Council by the Commission or a Member State, alleging failure to act upon treaty requirements; against the Commission or Council (and, as a result of case law, the Parliament) by one another or a Member State, calling for an annulment of action on grounds of lack of powers. Compared to preliminary rulings, direct actions are rare because procedures exist to encourage the resolution of disputes before matters reach the Court. But in the field of sex equality, there have been some notable actions against Member States both actually heard and withdrawn only at the last minute when agreement was reached (see chapter 6). In education, part of a Commission case was dismissed on grounds of procedural improprieties (see chapter 5). It was because of the Court that the Council of Ministers was finally forced to fulfil treaty requirements for direct elections to the European Parliament.

References for preliminary rulings are provided for by Article 177 of the EEC Treaty. National courts may request rulings from the ECJ when there are uncertainties in interpreting Community law (often in relation to domestic statutes; see below and further discussion in chapter 7). The ECJ does not make a substantive judgement about the particular case before a national court; it must answer the questions of interpretation put to it by national judges. The answers then form part of a further hearing in the national courts.

Because of increasing business and delays, straightforward cases have begun to be heard in chambers and, now, in the Court of the First Instance and its chambers. Originally conceived of as a place for the resolution of competition disputes, matters stemming from the ECSC Treaty and staff cases, the Court of the First Instance started life primarily as an administrative tribunal. All cases heard by it carry the right of appeal on points of law to the senior Court.

Nugent (1989: 142–3) explains that, like states, the European Community has to have an enforceable legal framework; without it effective Community decision-making would be impossible. And, in this respect, the EC 'state' is, indeed, a supranational one, its legally enforceable framework distinguishing it from all other international organizations. There are channels for statements of national interest in that governments, whether or not parties to a dispute, can enter submissions for consideration during cases. But so too can the Commission. The Court has acted like a constitutional court of a 'European state', as it were, not only by controlling the executive actions of its governing institutions and the Community's equivalent of statutes (Regulations and Directives; see next section) but also by using Treaty law, the equivalent of a written constitution, to do so. In carrying out its work, the Court draws upon common continental traditions in which law and politics are linked more explicitly than in the British version of the separation of powers. It also draws on legal methods and principles that are unusual in most Member States but are familiar in the United Kingdom; for example, precedents and certainty.

Although the ECJ is not strictly a constitutional court in respect of national legislation, its rulings have had the effect of review of national statutes and it is generally agreed that its rulings have contributed to the harmonization of national laws in various policy fields, including the social. The main impact of the Court, according to Nugent (1989: 150), has been in human rights, an area on which the Treaties are relevantly silent.

Sources and Instruments of Community Law: the
Relationship between Community and National Law

In addition to the Treaty provisions regulating institutions, others provide a kind of written constitution for Community policies. Nugent (1991: 168) points out that this makes the EC constitution different from national constitutions which do not usually regulate policies, except in terms of broad principle. Nevertheless, it can be said that Treaty policy articles do provide something like the general framework within which detailed policies are operationalized that has been recommended for the United Kingdom by, for example, Lord Scarman (1979). For our purposes, the most significant Treaty articles are those in the EEC Treaty that deal with the principles of free movement without discrimination (Articles 3, 7, 48), living standards (Articles 2, 117) and equal pay (Article 119) and those that refer to actions to be taken (e.g., Articles 118, 49–66). Some Treaty articles have 'direct effect' (see below) in the national courts. Article 119 on equal pay, being clear and unambiguous, has been ruled to be of this type (see chapter 6). Other Treaty articles have to be given effect through Community or national legislation; that is, by Regulations and Directives which are binding, and Decisions and Recommendations. Decisions are often about administrative matters; for example, requiring Member States to inform the Community about their vocational training programmes. Recommendations, though they are sometimes referred to in the ECJ, have usually been regarded as having no legal force;[2] for example, compliance with the Recommendation on Positive Action (see chapter 6) is treated as voluntary by Member States.

Social security and assistance for migrant workers are implemented by Regulations; workers' consultative rights and sex equality are covered by Directives (see chapters 5 and 6). Regulations contain details about the implementation of Community policy, are binding in their entirety (mainly) and, in Community language, are 'directly applicable' in the Member States without the need for national implementation measures. This produces what are usually known as 'direct effects', meaning they can be invoked by plaintiffs in national courts (Steiner, 1988; Usher, 1981). Directives call for the 'approximation' of national laws to meet specific Community objectives but allow this to be achieved by way of different national procedures. As such, they are addressed to national governments, requiring them to take the necessary steps. Thus, Directives are not applicable in the same way as Regulations. But parts of Directives which contain unambiguous policy objectives can also produce 'direct effects' and may be relied upon by plaintiffs in national courts in the absence of enabling legislation (or where national legislation is defective) after the expiry of implementation time limits (Steiner, 1988; Usher, 1981). This is not the same as being 'directly applicable' because governments can still, and ought to, legislate to give effect. It is 'a subsidiary remedy for individuals to counter the possibility of a state relying on its own failure to act' (Usher, 1981: 25). Whereas Regulations may impose duties on private individuals as well as governments ('horizontal effects'), Directives, being directions to governments to take action, have 'vertical effects'. Some significant consequences of these distinctions for social policy are discussed in chapter 7.

Development of the Supremacy of Community Law and its Applicability to States and Individuals

The idea that Community law creates rights and obligations in respect of states and individuals was first expressed in a reference in 1962 for a preliminary ruling (26/62 van Gend en Loos v Nederlandse Administratie der Belastingen; Usher, 1981: 20–1). The question from the Dutch courts was whether Article 12 of the Rome Treaty was 'directly applicable'. The ECJ answered that it was 'directly effective' because of its view that the question also raised the issue of whether nationals could claim individual rights under Community law. The Dutch, Belgian and German governments all argued that alleged breaches of Treaty obligations (stemming, in this case, from bilateral tariff changes after the entry into force of the EEC Treaty) should be resolved by institutions. In its reasoning, the Court held that the Treaty was more than an agreement that created obligations among states and that it called upon nationals to cooperate in enforcing the law. States had acknowledged that there was a need to place a duty upon the Court to ensure uniform interpretation of it. All these factors meant that a new legal order had been created which limited sovereign rights in certain areas and that Member States *and* their nationals were subjects of that order. In other words, obligations were imposed on Member States, Community institutions and individuals which gave rise to correlative rights which national courts were bound to uphold. Subsequent cases applied similar principles to cases arising from Regulations and parts of Directives (e.g. 41/74 van Duyn v Home Office; Usher, 1981: 22–4).

Such cases, then, give private individuals a role in safeguarding the Community's 'public interest' by contributing, through their cases, to the supervision of the actions of Member States and

Community institutions (Usher, 1981: 27). The effects of such judgements confirm, as Marbury v Madison did in the United States in 1803, the ultimate powers of review of the ECJ over national legislation as well as Community rules and action. This was explicit in 1964 when the Court said that the special and original nature of EC treaty law could not be overridden by national law without depriving the Community of its very foundations (6/64 Costa v ENEL; Usher, 1981: 30). This has been repeated often, and was forcefully so in 1978 (106/77 Italian Finance Administration v Simmenthal; Usher, 1981: 30).

Usher argues that there has been general acceptance of the supremacy of Community law and the constitutional function of the ECJ, even in the United Kingdom with its doctrine that Acts of Parliament cannot be overturned in the courts (but see note 3 in chapter 7 about a case heard recently in the UK). In other countries, of course, it is more common for legislation to be reviewed, though there were technical difficulties, now resolved, as to which level of judiciary was entitled to rule on inconsistencies between national and Community rules. In the United Kingdom, it has been accepted, with some doubts, that the European Communities Act (with its formula that all relevant legislation passed is to be construed as subject to the European Communities Act) is equivalent to acts which transfer power to former colonies; that is, that the EC Act is, in theory, reversible by a sovereign parliament, in practice, conditioned by political reality (Usher, 1981: 35–8; for similar arguments about other constitutional-type statutes, see Lock, 1989). As Usher points out, the reality of EC politics in the UK is that transfers of power back to the British Parliament would take place, not by laws being passed that were deliberately inconsistent with Community rules, but through negotiation – as, indeed, has happened over Maastricht.

The transfer of powers to a wider arena to regulate the duties and rights of states and nationals is not, however, unconstrained. Apart from the limits to the scope of the treaties themselves, the ECJ has ruled that certain guarantees have been transferred along with the powers. Usher (1981: 38) explains that this has come about as a result of questions arising from countries that have constitutionally guaranteed rights, as in the German Basic Law, and the possibility that EC rules may be incompatible. In such cases, the ECJ has examined the constitutions of the various Member States (and the European Convention on Human Rights) and reached conclusions about whether and how far EC provisions are seriously at variance with commonly guaranteed fundamental liberties; the Maastricht Treaty proposes that consistency with the

European Convention on Human Rights (ECHR) be formalized. It is through the Court's acknowledgement of the force of national constitutional law and conventions that it has developed the principle of legal certainty to justify restrictions on the effects of Community law and executive action (see chapters 5 and 7). It also takes account of international treaty law (Usher, 1981: 41–2) in connection with international agreements, such as the ECHR, which involve EC and non-EC countries; and bilateral agreements between EC and non-EC countries, though those between two Member States themselves are subordinate to Community law (for example, van Gend en Loos above).

Before discussing how this new legal order has affected the acquisition and implementation of social rights, it is necessary to explain how a social dimension came to be in the EC in the first place. This is the subject of the next chapter.

Notes

1   A Social Charter was appended in 1962 to the European Convention on Human Rights. The title of the Community's popularly called Social Charter is given in its Action Programme as: The Community Charter of Basic Social Rights for Workers (Commission, 1989c).

2   Nielsen and Szyszczak (1991: 127) draw attention to a recent ruling which may mean that measures that were thought to be non-binding might have effects in national courts.

4

Economic and Social Cooperation

Introduction

In chapters 1 and 2, I referred to two bodies of literature which I now discuss again because they are helpful in illuminating the growth of social policy in the European Community (EC). One is concerned with the development of national welfare states and the other is about theories of integration. By drawing on the former, I am not arguing that the EC is inevitably developing like or into a state. As noted earlier, the institutions of the Community have some state-like features and all that is being said here is that some elements of its social policy innovations have come about as a result of economic forces, political relationships and bureaucratic traditions that are similar to those identified in the literature as significant in the origins and expansion of welfare states. Policy-making in the EC, however, also takes place in a context that is quite different from that surrounding national welfare developments; that is, policy initiation, expansion and administration is also intergovernmental, bearing the hallmarks of national as well as common interests. This means that it is necessary to explain the different assumptions and expectations held by various architects and developers of Community economic and social policies. These rest – explicitly or implicitly – on different theories of European integration and it is through the interplay of different visions that compromises have been reached upon substantive policies. This chapter begins with accounts of welfare states, by no means comprehensive but paying particular attention to those features of analyses that are most relevant to social policy at the Community level. The chapter then outlines the theories of integration, showing that the approach which became dominant was not one in which a common social policy could flourish readily. Nevertheless, as the third section argues, the political contest over whether there should be a social dimension to the Community did not disappear. Here, it is argued that it was in the resolution of competing ideas about the nature of integration and the relationship between economic and social affairs that sex equality became a significant element of Community policy. Although the language of workers' rights is used now in the so-called Social Charter (see note 1 in chapter 3) and citizens rights in the Maastricht Treaty[1] the argument of this chapter is that social policy was not thought of by politicians in terms of establishing entitlements but in terms of removing anomalies and increasing the Community's legitimacy. This is in line with some theories of national welfare states in which welfare is functional to order and can be provided or not as is considered necessary. It is also compatible with the view that a limited theory of integration provides the best explanation of developments in the EC. Other theories about national development hold that, where welfare provision is thought of in terms of entitlements or rights, it is difficult for laissez-faire governments to dismantle them, even if elected on such a platform. In the European context, the translation from contingent provision to entitlement has been made most forcefully by the Court of Justice of the European Communities (ECJ) and this is discussed more fully in later chapters. For the purposes of this one, it is enough to note that it is partly because of the Court that social policy has come out of the realm of 'low politics', the only sphere, according to some theories of integration, where agreement is possible, into the realm of 'high politics' where union is unlikely. The difficulty of raising expectations by calling social provisions 'rights' and, by so doing, bringing them into an arena of political contest is discussed further in chapter 7.

Welfare State Developments

By tradition concerned with how social policies improve or harm social relations and the relationship between citizen and state, the welfare state literature also attends to systems and typologies: categorizing actual states by reference to their institutional features and particular arrangements for implementation; and categorizing types of explanation of the origin and expansion of welfare states. The main accounts of the origins of welfare states are neatly summarized by Skocpol (1988) as: the logic of industrialism (for which she cites Wilensky); national values or political culture (exemplified for Skocpol by Rimlinger and for King (1987a) by Stephens, Heclo and Taylor-Gooby); functional for capitalism (exemplified for Skocpol by Gough, O'Connor, Offe, Marklund and Mishra); and the social democratic model (exemplified for Skocpol by Korpi and Stephens and for King also by Epsing-Andersen). An alternative kind of explanation, based on Weber, is provided by Friedman (1981); since it is about the juridification of rights, it is discussed in chapter 7.

The first of Skocpol's types of explanation is a thesis that industrialization and urbanization need human capital development and make it more difficult for families to care for dependants, both inviting state intervention in education and the provision of health and social services and leading to convergence among countries with similar patterns of economic development. Dye (1975) includes employment and civil rights policies among those whose presence can be explained in the light of levels of development. That convergence of welfare and rights policies will automatically take place is disputed by Skocpol's second school. Rimlinger (1971) argues that different political traditions are warmer or cooler hosts to welfare innovations, paternalism explaining the pioneering position of Germany and laissez-faire liberalism making Americans resistant to the loss of the idea of self-help. Taylor-Gooby (1982, 1983b) argues that within one system different types of provision are more or less approved of because of attachments to both market and state-sponsored solutions. National and cross-national studies indicate that, although similar formal rights may exist – for example, to workers' compensation and in abortion laws – the ability of citizens to claim them varies according to the values of providers, the structures through which they operate and the influence and activities of groups and political parties in turning legal entitlements into tangible benefits (e.g., Lovenduski and Outshoorn, 1986; Norris, 1987; Thompson, 1981). These points are relevant to chapter 7 on the equal protection of the laws.

Capitalist development theories, like the logic of industrialism theories, are materialist but concentrate not on the transition to industrialization but on developments within capitalism. In these, the argument is similar in conception to the political criticisms, referred to in chapter 2, of liberal, legal and political rights. The welfare critique is that the state is increasingly required to promote accumulation and legitimacy. The two objectives have contradictory pressures on public expenditure but can come together, for a time at least, in policies that may simultaneously divert from individual employers some of the direct costs of reproducing suitable workforces and, through making the system seem fair, maintain social order. As noted in chapter 2, there is an argument that the development of the EC can be explained by the increasing inability of nation-states on their own to combine such objectives.

More empirically testable theories about national welfare states are proposed by those who attribute the welfare state to the growing strength of organized labour, but both Skocpol and King point out that there is very little evidence to support this social-democratic school in connection with the *origins* of welfare states.

Both point out that organized labour had very little active part in early innovations – that is, before the 1930s – though their presence had to be taken account of by élites. What Skocpol does argue, which is important to understanding the EC, is that bureaucratic and political structures and the interests and attitudes of public officials were critical in the timing and form of early welfare innovations. These are equally important in the young EC, as will be shown below. Both she and King argue that such factors remained important in the expansionary period of national welfare states after the 1930s but that it was also in this period that organized labour and their political representatives became more influential. Both deny that explanations of bureaucratic interest in welfare inspired by the public choice school of political economy stand up themselves. The latter propose that commitment to policy programmes is attributable to the defence of private interests in the public realm, through employment and security of tenure. For the former, this may play a part but there are other factors. For example, though the growth of public sector unionism may involve the cooperative pursuit of private interests, it also affects ideologies, encouraging collectivism and commitment to welfare. Together, unionism and approval of state-sponsored welfare make it likely that there will be cross-class alliances among professional administrators, clerical and manual public sector workers and a large number of recipients of services (including other middle-class citizens who may benefit more than the working class from the welfare state, see Le Grand, 1991). The breadth of such alliances makes it difficult for laissez-faire governments to devalue or dismantle welfare states (see also Foster, 1991, on evidence of this in opposition to privatization). As will be seen in this chapter, ideological attachments and alliance building among like-minded people are an important part of the story of Community social policy.

Before turning to theories of integration, it is perhaps worth mentioning the related, so-called 'new institutionalist' school. Like other welfare state theorists, they note that the arrival of the welfare state meant that it was no longer possible, as it once was, to make a sharp distinction between economic and socio-political affairs (King, 1987a; Steinmo et al., 1992). The consequences of the intermeshing worry politicians – particularly in the United Kingdom – of right and left; sometimes because of the control, benevolently exercised or not, that it affords the state over citizens, or because of what seems an unlimited personal dependency which has adverse effects on morality and the public purse. The response of the left to the ideas of the new right involves the possibility of redefining state–economy relations through workers' and citizens' rights along the lines of Scandinavian notions of citizenship and the modern German concept of the social-rights state. Both of these are thought to be devoid of the inequality of respect and the demeaning class ideology to which the British system is susceptible (Parker, 1975). The democratic socialism of the British Labour Party is taking on tones of continental social democratic parties and it now appears to be a more willing partner in Community alliances to promote a system of rights for European workers – in contrast to the post-Thatcher Conservative Party which emphasizes consumer rights in domestic industries and services.

Theories of Integration

George (1985, ch. 2) assesses the political power and analytic utility of three theories of European integration which guided advocates of a new European order or served observers as methods of understanding. These are: federalism, functionalism and neofunctionalism (or federal-functionalism). The first includes what Nugent describes as the political idealism of the utopian visionaries (1989: 11). Immediately after the Second World War, some people thought that unlimited nationalism was the cause of twentieth-century conflicts of tragic proportions. According to another strand of thought, Europe had always been a natural community, a community unnaturally interrupted but now capable of rediscovery. The idea of resuscitating a common destiny motivated Altiero Spinelli, one of the major founders of European integration (Nugent, 1989: 9), and the feeling that it had never quite been forgotten inspired Walter Hallstein, the first President of the European Commission (Nugent, 1989: 12). A federalist movement believed that, if federal European institutions were created, national loyalties would become European loyalties and this would bring about a natural federation (George, 1985: 17). In the same period, governments' perceptions of national interests – in reestablishing respectability after fascism, in consolidating liberal democracy in Western Europe in the face of communism in the East, in achieving economic recovery and growth in a world of increasing interdependence – appeared to flow in the same direction. Both internationalism and national interests contributed to agreements on the founding of the forerunner of the Organization for Economic Cooperation and Development (OECD), the Council of Europe and the European Convention on Human Rights (ECHR). But these innovations were pale reflections of the

federalist hopes of the idealists and indicated to Jean Monnet and
Robert Schuman (George, 1985: ch. 2) that ultimate integration
could be achieved only if frontal assaults on national sovereignties
were avoided in the early stages. Their plan for the European Coal
and Steel Community (ECSC) combined elements of federalism
and functionalism. It was 'a start', a 'basis for building the
concrete achievement of a supranational regime within a limited
but controlling area of economic effort'. It was an 'abnegation of
sovereignty in a limited but decisive field', possible because of a
common interest in re-establishing what, at the time, was a key
element in industrial re-development (Monnet, quoted by Nugent,
1989: 31–2). Chancellor Konrad Adenauer also saw its ultimate
importance as political not economic (Nugent, 1989: 32), but it was
to begin with the common direction of a common functional need.

George points out that functionalism of the type pioneered in
American political science, notably by Mitrany, is, like federalism,
concerned with how interdependence might be used to resolve the
problem of conflict (1985: 20). He describes functionalist integration as discerning and advocating the growth of *separate* international agencies, specializing and providing authority in specific
areas – a kind of international institutional pluralism which, like
national pluralism in Robert Dahl's political theory, is incapable of
giving rise to cohesive ruling power. States would be less and less
able to take independent action because they would be locked into
a web of separate international activities and agencies. But, unlike
the situation envisaged by the federalists, power would be dispersed
and interdependence would not lead to a single supra-state exercising authority over the whole range of normal public activity. As is
obvious in the Monnet quotes above, his neo-functionalism
contains an 'expansive logic of integration' (Haas, quoted by
George, 1985: 21) which *does* lead to political unification within a
single regime. George explains this as follows: the creation of a
common market needs the abolition of tariff barriers among
members; this can only work fully if national controls over
exchange rates are surrendered; this in turn diminishes the
possibility of using national instruments to control domestic
economies; moreover, a common external tariff impinges on
general external relations, encouraging a search for a common
foreign policy (European Political Cooperation or EPC); foreign
policy is increasingly difficult to distinguish from defence, or at
least security, policy. Thus, technical 'spill-overs' mean that a
common market leads to monetary union which leads to full
economic and political union. Other kinds of political 'spill-overs'
also occur. With economic integration, interest group activity

moves to the Community level; this increases the understanding of activists of the benefits of integration and the dysfunctions of remaining barriers; this leads to demands for further integration and interest groups themselves serve as bulwarks against any retreating by national governments. According to the theory, this will happen spontaneously but can be stimulated and encouraged by Community institutions. According to George, Walter Hallstein was prepared to accept that role and he and his staff behaved accordingly in the early years of the EC (1985: 23–4).

George argues that the Mitrany approach has been a robust predictor of what has happened in the Community in that functional integration in one area has encouraged functional integration in another, albeit not in a multiplicity of organizations. But, like Aron, his view is that the optimistic assumptions of the neo-functionalists about political 'spill-overs' have not been borne out by experience. Further integration, as in agriculture, has happened not because of a decline in national loyalties, resulting from a limited experience of integration, but for the opposite reason that perceptions of national interest seemed to require it, pressure groups' politics remaining essentially national. Neo-functionalists misunderstood the nature of nationalism, the complexities of different domestic pressures, different kinds of economic interests and their various international contexts. In the face of such mistakes and the inevitable assertion of national interests at the Community's political level (see chapter 3), neo-functionalism died in the Commission and, according to George, cannot revive even though, once again, it has strong leaders. In 1985, George accepted Hoffmann's view that, in matters of 'low politics', integration is possible but not in the 'high politics' of political union and defence. Welfare policies were thought to fall into the category of 'low politics' in this view (George, 1985: 31). In one sense Hoffman is vindicated in the story of Community social policy; the 'Veldkamp Compromise', discussed in the following section, represents what national politicians thought were low level agreements on matters of technical 'spill-over', with interests regarded as 'core' being left, against the wishes of the Commission, untouched. But it is also possible to see technical 'spill-overs' in social policy as political (as George does in his 1991 edition) because they are also about legitimacy; Hartwig (1978), for example, argues that policies almost always combine technical and political rationalities. Moreover, policy approaches compatible with the neo-functionalist view continued in the Commission and did have an effect on events following the Veldkamp Compromise. And, indeed, social policy, now redefined as rights, is indubitably in the realm of 'high politics'. It was a key area of bargaining in the period leading up to the Maastricht Treaty of economic and political union, it was a significant factor in part of the Danish referendum campaign (see note 2 in chapter 6) and, whatever the outcome of Maastricht, its rationale is informing debate about political rights (see chapter 8).

The Development of European Social Policy

Social security is listed separately from social policy in European documentation because the former, deriving from the Treaty principle of freedom of movement, is applied to migrant workers while the latter, except in the case of equal pay, is not directly authorized by the Treaty and provides protection for workers within Member States. They are taken together here because it is inconceivable to think of welfare systems without including social security. Moreover, the two sets of policy are linked in Community history.

Gough and Baldwin-Edwards (1990, 1991) point out that, before the establishment of the EC, there already existed a complex pattern of multi- and bilateral agreements on social security. The ECSC began to try to make things more orderly but it is the Treaty of Rome on the Common Market that provides the bases for current policies. The first Regulations (3/58 and 4/58 on related administrative matters) were about social security for migrant workers insured under general schemes. Assistance for migrant workers and families was dealt with in Regulation 1612/68. Court rulings and implementation difficulties led to the replacement of the first social security rules by Regulations 1408/71 and 574/72 which rest upon insured status rather than employment. In 1981, they were extended to cover the self-employed (Commission, 1983a). Further discussion of these is provided in chapter 5. Social policy measures were taken in the 1970s and 1980s to deal with workers' participation and sex equality and in both fields there are further proposals which remain disputed (see below). Directive 75/129 covers consultations over mass dismissals, Directive 77/187 deals with consultative rights in the event of transfers of business, and Directive 89/391 with involvement in health and safety procedures (see also chapter 5). Sex equality is the subject of Article 119 of the Treaty of Rome, which originally required equal pay for the same work. This has been augmented by Directives 75/117, 76/207, 79/7, 86/378 and 86/613. The first re-defines the principle of Article 119 by requiring equal pay for work of equal value. The second requires equal treatment in other conditions of employment. The third deals with statutory social security schemes, the fourth with private occupational schemes and the fifth covers the self-employed. These are discussed more fully in chapter 6.

George's arguments, noted above, about the limited 'spill-overs' of a common market seem vindicated by early interpretations of the link between freedom of movement and social security. Freedom of movement of labour was not necessarily thought of as conferring upon workers the right to move without hindrance or disadvantage; it was also possible to define the principle as a means of eliminating labour market distortions by allowing employers to move workers around freely (Collins, 1975). It seems clear that the second conception was dominant among politicians. Holloway (1981: 41) quotes the observation of the former Dutch Minister of Foreign Affairs, Herr Veldkamp, that the authors of the Treaty based themselves on the principle that all artificial economic distortions must be eliminated but that regulating social conditions that were not essential to economic unity was not necessary. Such views are also evident in disputes between the Commission and Council of Ministers about whether Community social security objectives should be achieved through 'harmonization' or 'coordination'.

Harmonization can mean the upward development of common standards through the 'approximation' of national laws. It can also mean simply the bringing about of common minimum standards by the same means. Either way, it implies a degree of uniformity of material and legal protection across the Member States. In contrast, coordination means that national laws can continue to differ provided that they do not undermine Community policy and provided that some mechanism exists to prevent differences from discouraging the free movement of labour. The legal basis for harmonization of social security is unclear. As Watson (1980, 1981) and Holloway (1981) point out, the Treaty is susceptible to various interpretations, and different legal scholars have arrived at conflicting conclusions which have been relied upon by the contending parties to justify enthusiasm for or caution about further integration.

Harmonizing social security was first proposed by the French during negotiations over the ECSC Treaty of Paris, not to ensure common European rights, but because of fears that wage levels and social charges that were higher in France than elsewhere would distort competition. Other Member States regarded harmonizing social security as impractical and unnecessary. The question was raised again during the negotiation of the Common Market Treaty of Rome. By that time, other States were able to refer to the Ohlin report, published by the International Labour Organization in 1956, which argued that social charges had little impact on production costs (Holloway, 1981: ch. 3; Watson, 1981). The report also pointed out that social security was funded in some countries out of a payroll tax and, in others, out of general taxation. However funded, the costs ultimately fell on consumers and, in any case, where there were heavy social costs on employers, there were likely to be compensating factors such as low general taxation. So, even though the Treaty of Rome deals more extensively than the Treaty of Paris with social security, Germany and the Benelux countries were able to use the analysis to justify the exclusion of very explicit statements about common policies.

The French also feared being uncompetitive because of the relatively high pay of French women compared to men (nominally equal, though not in practice) while the difference was much larger in the other countries. This was one of the main reasons for the clear and unambiguous Article 119 of the Common Market Treaty of Rome. It was regarded as so significant that unwillingness on the part of the United Kingdom's negotiators in 1962 to commit themselves to immediate legislation proved to be one of the major reasons for the UK's application for membership being turned down (*Daily Telegraph*, 26 May 1966).

Despite the greater directness of Article 119 than those dealing with social security, the Commission devoted most efforts until 1966 to bringing about common living standards *across* the Community, doing little at first to make Member States enforce common standards as between men and women *within* each country. Sex equality became the cornerstone of Community social policy after the failure of the Commission's social integration approach to social security. One of the reasons for this approach was, as noted above and in the previous chapter, that Commission leaders and staff had a more visionary conception of integration than Member State governments; this was especially true of the direct recruits compared to those on secondment (Coombes, 1970). Holloway (1981: 52, 87) draws attention to the analysis of Ribas and to the words of Levi Sandri (Commissioner then responsible for social affairs) in his report to the European Parliament in 1967. For the first, it was necessary that 'countries that had linked their destinies . . . should reduce their differences . . . that their peoples should feel part of the same community . . . [and] that their social levels are equivalent'. For the second, 'the Dutchman should feel he shares something with the Frenchman', the Frenchman with the German and so on and all 'should be aware that their common fortune is attributable to the Community'.

In common with accounts of domestic welfare expansion, the Commission used the influence of the trade unions, one of the 'social partners', to promote its social vision – to 'Europeanize' the work of the Economic and Social Committee and to provide a 'constituency' from which to press its approach upon the Council of Ministers (Holloway, 1981: 49, 51, 86–7; Kirchner and Schwaiger, 1981). Both the Commission and unions rejected the limited approach to integration and argued that, even if extensive harmonization was unnecessary to eliminate distortions, common improvements in living and working conditions were desirable ends in themselves. In 1962, a report was presented by a French trade unionist, M. Veillon, saying that harmonization should be achieved by 1970 through the raising of all benefits in each country to the highest in existence elsewhere (Holloway, 1981: 49, 51, 86–7). The Commission and other trade unions were less radical, arguing instead that small national differences, such as qualifying periods for maternity benefits, should be harmonized immediately and that further common standards should come about as a result of learning through the cross-fertilization of ideas. The enthusiasm of the Commission brought it into collision with the Council of Ministers even over its modest proposal to harmonize schemes to deal with occupational diseases.

This conflict was taking place at the same time as the general political crisis referred to in chapter 3. Rulings in the Court of Justice were clarifying the existence of a new order which involved some loss of sovereignty, a loss that meant existing social security provisions, let alone extended ones, were more expensive than anticipated (see chapter 7). More direct explanations for ministerial opposition lie in the attitudes of both 'social partners'. Employers' associations were voicing strong objections to the closeness of the relationship between the Commission and the trade unions. In addition to contributing to rising costs at the Community level, the unions were also, according to Holloway (1981: 51, 87), using the opportunity afforded by the Commission as an extra lever in the pursuit of improved living standards at home. He draws attention to actions by the British Trades Union Congress (TUC) and to writings by Richard Titmuss which, he argues, were ostensibly about European integration but were really castigations of British governments. He suggests that similar things were going on in other countries. These domestic pressures led to accusations by governments that the Commission was using trade unions as pressure groups against them. With mounting resistance from Member States to the idea that the Commission might usurp their sovereignty in social affairs, a complete breakdown in communications between governments, with the exception of Italy, and the Commission had occurred by 1966. Following the political

'Luxembourg Compromise' in January 1966, a social compromise was reached in December of that year through Herr Veldkamp whose country, the Netherlands, was then chairing the Council of Ministers.

The main components of this compromise were that the initiative in social policy should pass from the Commission to the Council, the latter determining the Commission's programme of studies and action and choosing the independent experts consulted by the Commission. Recommendations for action were to proceed only on the basis of unanimous agreement among ministers. Contacts between the Commission and trade unions and employers' associations were to be restricted. Thereafter, the Commission was obliged to accept the view that social security systems should vary according to national priorities and that common policy should be restricted to coordinating these different schemes.

As part of this coordination, the idea of the European Social Budget came about. In one sense, this can be seen as a triumph for the Council's economistic view of integration. It can be seen as a regional means to what Member States were trying to do at national levels. Holloway (1981: 58–83) suggests that it was a means of keeping down the aggregate costs of social security. By the late 1960s, all Member States were trying to cope with economic difficulties by restricting labour costs, including indirect incomes, by controlling the costs and benefits of social security. However, the European Social Budget can also be seen as retaining a vestige of the idea of harmonization because, as Watson (1981) points out, it embodies the idea of common indicative planning. Moreover, the possibility of spontaneous harmonization was also present in some of the measures of the First Social Action Programme agreed in 1972 and operational from 1974.

Despite the conflict leading to the Veldkamp Compromise, Member States found themselves unable to confine 'spill-overs' as narrowly as they might have wished. Some of the features of 'nation-building' (chapter 2) or of the capitalist development school of welfare are evident here. Community politics seem to corroborate the ideas of Habermas (1976) that states in capitalist societies are obliged both to restrict public expenditure to assist in accumulation and to spend money on welfare in order to maintain legitimacy. By 1972, ministers were, in their own way, acknowledging the existence of a legitimation crisis in the Community. In October, Herr Brandt proposed a gradual approximation of European social policies and the reason for some such steps was outlined by the French Prime Minister, M. Messmer. Ordinary people had a bad impression of the Community which was threatening the realization of a common market. To counteract the problem, he recommended the 'construction of goals which would attract popular support' (quoted by Holloway, 1981: 79). The European Social Budget can be seen as the first step in arriving at a compromise to meet the two objectives discussed by Habermas; that is, it envisaged *controlled* public spending. In December of 1972, however, the meeting of the Council of Ministers again emphasized that social policy goals should be limited to those that were related directly to economic competitiveness. The French Minister of Social Affairs, M. Faure, said that economic and monetary union could not be achieved without a social policy but that social security expenditure had reached budgetary limits (Holloway, 1981: 80). Nevertheless, the meeting acknowledged what had been disputed in 1966; that is, that unification into a single market must mean some loss of sovereignty in social affairs.

To give the Community its 'human face', four main objectives were adopted: first, to attain full and better employment; secondly, to improve living and working conditions; thirdly, to involve management and workers more in the economic and social decisions of the Community; and, fourthly, to involve workers in the lives of the undertakings in which they worked. In the social security field, this was to have meant extending protection to everyone not covered, or inadequately so, by existing schemes, linking prices and earnings ('dynamization of social benefits') and better coordination through more elaborate social indicators in the Social Budget, developed through consultation among experts from different countries. It was this pooling of ideas that Watson (1981) believes could have led to 'spontaneous harmonization'. Progress in cross-national expert collaboration has been made; for example in the completion of a cross-national anti-poverty research programme, coordinated by Graham Room of Bath University, in the European Centre for the Development of Vocational Training (CEDEFOP) and in various fields commissioned by the European Foundation for the Improvement of Living and Working Conditions (Baldwin-Edwards, 1992b; Lodge, 1989). Such research may involve activists (for example, trade unionists as well as sociologists in CEDEFOP) or lead to the formation of networks of non-governmental organizations (for example, Carroll (1992) on the European Anti-Poverty Network).

But the issue of workers' rights of participation at work and in Community institutions has been bedevilled by controversy. The recognition in 1972 of the need for some kind of social union led to the Commission's drafting a Directive (the Fifth, of 1983) on Company Law which, while being mainly about harmonizing labour markets, also included the idea of a common model of worker participation in places of employment. Grahl and Teague (1990: 199–208) describe the Commission's conception of this policy as integrationist, which provoked immediate and ferocious opposition from governments and employers' associations. Such opposition, particularly from the United Kingdom behind whom other governments could hide their reservations, persisted into the 1980s against the so-called Vredeling draft Directive (Herr Vredeling was then Vice-President of the Commission). This was more directly and extensively about workers' rights to be informed and consulted about company policy on its structure, economic situation, production, sales, employment and investment (see also Brewster and Teague, 1989: 338). In the meantime, the Commission became concerned about the effects on workers of restructuring by multi-national corporations and, here, it met with greater success when the Directives, referred to earlier, on consultation in situations of mass dismissals and transfers of undertakings were passed (as well as one on financial arrangements in insolvencies). This time, Grahl and Teague point out, Commission proposals reflected what Member States more or less intended to do in national legislation.

Despite the strictures in 1966 on Commission contact with the unions, contacts were permitted in the early 1970s to realize the objective of bringing workers into decisions about Community policy. This time, the Commission was ·careful to ensure that employers were included (Grahl and Teague, 1990: 214–16). These meetings, intended by the Commission to produce sectoral labour agreements that would become Community policy, were 'lacklustre' (1990: 215) and discussions with the 'social partners' fell into abeyance until the presidency of Jacques Delors which began in 1985. His ideas involved social dialogue between the 'peak' transnational organizations of labour and employers (European Trade Union Confederation, ETUC, and Union of Industries of the European Community, UNICE). From the beginning of these 'Val Duchesse' talks (held in Val Duchesse château, near Brussels), employers sought an undertaking from the Commission that there should be no proposals for legislation arising from any agreement that might be reached (Grahl and Teague, 1990: 216). The Commission agreed but, since such a stipulation undermined the whole point of the exercise, the idea has not lived up to its promise and very few agreements exist.

Participation in places of employment has been reactivated in the Social Charter, which also, and more extensively, deals with conditions of employment, and in other Community instruments. These are discussed below. In the meantime, it is necessary to turn to the other objectives of the agreement reached in 1972. Improvements in living and working conditions were expressed most concretely in the Directives on sex equality and these are generally agreed to have been the most significant Community achievement in the First Social Action Programme.

Harriet Warner (now Jones) (1984) cites the view of Vice-President Vredeling in 1980. He confessed that 'the picture . . . of the European Community is not inspiring and is hardly likely to create converts'. But he felt that sex equality was 'one area of the Community's work' which was 'a pioneering one', where the Community was ahead of the Member States. Other observers are less optimistic and their analyses reveal the same kind of division between Commission and Council of Ministers that we have already discussed in connection with social security. Despite the severity with which the UK was questioned on its commitment to equal pay in 1962, the then Member States had done very little, despite a series of adverse commentaries from the Commission, to implement Article 119 by the expiry of the deadline in that same year (Warner, 1984). During the 1970s, Member States passed or amended legislation about equal pay and equal treatment at work. Partly, this stemmed from feminist and trade union pressures in domestic polities but these influences were also facilitated by a view increasingly held in political circles that there was an economic justification for rationalizing workforces and that it was proper for governments to encourage this. As in Ohlin's arguments about the costs of social security, it was possible to believe that, if there were sex equality costs, they would fall on consumers. Not falling directly on public expenditure (except for the major fact that governments are large employers of women – see chapters 6 and 7), sex equality at the European level may have seemed a cheaper way than common social security standards of giving the Community its 'human face'.

Such a possibility is corroborated by the fact that, when Vredeling made his remarks, Community legislation was mainly limited to equality at work. Some Member States have shown a marked reluctance to implement the Directives on social security, one of which directly affects public expenditure and the other indirectly. Belgium and the Netherlands insisted on a very long implementation period for the Directive on statutory social security, the former also making some provisions *more* discriminatory during the period (Warner, 1984). The Directive on private occupational schemes (whose implementation has led to increased pressure to equalize retirement ages in those countries where they are different) and the

Directive on the self-employed were agreed to by the Council of Ministers only in weaker forms than the drafts put to the Council by the Commission. In both Belgium and the Netherlands, direct discrimination in social security has been reduced but in ways that increase indirect discrimination (see chapter 6). The United Kingdom has been accused of amending all its equality legislation within the letter but not the spirit of Community law, most recently in connection with the interface between disability benefits and state pensions (*The Independent*, 31 August 1992).

Further steps to bring about real rather than formal equality at work have proved controversial. Commission proposals on part-time work, parental leave and the burden of proof in discrimination cases have all been blocked, mainly by the United Kingdom, and one on positive action was rendered ineffective by German insistence that it take the form of a Recommendation and not a Directive. The view that governments might have turned away from sex equality because it is not after all such a painless way of giving the Community its 'human face' is also supported by the fact that rulings in the Court of Justice have thrown the costs more directly on to governments, as employers and social security legislators, bringing about, as in general social security, the possibility of unexpected expenditure.

On sex equality matters, as in social security, at least some Commissioners and staff seem to have a fuller vision of integration than the Council of Ministers and the Commission's cooperation with 'constituents' continues despite ministerial reluctance for further action. Hoskyns (1985, 1986, Hoskyns and Luckhaus, 1989) describes the efforts of a few key personnel in the Commission to promote sex equality and to persuade the Committee of Permanent Representatives (COREPER) to recommend to the Council of Ministers important components of the Commission's programmes, dimensions which are significant to feminists. This is not to say that Commission proposals prevail in full over ministerial wishes. But it is the case that some matters might never have been agreed to at all, albeit in weakened form, had it not been for the persistence of the Commission; the Commission has not been so decisively defeated on sex equality as it was in 1966. Nor is it to say that the Commission as a whole has a programmatic commitment to women's rights. Indeed, Community institutions are themselves no better than many other employers of women and there is a tendency for the women's rights section of the Commission to be marginalized (Interviews). But its need for a popular basis of support, perhaps less controversial than that with the unions, has led to continuing contacts with feminist organizations, particularly trans-European ones, and related movements. Trans-European groups, like these and the sectional ones referred to above, are generally thought necessary for neo-functionalism to have been borne out.

Despite all this, the innovatory role of the Community has been said to have run into the ground by the middle of the 1980s. Hoskyns (1988) explains this in terms of the growing preference among Member State governments for deregulation and non-intervention and, as noted earlier, sex equality was becoming a more expensive way than expected of popularizing the Community. Opposition to further action on sex equality, as in the case of workers' rights, came most vocally from the United Kingdom, the most overtly deregulatory Member State. Sex equality was also affected by Jacques Delors's focus on the resurrection of general participation and social rights. Nielsen and Szyszczak (1991: 31-7) suggest that the Val Duchesse talks and the origins of the Social Charter reflect his determination to break deadlocks in social policy arising from the frequent use by governments of the veto (see chapter 3) in this field. A coherent social policy was necessary in his view to circumvent problems in the transition to the Single European Market.[2]

Information and consultation initiatives (the Fifth Company Directive, the Vredeling Directive and the Val Duchesse talks) having led to controversy and disappointment, the Council adopted a Resolution in 1986 on worker participation that 'emphasized the importance of the social area in the context of the completion of the Community Internal Market' (Nielsen and Szyszczak, 1991: 169). This social dimension was also introduced in the Single European Act of 1985, which prepared the way for the internal market, and it began to take shape in 1987, with recommendations from the Economic and Social Committee in 1988 that formed the basis of a Commission proposal for a set of social rights that would entail Community action. The Committee and the European Parliament were enthusiastic advocates of the idea of 'a binding legal framework of Social Rights to form the basis of legal remedies' (Nielsen and Szyszczak, 1991: 33). The Parliament proposed that the provisions in the Single European Act for cooperative decision-making and qualified majority voting (see chapter 3) should be applied to the social aspects of the internal market (1991: 33). Although there were governments that were sympathetic to the Commission, employers and the UK government opposed the idea of what Grahl and Teague (1990: 212) call 'a social constitution' of rights. The United Kingdom rejected the Commission's first draft of the Charter in the spring of 1989, with

Denmark abstaining on a technicality (Nielsen and Szyszczak, 1991: 33–4). To try to maintain consensus, it was agreed that the Charter should not, itself, be legally binding but should be a 'Solemn Declaration' (1991: 210). This was signed by all Member States, except the United Kingdom, in December 1989. Since a 'Declaration' has only moral, not legal force, the Commission drafted an Action Programme of implementation measures, which, given the rejection of a Community 'social constitution', would have to be taken by Member States under Directives. In effect, then, the Social Charter is really the recommendations of the Action Programme and subsequent Directives that arise from it and its potential has been 'enormously limited by the development of support for the concept of subsidiarity' (Spicker, 1991: 11) which, in the Community context, is intended to reassure Member States that the competence of common institutions, primarily the Commission, is limited to action where it would be difficult for national governments to act effectively (see also chapters 3 and 8).

Because of the United Kingdom's hostility to the whole idea of social rights being regulated at the common level and UNICE's similar insistence on economic rather than social cohesion, the Commission's Action Programme made concessions that infuriated the European Parliament and the ETUC. Both were critical of commitments that had become 'fragile and uncertain' (Nielsen and Szyszczak, 1991: 34), and the Parliament of the failure to revive the enforceable measures for women, previously vetoed by the United Kingdom. As noted in chapter 3, seeking consensus among governments can be sensible since policies that are willingly adopted may be implemented more effectively. But this instance of it is ironic. Not only did the United Kingdom vote against the 'Solemn Declaration' and Action Programme in 1989. Now, the Social Charter, diluted from being a 'Community constitution of rights' in order to try to win UK support, forms the Social Chapter of the Maastricht Treaty of Union. But, the United Kingdom made its acceptance of the Treaty conditional upon exemption from the provisions of the Social Chapter (as well as on special arrangements for economic and monetary union). Thus, the other members have agreed by Protocol to 'borrow' Community institutions to implement a Charter whose present content is as it is for the sake of a non-participant (unless, on specific topics, the UK wishes to be included).

The United Kingdom is, however, still bound by the regulations that are discussed in the following three chapters.[3] The others may be more able, without the UK, to resolve matters that have remained on the agenda without agreement since the early 1980s;

for example, the issues now contained in the 1991 Draft Directive proposing information and consultation in Community-scale undertakings through a European Works Council and in the Draft European Company Statute proposing employee participation 'in the supervision and strategic development' of a proposed new form of organization – European public limited companies (Nielsen and Szyszczak, 1991: 169–80). Despite the United Kingdom's exemption, it may be possible that UK social practice will be brought involuntarily within the ambit of the Maastricht Treaty, if it is ratified. This is because UK companies operating in other EC countries will have to abide by what other Member States agree upon and this may mean that such employers will find it too irrational to operate under different sets of rules at home and away – especially if their employees are mobile amongst the various locations. This suggests that, while the Community is in a serious political crisis for the time being, the dynamics which give it its raison d'être continue and that, even if Maastricht were renegotiated, something recognizably like a continuation of previous developments would take its place. The enforcement of what has been agreed so far is discussed in the next three chapters and the political future is the subject of chapter 8.

Notes

1 The shift from rights based on working status to rights for human beings is discussed more fully in chapter 8.

2 Such dislocations include 'social dumping' – the relocation of production, particularly that which uses semi- and unskilled labour, to countries with weaker forms of protection and rights for workers and, hence, where labour costs and social charges are lower. Such relocation is expected to take place from the centre to the poorer, peripheral countries. Another dislocation might be mass migration from the poorer countries as workers search for better occupations, which could lead to heavy demands on unemployment and social provisions in the centre. References made in chapter 7 and a special edition of *Women's Studies International Forum* (1992) discuss the implications for women of change in Europe. Rhodes (1991a, b) and Michon (1990) discuss the difficulty of achieving a coherent social policy that takes account of different kinds of labour market, different forms of representation and different social security systems. See also Butler (1991) and Mazey and Richardson (1992).

3 Thus it is that the Community is still able to debate, and the UK to resist, current proposals for the 48 hour limit on the working week and protection for pregnant women workers. Though proposals for action in these areas were in the Action Programme to implement the Charter, they have since been developed under the auspices of the 1989 Health and Safety framework authorized by the Single European Act which binds all Member States. Health and safety was an area in which it was agreed to use qualified majority voting (see chapter 3). The UK government has been trying to argue that, properly speaking, these measures are not health and safety ones but are matters relating to workers' rights and protection and therefore require unanimity.

5

Class and Citizenship

Introduction

The idea that civil and political rights are illusory for subordinate groups and classes has been proposed from within the liberal tradition and from without. Socialists in the Marxist tradition argue that the language of universalism obscures an unequal distribution of political power stemming from class relations in civil society; citizenship is attached to property, those without property are subjects. Proponents of the welfare state argue that property relations are not inevitably a cause of unequal citizenship but it is likely that, without intervention, unequal social conditions will make it more difficult for the poor than for the rich to exercise their rights. Put baldly, the first kind of critic will find nothing in Community arrangements that will contribute to real equality because that cannot be done without a transformation of property relations, while the EC Treaties uphold and promote private property. But, neither the criticism nor the constitutional position are quite as clear-cut because of modifications in theory and practice which temper ownership with the notion of control. For the second kind of critic, it must be the case that the Community has some egalitarian promise – if only on the ground that its policies, existing and proposed, are contested and that opposition would be pointless if no real transfers of resources or extensions of rights were at stake. Community policies are predominantly, as might be expected, in the tradition of the welfare critique of civil and political rights but pay some attention to matters of control.

This chapter expands upon ideas introduced in chapter 2 about property ownership and control and their connection with political participation. It then turns to the contention that entitlements to welfare can compensate for class inequalities when it comes to the practicability of exercising civil and political rights. Finally it explains what has happened in the Community with respect to the entitlements of 'industrial citizens'. Bearing in mind the political controversies in chapter 4, the argument here is that the practical transformation of benefits into entitlements or rights is attributable to the Court of Justice (ECJ) – at least until the mid 1980s.

Ownership, Control and Political Participation

In chapter 2, it was pointed out that property rights bias citizenship rights in two ways. One is obvious; bodies of thought and actual systems of law explicitly excluded certain categories of people from citizenship on grounds of a connection between a lack of property and moral unfitness. In the other, even when the formal barriers are removed, a language of universalism disguises class or group inequalities.

Even though their ideas were based on the natural equality of all individuals, the English Levellers, for example, wanted 'rights for well-affected people and their representatives' (Lessnoff, 1986: 43); Locke's active citizens were those capable of disinterested rationalism, indicated by an ability to accumulate property (chapter 2); and Kant thought that the qualification for citizenship should be an 'ability to support oneself without being dependent on others' (Lessnoff, 1986: 92). The interests of others, more like subjects than citizens, were to be protected by the obligations of active citizens and rulers to make laws that could be consented to by all (1986: 92).[1] In the obvious argument about bias, the language of universalism can be made real. Knowledge about actual people, instead of abstractions of the individual, can correct theories of human nature that equate rationalism and property and, hence, can be used to alter political practice. It is on such a basis that political rights in most countries have been universalized. In expanding the franchise from the propertied to rate-payers and to all adults, voting rights have been emptied of explicit discrimination against former slaves, the working class and women. In the granting of rights of assembly and combination, an organized working class has acquired a means through which they can influence what is to count as the public interest. With equal legal and political rights for virtually all adults, reformers might be said to have succeeded in turning ideas about the natural equality of all individuals into the reality of universal citizenship.

But in the more complex account of property, class and citizenship, the bias is more deeply and even structurally embedded. Chapter 2 referred to Macpherson's critique of Hobbes and Locke in which he argues that their individualism was based not, as purported, on how humans would have behaved in the state of nature but on how they had to behave in emerging capitalist society. In the case of Hobbes, it is the market not nature that creates unlimited wants and insecurity against the pursuit of wants by others; it is the market that 'requires men to compete to exercise power by controlling other men' (Lessnoff, 1986: 107). In

Macpherson's view, Hobbes' advocacy of a near absolute state is the most coherent version of the social contract, given the 'brutishness' of natural or, in Macpherson's interpretation, capitalist society. In Locke's case, control is rendered more obscure or palatable as a result of his more benign view of human beings and their cooperative rather than competitive instincts. Although some early French socialists, influenced by Rousseau (Gough, 1956), believed it was possible to construct a contractarian body politic that was genuinely egalitarian, most Marxist socialists have maintained that unequal property relations carry over into the political sphere. However, some revisions to Marxism introduce the possibility that citizenship rights might be made more effective for those without property. This is because control of property might be more significant than ownership of it.

Burnham's classic managerial revolution thesis (1941) was that, in modern conditions of capitalism, ownership has become divorced from control. Owners are relatively anonymous and distant collections of shareholders, while control over production and labour processes is exercised by salaried employees. The idea that management, not property systems, determines the working and social lives of employees is present also in arguments by Trotsky (1973 [1936]) and Djilas (1957) that revolutions in their countries did not result in classlessness but in systems of 'state capitalism' managed by state functionaries. It has also been supported by social democratic thinkers such as Crosland (1964 [1956]) who argued that nationalization had no discernibly different impact from that of private corporations on working conditions, culture and political consciousness.

It is on the significance of control that sociological theories of class and political theories of participation (see chapter 2) come together. In both bodies of literature, the ideologies that maintain distance between managers and the managed and rulers and the ruled are described in a similar way; that is, that both positions of dominance are justified by the alleged possession of craft and wisdom that is not, by nature, evenly distributed among people. The call for 'opening the books' and a 'social audit' (Coates and Topham, 1974) represents the idea that micro- and macro-level management skills, like political arts (Pateman, 1970), can be learned if participatory opportunities are provided. The point is not merely that the two sets of ideas are similar or that one inspired the other; it is structural. One aspect was mentioned in chapter 2; that systems of workers' control could be an alternative, in complex society, to the city-state as the means of expressing essentially political natures.[2] Secondly, democratic practice at work would provide the intellectual and practical bases for transforming politics (Pateman, 1970). The third is more fundamental; that is, if control *is* a constitutive element of class domination and if political power stems from class relations, transformed systems of control would mean equal citizenship.

Both bodies of literature, however, also provide similar grounds for caution. If political theory often provides a justification for disobedience on grounds of unjust laws or arbitrary exclusion from the making of them, the corollary is that people who *have* participated will be bound by decisions even if they are bad, contrary to their interests or unjust. Pale reflections of workers' control, consultation or job enrichment, are sometimes proposed by managers themselves in order to deal with production problems, which might require unpalatable solutions. Participatory democrats are often criticized for not taking into account the trivialization of matters that are allowed to be decided jointly. Moreover, it has been shown that where accessible opportunities for political participation do exist in Britain, they are more commonly used by those who already possess advantages in the civil and private spheres (Parry et al., 1992). The same might happen in the workplace. While the orthodox Marxist would have anticipated this, the participatory democrat or the Gramscian might argue that apathy was not inherent but precisely an indication of defective institutions.

As indicated in chapter 4 and discussed more fully later in this one, Community policies so far for worker participation resemble the illusory versions in that they embody the right to be consulted, but not yet the right for workers to make decisions affecting the collective life of their enterprise. However, they are not trivial matters that are required to be the subject of consultation. More substantial participation has been on the agenda since 1980 (see chapter 4) and the fact that there has been so much intergovernmental dispute about these proposals suggests that they are not vacuous concessions to workers.

Welfare and Citizenship

The other allegation about unequal citizenship, mentioned in chapter 2 and at the beginning of this one, is that civil and political rights cannot be exercised equally effectively because of unequal distributions of wealth and incomes. Obviously, if a person cannot afford to pay for legal advice when a contending party can, in a system of justice that requires expert representation, the equal protection of the laws is undermined. If education is neither affordable nor provided by the state, many citizens would be unable to read manifestos or newspapers and their capacities to vote and to judge governments would be diminished. Although it is generally acknowledged that there are social inequalities, there are disputes about whether this implies rights to be imparted, as in the directly civil and political spheres, by the laws of the state. Some of the most influential libertarians, who oppose the idea of social rights, nevertheless admit the possibility of some distributive state intervention, though not in the name of rights. Some who argue that social rights *can* be justified also have individualistic assumptions, others are Aristotelian.

The libertarian view stems most strongly from the state tradition identified by Dyson (see chapter 3) as Anglo-American. It is the duty of the state to provide the conditions under which citizens may exercise their lawful liberties. Its role is essentially negative – to remove arbitrary legal impediments and physical coercion and to maintain their absence. It is not proper for the state to provide the positive means that might facilitate the exercise of civil and political rights. On the one hand, the constraints of poverty cannot be attributed to the actions of any particular person, as physical coercion could be, but arise from the impersonal operations of the market (Berlin, 1958; von Hayek, 1960). On the other, depriving one person of part of what he or she earns to enable another to do something, as happens in taxation and social security payments, is coercion carried out by the state (Nozick, 1974). Compensation for inequalities generated by the operation of a lawful order requires a departure from the equal protection of the laws (Hayek, 1960). Specific forms of legal treatment for identifiable people cannot be rights since rights are, by definition, universal (Cranston, 1973). Moreover, in this view (though see discussion of Friedman in chapter 7), specific treatment can give rise, not to a socially valued state of affairs, but to arbitrariness. It is also impracticable to expect governments to be able to guarantee, for example, jobs and minimum incomes.

Nevertheless, Hayek suggests that there may be some scope for state encouragement of schemes of insurance of social risks and Berlin that income maintenance may be proposed legitimately on grounds of justice instead of liberty or rights. Critics of Nozick, drawing on Rawls's theory (1971) of distributive justice, hold that, even within Nozick's own framework, it need not be out of order to find some state-sponsored means of meeting need, if a majority values economic security highly (Lessnoff, 1986).

The case for social rights made by the non-libertarians is based on what Aron categorizes as human rights, arising from a belief in natural equality. Though social rights may be declared by bodies other than nation-states (Aron, 1974) and granted by nation-states to non-citizens (Leca, 1990), they are, it is argued, inseparable from the abilities of citizens to exercise civil and political rights. Watson (1977), for example, argues that individuals need fair trials and material assistance because both are necessary to them as human beings. But, contrary to Aron's view that believing in natural human equality gives rise to two different orders of rights and to the libertarian insistence that it implies only negative freedoms, Watson argues that welfare entitlements can be conceptualized according to the same principles as civil and political rights, strictly defined. In a system of equal civil rights, states are not, in practice, guaranteeing all people a fair trial all of the time but to citizens as and when they are accused. If citizens are not constantly needing a fair trial, they are also not at all times requiring the state to give them a job, re-training or an alternative form of income – but only when they become ill or involuntarily redundant.

Though T.H. Marshall's arguments entail positive provision while those of the libertarians do not, universalism and equal protection are equally central to his ideas. Indeed, he thought it critical that social rights to health and education services, for example, were couched in universalistic terms because this conferred equal status. However, not all benefits are framed in universalistic terms because 'informational constraints' (Sen, 1977) have an adverse impact on the effective delivery of benefits and services, a problem acknowledged by governments committed to welfare as well as those not (see chapter 7). Even so, Parker (1975) argues that entitlements arising from insurance are compatible with universalistic principles because they can be claimed by anyone who finds himself or herself in the circumstance that activates them. Departures from the principles of natural equality and equality of respect may arise from the method of disbursement and are very likely in the case of discretionary assistance. Devising welfare schemes on the basis of some principle other than equality invites the stigmatization of those in need and encourages providers to make specific judgements about the moral worthiness of particular individuals. Since the presence of deprivation can be construed impersonally as a breakdown in the system of entitlements, social rights can be argued to be another type of civil right, subject to the same tests (see chapter 7). As noted in chapter 2, the actual provision of welfare can be said to serve the same function as the civil right to hold property in providing the material basis for rationality and, hence, political participation.

Though T.H. Marshall has inspired many supporters of social rights, he has also been criticized for being too rooted in the same traditions as those who refuse to accord social rights the status of citizenship rights. Jordan (1989) argues that, though Marshall believed that social rights gave people something in common, his moral vision retained the idea that the good society was one of self-interested economic participation (1989: 79). In his view, the moral dimension of citizenship was stronger in Richard Titmuss's view that social welfare was about the universalization of humanistic ethics, the good of all citizens. Titmuss saw in the communalism of working-class societies the possibility of re-uniting ethics and politics on a more inclusive scale (1989: 79–80). The idea that forms of citizenship rights and the nature of government interventions arise from and contribute to a moral order in which individuals are not private was also present in the work of T.H. Green (Vincent and Plant, 1984) and Leonard Hobhouse (George, 1977, 1981). The works of Idealists were part of an intense public debate in Britain at the turn of the century about the ethics of citizenship and public life (Harris, 1989). Such sets of ideas bring these advocates of social rights close to the participatory democrats in the sense that neither is proposing arrangements to bring about the more effective representation of private interests but institutions and practices that foster genuine consensus about the nature of politics and society. That this has been an enduring preoccupation of political thinkers from the Greeks to the present is clear in Parry's account of citizenship and knowledge (1978). But, today, it is only in Scandinavia, according to Jordan, that 'integrative social policies' deal with the moral and common dimension of citizenship. The Scandinavian tradition is particularly relevant to discussion of women and is influencing women in non-Scandinavian EC countries; consequently, discussion of it will occur in chapter 6. Suffice it to say here that central to it is the notion of solidarity between classes over the nature of society.

In so far as social rights theories do not propose a revolutionary transformation of property relations, they remain, like their libertarian critics, in a liberal tradition – even though some of them relate social rights to the commonality of human beings and the need for institutions and practices through which that characteristic can be expressed. Individualistic social rights theorists, in particular, have been criticized for being ambiguous about whether they think social rights alter class relations or generate a false sense of the common good that minimizes the risk of the outbreak of conflict (Barbalet, 1988; Chirkin, 1985).

Welfare and Industrial Citizenship in the EC

In a chapter on class and citizenship, the rights of nationals of Member States of the European Community can hardly be said to be strengthened by the existence of the Community if the classic Marxist concept is insisted upon. As noted earlier, the Treaty of Rome confirms pre-existing property systems in Member States, provided that there is no national discrimination in their operation[3] and the general purpose is to promote market society on a European scale. Conversely, the libertarian element of modern British Conservative ideology believes that the Community is resuscitating the socialism they, or Margaret Thatcher, had sought to destroy. What is present is something in between. If control can be said at least to modify ownership as a fundamental source of political inequality, there are some signs of an institutional basis for equal citizenship. For those with a continental sense of democracy and the state (see chapter 3) and a Weberian idea of class (an occupational structure in which mobility is possible and where rights to services and income maintenance can assist mobility or compensate for deprivation) elements of a material basis of equal citizenship, at least for men, exist at the Community level. Whether or not the Community promotes an individualistic concept of social rights or an EC-wide, communitarian one is an open question. As noted earlier, trade unionists and analysts of their role have sometimes been said to have used the Community as a lever with which to resist the undermining of domestic welfare states. On the other hand, the preambles to Community policies, as also noted before, refer to common standards and social cohesion. Moreover, there is now a web of specialists and activists who operate on a cross-national basis which cross-fertilizes analyses and expectations – and this feeds into the Community machinery.

The rest of this chapter deals with Community Regulations and Directives, and their enforcement, that cover the kinds of rights most closely associated with a social conception of citizenship. Historically, those dealing with social security and assistance are more long-lived and more entrenched than those dealing with participation and will be dealt with first here. Both sets apply to women as well as men in their capacities as migrant workers in their own right or as members of the families of migrant workers; but they are essentially about the abolition of national, not sex, discrimination. Indeed, as is shown in the next chapter, systems of welfare based on Marshallian concepts can be as blind to women's equality as liberal theory.

1 Regulations 1408/71 and 1612/68

The first Regulations (3/58 and 4/58 on related administrative matters) were about social security for workers insured under general schemes. Court rulings and implementation difficulties led to the replacement of the first social security rules by Regulations 1408/71 and 574/72, which rest upon insured status rather than employment. In 1981, they were extended to cover the self-employed. Social assistance, outside Community competence to start with, was introduced in Regulation 1612/68. Regulation 1612/68 is intended to assist workers and their families to integrate into host countries, so that mobility is not impeded. Among forms of social assistance, the Regulation refers specifically to access to housing and education – though the content of general education, as distinct from vocational training and student exchanges, is theoretically outside the scope of Community competence.[4] Regulation 1408/71 deals with the coordination of different national social security benefits relating to sickness, maternity, invalidity, old age, survivors, accidents at work, occupational diseases, death, unemployment and family responsibilities. Schemes subject to this regulation may be contributory or non-contributory but they must be based on insurance, not need. Member States are required to submit lists of benefits categorized in this way. The Regulation excludes the right to 'overlapping benefits' (two or more benefits payable in different Member States based on a single period of insurance) and determines the method of calculating the level of a single benefit arising from insurance periods completed in more than one country. Provided that a worker would not gain less from the application of Community rules than from national legislation alone, periods of insurance are aggregated and obligation to pay is apportioned to the 'competent' institutions in the different Member States ('pro-ratarization'). Under this Regulation rights to most, but not all, benefits are payable ('exportable') to workers who no longer reside in the country responsible for payment.

2 Social Security and Assistance in the ECJ

In contrast to the Council of Ministers, the Court has played a major part in developing the idea that EC policies embody entitlements for individuals in Member States. For nearly thirty years, in conforming with the Treaty principle of no national discrimination, it has insisted that there is a fundamental right to social protection. Examples of its rulings are grouped here as: a miscellaneous set involving freedom of movement and the provision of professional services; and disputes directly about social security and social advantages.

Freedom of Movement and Service Provision   Many, though not all, of the cases in this set stem from the application to migrant workers and their families of inconsistent national social security schemes. Several times in the 1960s, the Court made clear statements that there must be 'no discrimination when exercising the right of freedom of movement' (4/66 Labots v Raad van Arbeid) and that there must be 'equal access for migrant workers to national law' (1/67 Ciechelski v Caisse Régionale de Sécurité Sociale du Centre d'Orléans). Its continued upholding of the Treaty has been reiterated in the 1980s; the 'largest possible degree of freedom of movement of migrant workers is one of the fundamental principles of the Community . . . [and it] is not achieved if, as a result of exercising the right of free movement, workers lose social security advantages' (43/86 Bestuurvan de Sociale Verzekeringsbank v de Rijke and de Rijke-van Gent). 'All the Treaty Articles . . . on free movement . . . are designed to make it easier for nationals of a Member State to pursue gainful activities of every kind throughout the territory of the Community and are opposed to national legislation which might be unfavourable to nationals . . . [wishing] to pursue their activities beyond the territory of a single nation state' (154 and 155/87 Rijkinstituut voor Sociale Verzekeringen der Zelfstandingen v (a) Wolf and Microtherm Europe N.V. and (b) Dorchain and Almare PVBA). In consequence of this view, the Court declared void a section of Regulation 1408/71 in which Community law itself made an exception of certain benefits for migrant workers in France, saying that it 'added to disparities caused by different national legislations . . . [and] impeded Articles 48 to 51' (41/84 and its follow-up 359/87 Pinna v Caisse d'Allocations Familiales de la Savoie).

The substantive outcomes of freedom of movement/no national discrimination cases have been broad in scope, through dealing with 'social advantages' also touching upon matters which arguably fall within Aron's rights of citizenship (see chapter 1) or at least in a 'grey area' between his civil and political rights on the one hand and human rights on the other. For example, the Court has reduced the significance of residence permits, though states are still allowed to impose minor penalties for non-compliance with immigration formalities and border checks are permissible – until the imminent completion of the opening of internal frontiers – if carried out randomly.[5] Community nationals have rights to own immovable property and of access to mortgages in Member States other than their own.[6] Migrants have the same right as nationals to compensation following criminal assault even though travel may not have been connected with work; and they have the right to be sure of understanding judicial proceedings, generally through translations but, in certain circumstances, by the use of a specific language in their trial.[7] The Court has argued, too, that though the Treaties exempt employment in public institutions from the principle of no national discrimination where there are questions of national security and public order, the term 'public service' must be construed as narrowly as possible; it cannot justify the exclusion of migrants from teaching and research posts simply because such occupations are classified in this way in several countries.[8]

The Court has considered a number of disputes involving a motley collection of providers of professional services; doctors, nurses, dentists, pharmacists, clinical biologists, lawyers, accountants, tutors, researchers, journalists, architects, surveyors, engineers, specialists in transport, travel and tourism, storage and warehousing, football and sports trainers and artists. In many of these cases, the issue at stake was the mutual recognition of diplomas, not always social security. But they are mentioned here because they emphasize the strength of the Court's view that 'the main aim of [Articles 59–60 of the Treaty of Rome] is to enable a person wishing to provide services to pursue his [sic] activities in the host state without discrimination in favour of the nationals of that state'.[9]

Social Security and Social Assistance for the Self-employed and Migrant Workers and their Families Key features in these cases are, as in those above, freedom of movement and the principle of no discrimination based on nationality. In the absence of 'harmonized' (see chapter 4) national schemes, the Court has to steer between the Scylla and Charybdis of legitimate national variations and the need to ensure that their coordination causes no disadvantage to workers who migrate.[10] Its general philosophy is exemplified in two rulings made in 1983; that 'it had repeatedly upheld the inviolability of rights in matters of social security' (149/82 Robards v Insurance Officer) and that it 'had evolved a very broad concept of social security which encompasses both the satisfaction of an individual's primary needs and the guarantee of a given standard of living' (139/82 Piscitello v Instituto Nazionale della Previdenza Sociale). Its dual acknowledgement of national sovereignties and the rights of migrants is evident in recent rulings about 'overlapping benefits' (see above). In such cases, the Court has said it has no jurisdiction over the classification by one Member State of the benefits of another for the purposes of dealing with overlapping benefits and that, when a worker receives a pension solely by virtue of national legislation, Community rules do not prevent the application of national rules against overlapping benefits.[11] It has also said that it is 'for national legislation to determine the conditions governing rights or obligations to become a member of a social security scheme'.[12] But the Court insists that the application of national rules must not be less favourable to the recipient than the application of Community rules; workers must be protected against the substitution by the host country of its benefits by *lower* benefits payable in the country of origin.[13]

In giving effect to its values, the Court has extended the category of person entitled to benefit and has broadened the category of benefit to which he or she has a right. Often cases are ruled upon in the light of *both* Regulation 1408/71 (insurance-based benefits, including family benefits, for workers) and Regulation 1612/68 (assistance for workers and their families) because it is difficult to distinguish between workers' rights and families' rights since a denial of either would constitute a loss and thus frustrate movement (Steiner, 1985: 37–8; see also chapter 7 for further discussion of overlapping benefits and legal techniques).

Definitions of 'worker' and 'family member' Although Community rights stem from a person's status as a worker (or insured person) or as a member of a worker's family, the Court does not give a literal interpretation to these terms. Provided that insured status has been established in one country,[14] migrants count as workers if not fully employed (139/85 Kempf v Staatssecretaris van Justitie) and even if their travel is not connected with work (186/87 Cowan v French Treasury). Unemployment may reduce rights but does not deprive migrants of them; however, certain kinds of work do not count as employment in the Community sense.[15] The Court has defined 'family' as not only spouses living together and with elderly and minor dependants; undivorced spouses living apart count as 'family' and, if there has been divorce and there are children, the person with parental responsibilities is still a member of the family of a migrant worker.[16] The Court takes the view that 'spouse' cannot include the unmarried companions of migrant workers but they may not be discriminated against if there is no similar discrimination against the unmarried companions of national workers (59/85 Netherlands v Reed). 'Family' includes the foreign spouses or children of Community nationals[17] but there is no legal protection against discriminatory national legislation about residence and assistance if dependants have not migrated within the Community.[18] Subject to certain restrictions, the children of migrant workers are entitled to assistance even if their parents have died or moved away from the country in which a claim is made.[19]

Regulation 1408/71: Insurance-based Benefits In those cases where the Court has extended what is to count as social security, one of the tests applied is the practical purpose of a benefit or advantage, even though it has not been classified explicitly as social security by the Member State which grants it. Steiner discusses several cases involving workers' benefits.[20] In one, involving a claim by an Italian worker for a Belgian non-contributory, need-based supplement to the old age pension, it was ruled that the supplement performed the double function of guaranteeing a minimum for persons outside the social security system *and* of supplementing inadequate insurance-based benefits. Because of the latter, it had to be payable to a worker covered by Regulation 1408/71. In another case, a French woman worker in Belgium claimed a special supplementary grant for the handicapped and similar reasoning was used.

Insurance-based benefits may also cover families as well as workers themselves, though their access to them depends, of course, on the contributions or status of the working member of the family. In cases of this sort, the Court has struck down residence conditions. For example, in the case of an Italian in Germany whose wife and family were in Italy, the Court confirmed that a worker's benefits for an absent family should not be suspended if the family were ineligible for benefits in the country of residence (153/84 Ferraioli v Deutsche Bundespost. And, if they *were* eligible but the benefit was of a lower value, then the rule noted in note 12 would apply). But, though the Court similarly required family allowances to be paid to an Italian worker in France (because it would be paid to French workers whose children were temporarily absent; 41/84 Pinna v Caisse d'Allocations Familiales de la Savoie), it has insisted that only family allowances 'properly called' can be claimed by absent parents. It upheld the French rule that other, related benefits, namely single salary allowances and in this case, though generally unlikely, schooling allowances, were payable only to parents in receipt of the old age pension and resident with their children in France (313/86 Lenoir v Caisse d'Allocations Familiales des Alpes-Maritime).

As with insurance-based benefits for workers themselves, the Court has extended definitions and eligibility in insurance-based family support. For example, an Italian wife of a Belgian worker tried to claim the Belgian grant for handicapped workers, referred to above, even though she was *not* employed (39/74 Costa v Belgium; see Steiner, 1985: 28–9). Consequently, in the opinion of the Advocate General, although she was a member of a worker's family, the benefit in question was not a family one and she had no right to it. The Court, however, took the view that she was so entitled because it conferred a legally defined position on recipients, it did not have the discretionary character of assistance and could be assimilated to an invalidity benefit. In a third case, it was ruled that a teenage son of an Italian worker was eligible for the Belgian grant for the handicapped (7/75 Fracas v Belgium; see Steiner, 1985) and, in a case about a similar benefit in France, a claim by an adult son was allowed (63/76 Inzirillo v Caisse d'Allocations Familiales de l'Arondissement de Lyon; see Steiner, 1985: 28–9). Steiner (1990: 217) describes these benefits as having 'extremely dubious status as social security benefits' and suggests that, while it is an admirable desire to imbue all benefits with equality, it is illegitimate to do so by defining away the exclusion of social assistance from the rules about social security. However, since these rulings on workers and family members, the Court has said that even though a benefit 'grants a legally defined position to those entitled to it', its essential criterion may be 'need'. For example, it accepts that a Belgian benefit guaranteeing a minimum means of subsistence, *Minimex*, is of this nature. Nevertheless, Dutch and British nationals have been able to claim it because, in the Court's view, it constitutes a 'social advantage' and is subject to the rules of Regulation 1612/68 (249/83 Hoeckx v Centre Public d'Aide Sociale de Kalmthout and 122/84 Scrivener v Centre Public d'Aide Sociale de Chastre). In the Dutch case, it was held that a period in France could not deprive Hoeckx of this right as there was no residence requirement for Belgian nationals. These cases represent a new trend since the mid 1980s; that is, instead of assimilating assistance into social security, the Court is increasingly expanding what should count as assistance, or 'social advantage' (Steiner, 1988: 197; see also further discussion in chapter 7).

Need-based Assistance or 'Social Advantage': Regulation 1612/68
It has been noted already that workers have benefited from the Court's interpretation of what is a 'social advantage' and covered by Regulation 1612/68 so as not to inhibit freedom of movement; for example, compensation, trial language and the Belgian *Minimex*. Assistance for families has also been extended by the abolition of different residence conditions for nationals and

migrants in a growing range of types of benefit. For example, in 1976, an Italian woman was able to acquire a family rail-card normally only available to French parents of large families (32/75 Fiorini, neé Cristini, v SNCF; Steiner, 1985: 36–7) and, in 1982, an Italian couple were allowed to claim a discretionary childbirth loan normally restricted to resident German nationals (65/81 Reina v Landeskreditbank Baden Würtemberg; Steiner, 1985: 36–7). Now, elderly mothers of migrant workers who come to live with their families can claim special old age pensions (157/84 and 256/86 Frascogna v Caisse des Dépôts et Consignations), unemployed children can claim benefits (*Deak*; see note 17) and migrant workers and their families cannot be discriminated against in access to not only social housing, but also reduced-rate mortgages (63/86 Commission v Italy) – if such provisions are available to national workers and their families.

As a result of Court rulings rights to further and higher education may include not merely admission but grants and fees. According to the Court, maintenance awards are a 'social advantage' which should not be applied discriminatorily to genuine migrant workers or their dependants; though they are not a general right of all EC students (and, now, EFTA students in the Erasmus student exchange scheme) or of nationals who move to another country solely for education.[21] The general question of national discrimination in the level of registration fees was first tested in 1985 in the case of a French art student admitted to a course in Belgium who succeeded on the basis that Community laws about freedom of movement and vocational training (not social assistance) prohibited discrimination against all EC nationals on grounds of nationality or residence (293/83 Gravier v City of Liège).[22] In 1986, the question was raised by veterinary students with respect to Belgian universities which were funded on the basis that students from outside Belgium and Luxembourg paid a special fee, the *Minerval* (24/86 Blaizot and Others v Université de Liège, Université Catholique de Louvain, Université Libre de Bruxelles and Facultés Universitaires Nôtre Dame de la Paix de Namur). Here, the Court said that vocational training could not be conceived so narrowly as to exclude university courses and, subject to a time limit, Belgium was required to repay fees improperly charged (also, but without a time limit, in 309/85 Barra and Others v Belgium and City of Liège).[23]

Summary Workers have been able to augment 1408/71 benefits for themselves by benefits with a need criterion if the latter are intended to supplement inadequate insurance-based social security.

This is important because it widens the range of 'exportable' benefits possible under Regulation 1408/71 but not Regulation 1612/68. Workers have been able to claim insurance-based family benefits denied to them because of the absence of their families where no similar residence condition is imposed on workers and their families who are nationals. Families have been able to claim benefits that do not appear to be classified as family benefits. And workers and their families have been able to claim assistance not explicitly referred to in 1612/68, because it constitutes a 'social advantage' which should be applied without national discrimination. Noting particularly the effect of assimilation on 'exportation', Steiner (1985: 40) has argued that the Court's habit of remedying the defects of the one Regulation by reference to the tests and standards of the other, in order to give the fullest effect to the freedom of movement principle, has blurred customary distinctions between security and assistance so much that discrimination in almost any welfare benefit might be regarded as contravening Community law. Although the Court now seems less inclined towards assimilation, its expansion of 'social advantages', albeit with some restrictions, means that its methods still have significant financial and, hence, political consequences that will be referred to again in chapter 7.

3   Directives that Include Provisions Requiring Participation or Consultation

Nielsen and Szyszczak (1991: 161) point out that two different models of increasing worker participation have been tried. In one, workers would participate fully in the strategic management of their enterprises in ways that were common throughout the Community, as embodied in the draft Regulation for a European Company Statute and in the draft Fifth Directive on European Company Law. The other approach, they point out, requires workers to be informed and consulted in advance of important decisions but leaves the structure of representation to national practice. This has been applied in Directive 75/129 on collective redundancies and Directive 77/187 on the safeguarding of employees' rights in the event of transfer of undertakings, which are the main provisions that have reached the Court. The model is also present in the Third and Sixth Directives on company law, Directive 89/391 on health and safety and various other draft Directives on cross-border mergers, part-time and atypical work, in the controversial Vredeling Directive and in the draft Directive on a European Works Council for Community-scale undertakings.

Directives 75/129, 77/187 and 89/391   These directives are a weak attempt at convergence in the face of the strength of German unions in such situations and of the influential role of public bodies in France and the Netherlands, compared to other Member States (Nielsen and Szyszczak, 1991: 133–4; see also Butler, 1991 and Rhodes, 1991a and b). The first deals with the conduct of mass dismissals or collective redundancies.[24] Its consultation aspects state that employers must consult workers' representatives, with a view to reaching agreement, when collective redundancies are contemplated. Agreements should try to minimize redundancies and mitigate their consequences. So that representatives are in a position to make proposals, employers must provide, in writing, information about the reasons for the proposed action and the numbers to be affected. At the same time, employers must inform a public authority in writing, copied to workers' representatives, that redundancies are impending, giving thirty days' notice. The public authority must also be sent copies of information given to the representatives and the latter may make comments to the former.

Directive 77/187 deals with the transfer of an undertaking, business or part of one to another employer, as a result of a legal transfer or merger. It aims to make it possible for workers to continue to work for the new employer under the same conditions as in their original situations ('acquired rights'). Including rules about social security entitlements, it has consultative sections which require workers' representatives or workers themselves to be informed in good time of the reasons for the transfer, its legal, economic and social implications and the measures envisaged in relation to employees.

In view of the fact that one of the Danish objections to the Maastricht Treaty is a fear that Community standards of citizenship are often lower than those in Denmark, it is worth noting that these Directives state explicitly that they do not preclude more favourable national legislation. Most cases in the ECJ arising from these Directives deal with issues that do not bear directly on consultation. But, in one, the Court ruled against the Italian government's failure to require written notification of redundancy to workers and to impose a duty to inform a public authority. It has emphasized the general importance of redundant workers' rights by insisting that provisions apply, even in situations of a small number of redundancies (215/83 Commission v Belgium; Nielsen and Szyszczak, 1991: 135) and that there can be no excuse for failure by Member States to fulfil obligations (215/83 Commission v Belgium; 1991: 136; and 131/84 Commission v Italy (No. 2); 1991: 139). A similar strictness was evident in a ruling about the transfer of an undertaking in which the Court held that there can be no disadvantageous derogation even on one point and in a situation where the contract as a whole is favourable (324/86 Foreningen af Arbejdsledere i Danmark v Daddy's Dance Hall A/S; 1991: 143).

Directive 89/391 states that workers must be informed about health and safety risks and protective measures. Workers or their representatives have the right to make proposals and to be brought into balanced participation in accordance with national practices. Representatives vary in different countries according to whether unions or separate health spokespersons are customary. Whoever they are, they are also specifically protected in this work by the Directive. Because it is so new, a number of important factors are still to be interpreted; for example, who would count as the employer in a multiple or cross-border company (Nielsen and Szyszczak, 1991: 160–7).

Conclusion

Obviously the Directives just discussed are very small steps towards the institutionalization of participation. Those in force deal with the immediate interests of the individuals protected by them. Important though this is to people who find themselves in uncertain or hazardous situations, the Directives do not meet the intention, referred to in chapter 4, to include workers in decisions about the lives of their undertakings and in Community policy-making. Though, given their protective intentions, it might be wrong to dismiss them as illusory, they are not the kind of workers' rights that can be said to alter systems of control in the economic sphere and, hence, to contribute to the realization of equal citizenship. Indeed, measures such as strategic management and equity-sharing which would be more convincing evidence of equal citizenship to the participatory democrats, are still controversial – though perhaps less so among those Member States who will cooperate with one another without the United Kingdom, if the Maastricht Treaty is ratified.

On the basis of a review of cases, it is not possible to know whether the experience of claiming Community social security rights has had an impact on people's idea of citizenship. We cannot know whether they see the Community as an instrument for a better deal in their patrial or adopted societies; whether they see common policies as enabling them to lead more cosmopolitan lives in the civil society of the Community; or whether they have acquired the more collective sense of a common moral order present in the words of Levi Sandri and others, quoted in chapter 4. On the other hand, that they claimed entitlements has had an impact on the public space in the sense that the rulings promote a common civil society. And, since the expansiveness of those rulings takes the scope of social rights far beyond what governments had intended, they imply, much more obviously than workers' rights, some redistribution of power.

Many of the social security claimants, or those affected by the rulings, were women, sometimes as paid employees, often in their roles of partner and mother. But, even so, the assumptions that underlie conventional welfare rights systems, and in radical ideas about workers' participation, do not usually have the capacity to contribute to equal citizenship for women. Whether or not this can be overcome by policies that are explicitly about sex equality is the subject of the next chapter.

Notes

1 It might be said that they were expected to anticipate Rawls's 'veil of ignorance' (1971) in which people would choose a distribution of justice on the basis that choice should be made on the assumption that they would not know their place in society.

2 Gorz (1967), too, argues this to be a human need after the satisfaction of material needs.

3 Before the Danes rejected the Maastricht Treaty, their leaders had negotiated an opt-out clause which exempted them from this requirement in rules about the purchase of second homes – mostly by Germans.

4 There are schemes to promote Community languages and knowledge about the Community.

5 Judicial general developments over residence permits are explained in *Periodical 4/83* on the Court (Commission, 1983b: 33–4). See also 321/87 Commission v Belgium on border checks. But residence and other rights are weaker for the unemployed; see 39/86 Lair v Université de Hanovre; Steiner (1988: 146, 152, 160–4, 180–3); and Wilkeley (1988). There are intergovernmental conventions in this area on foreigners, following the Schengen Agreement (Baldwin-Edwards, 1991; Brubaker, 1989; Loescher 1989; see chapter 8 for further discussion of the agreement).

6 305/87 Commission v Greece dealt with property and 63/86 Commission v Italy with access to concessionary mortgages. But see proposed new exception for Denmark at note 3 above.

7 In 186/87 Cowan v French Treasury, as Mr Cowan was a tourist, not a worker, the French had applied a rule which stipulated the possession of a residence

permit as a condition of access to criminal compensation, in this case for assault on the underground railway. The Court held that, if there was a freedom to provide services across the Community without national discrimination, there must be a corresponding right to consume them. In 137/84 Ministere Public v Mutsch, which involved criminal proceedings and a migrant worker from Luxembourg living in a German-speaking municipality in Belgium, the Court held that the right to use one's own language fell within the category of 'social advantage', regulated by Community standards. If accused German-speaking Belgians were entitled to have criminal proceedings in German, the same must apply to migrants.

8 See 307/84 Commission v France; nurses classified as public servants. 66/85 Lawrie-Blum v Land Baden Würtemberg; teachers classified as public servants. 225/85 Commission v Italy; researchers in Consiglio Nazionale delle Recerche (CNR), deemed by the Court as not responsible for safeguarding the interests of the state. 33/88 Allué and Coonan v Università degli Studi di Venezia; foreign language *lektors* classified as public servants. See also discussion of Marguerite Johnston and the Royal Ulster Constabulary in chapters 6 and 7.

9 The quote is from 427/85 Commission v Germany on lawyers. Other professionals mentioned here were considered in the following cases. 29/84 Commission v Germany; nurses' diplomas. 197/84 Steinhauser v City of Biarritz; artists. 96/85 Commission v France; doctors and dentists. 307/84 Commission v France; nurses. 168/85 Commission v Italy; journalists, writers, tourist and travel specialists, pharmacists. 98, 162 and 258/85 Bertini di Santo, Pugnaloni and Others v Regione Lazio and Others; doctors and set intake figures. 306/84 Commission v Belgium; doctors. 221/85 Commission v Belgium; doctors, pharmacists, clinical biologists. 225/85 Commission v Italy; employment conditions of CNR researchers. 222/86 Union Nationale des Entraîneurs et Cadres Techniques Professionels du Football v Heylens; sports trainers and reviewability of the equivalence of diplomas. 147/86 Commission v Greece; teachers in 'crammer' and private technical schools, private tutors. 283/86 Commission v Belgium and C-306/89 Commission v Greece; transport, travel, storage and warehousing specialists. 309/90 Commission v Greece; architects, civil engineers, surveyors, lawyers. In 292/86 Gulling v Conseil de l'Ordre des Avocats du Barreau de Colmar et Conseil de l'Ordre des Avocats du Barreau de Saverne, the Court agreed that the decisive factor that excluded a lawyer from practice in another country had been unprofessional conduct, not nationality.

10 There are two types of Community migrant; frontier workers who cross borders regularly, perhaps living in one country and working elsewhere, and those who settle for periods away from the country of origin. Migrants from outside the Community are often called 'third country migrants'.

11 In 197/85 Office National des Pensions pour Travailleurs Salariés (ONPTS) v Stefanutti, the Italian widow of an Italian worker in Belgium had been denied a Belgian survivor's benefit because she received, in her own right, an Italian invalidity pension. In 128/88 di Felice v Institut National d'Assurances Sociales pour Travailleurs Indépendants, an Italian who had worked in Belgium had been denied a Belgian early retirement pension, despite having completed the necessary period of insurance, because of receiving an Italian invalidity pension. On the other hand, these rulings refer only to multiple benefits possibly payable to one person and not to a family unit. In 151/87 Bakker v

ONPTS, a pension paid to a wife as the result of the entry into force of the Dutch reforms to equalize social security for men and women was not allowed to count as a reason for reducing her Belgian husband's family-based pension.

12 The Court did not uphold a claim to be allowed to make retrospective payments in Germany so as to qualify for a Belgian invalidity pension in 29/88 Schmitt v Bundesversicherungsanstalt für Angestellte. The principle was also stated earlier in 43/86 Bestuurvan de Sociale Verzekeringsbank v de Rijke and de Rijke-van Gent.

13 If there is a difference, this is payable by the more 'generous' state (Steiner, 1990: 214). See also *Stefanutti* and *di Felice* at note 11 above and cases: 1/88 Baldi v Caisse de Compensation pour Allocations Familiales de l'Union des Classes Moyennes and 24/88 Georges v Office National d'Allocations Familiales pour Travailleurs Salariés. In the first, Belgium had ruled that an orphan's supplement to the family allowance claimed in respect of a child abroad for a period – in Italy – could be paid only if the deceased parent, unlike Signora Baldi, had been a worker; moreover, the surviving parent, who had been an insured worker, was eligible for an Italian benefit during the period of ineligibility in Belgium. In the second, France had demanded the repayment of family allowances on discovery that the Belgian claimant was also self-employed in Belgium, where the family lived. The Court held that if the allowances in the state of residence were less than those in the country of employment, the latter should make up the difference.

14 Established in 75/63 Hoekstra (née Unger) v Bestuur der Bedrijfsvereniging voor Detailhandel en Ambachten, Utrecht, a case which contributed to the replacement of Regulation 3 with Regulation 1408/71. Here a German migrant in the Netherlands returned to visit her family when she fell ill. On return to the Netherlands, she tried to reclaim medical expenses (Watson, 1980: 59–62 and, for later cases, 90–1. See also Steiner, 1985: 26).

15 For example, remedial work in a drug rehabilitation centre (344/87 Bettray v Staatssecretaris van Justitie) and short-term work undertaken by students for their sponsors in preparation for university (197/86 Brown v Secretary of State for Scotland – in contrast to the situation in 39/86 Lair v Université de Hanovre, to be discussed later). Gough and Baldwin-Edwards (1990) point out that the need for insured status constitutes the normal barrier against social security claims by students. This, of course, does not apply to social assistance which has been successfully claimed in respect of unemployment even by a non-Community national (see note 17 below).

16 In this, the Court has extended Member States' definitions of 'member of the family' in order to promote the free movement of workers (see Steiner, 1990: 212 on 139/82 Piscitello v Instituto Nazionale della Previdenza Sociale). See 267/83 Diatta v Land Berlin and 249/86 Commission v Germany, on spouses living apart, and 149/82 Robards v Insurance Officer on divorce and responsibility for children.

17 In 94/84 Office National de l'Emploi v Deak, Deak, who as a Hungarian national could not rely on 1408/71, was, as the son of an Italian worker in Belgium, entitled to the 'social advantage' of benefits for young people unemployed after completing studies.

18 Deak, as noted above, was able to claim assistance. In 147/87 Zaoui v Caisse Régionale d'Assurance Maladie de l'Ile de France, it was stated that assistance could be claimed only if dependants move within the Community. It remains

to be seen if assistance is affected by divorce (Steiner, 1990: 169 on 267/83 Diatta v Land Berlin where Diatta was the Senegalese spouse of a worker in Germany). The philosophy of the ECJ about residence and foreign family members in *Diatta* was not acknowledged in the UK appeal courts which upheld a deportation order; see note 3 in chapter 7. In 12/86 Demiral v Städt Schwäbisch Gmüd, the Court said there were no social rights for Turks because the Turkish/EC Association Agreement was strictly economic, but there is 'now enhanced legal protection' (Baldwin-Edwards, 1992a: 215). The European Commission was challenged by Member States when it tried to bring about a Directive on the rights of non-EC migrants and now Member States are simply recommended to treat 'third country migrants' in the same way as Community migrants (Baldwin-Edwards, 1992a; Cunningham, 1992).

19 Brown (see note 15 above) was not only unable to establish himself as a worker but was also unable to count as a family member because, though his family had migrated at one time, they had not lived with Brown in Scotland. In 263/86 Belgium v Humbel and Edel, it was stated that non-discrimination in secondary education fees was obligatory only with respect to migrants living within the territory where the education was being provided; not, as in this case, where French workers in Luxembourg sent their children to school in Belgium – even though there was no discrimination between Belgian and Luxembourg nationals. In 389/87 and 390/87, Echternach and Moritz v Netherlands Minister for Education and Science, it was held that children's rights were not eliminated by parents' absence or diplomatic status but that decisions about the conditions of access to education should take account of whether or not it would cause intolerable discontinuity if the denial of equal rights meant that children needed to be returned to their country of origin.

20 Steiner (1985: 27–8) says that the Court counts a benefit as social security if governments say it is but does not exclude benefits which are not listed by Member States. Note the contrast with the Court's deference, referred to earlier, to how one state classifies the benefits of another for the purposes of dealing with overlapping benefits. The cases here are 1/72 Frilli v Belgium and 187/73 Callemeyn v Belgium.

21 9/74 Casagrande v Landeshauptstadt München involved a grant for the child of a migrant worker (Steiner, 1990: 174). See also 42/87 Commission v Belgium on not confining grants to nationals of Belgium and Luxembourg and ensuring their availability to orphans of migrant workers and the children of migrants formerly in Belgium with their children but who had now moved away. In 39/86 Lair v Université de Hanovre, the applicant, like Brown (see notes 15 and 19 above), had been denied a grant. She was not a dependant of a migrant family but had worked intermittently in Germany for several years, in contrast to Brown's pre-Cambridge employment with Ferranti in Scotland. But, by going to university, would she be making herself unemployed and ineligible for assistance for workers? The Court held that she must still count as a worker if the proposed course and resultant qualification related to her employment. If there were a close connection (and this was a response to the representations of Member States that there would be abuses; Steiner, 1990: 176), she was entitled to the same advantages as German nationals.

22 152/82 Forcheri v Belgium involved the special situation of the wife of a Community employee who challenged higher fees for non-nationals of Belgium, who also appealed on the basis of vocational training policies

(Steiner, 1990: 178). Gravier based her claim on freedom of movement and access to vocational training and her case was accepted, despite the concerns of Member States – particularly those of Belgium where the *Minerval* (see text) was said to constitute 50% of the costs of education provided (Steiner, 1990: 198).

23 In these cases the claims for repayment were for periods that preceded Gravier. Since there was no dispute about the vocational nature of Barra's college and gunsmithery course, the Court said that the Gravier ruling could be applied retrospectively. But Blaizot raised the new issue of university courses being construed as vocational training and, given the significance of the *Minerval* to university funding, the Court placed a limit on university students claiming repayments to the date of the Gravier decision. The Commission was also held to be at fault in dealing with Belgium and its legitimate interest in legal certainty over the method of funding its universities (293/85 Commission v Belgium; Steiner, 1990: 274).

24 There is another Directive on funds for workers in insolvencies, Directive 80/987.

6

Sex and Citizenship

Introduction

In chapter 2 it was noted that the acquisition of citizenship rights by women was both similar to and different from the inclusion of working-class men. There, the discussion of women was mainly about their lack of legal and political rights and their struggle to be included as citizens in these senses of the term. Chapter 2 and, more extensively, chapter 5 dealt with ideas that social, civil and political rights must form an indivisible triad for universal citizenship to be a reality. These chapters pointed out that social rights might be construed individualistically or as a cause and reflection of a solidaristic moral order. As in the case of civil and political rights, it can be argued that, if social rights do universalize citizenship, they do so for men but not women.

Chapter 5 drew attention to Jordan's view (1989) that it was only in Scandinavian countries that concepts of citizenship included not only social rights through which to enjoy private liberties but also something of a shared moral order. It is these countries that have produced and inspired much theorizing about women and citizenship. Such work involves more than and differs from Richard Titmuss's hope that the ideal of class solidarity might become the touchstone of society as a whole; criticizing the 'maleness' of this basis of social rights, some feminist work on citizenship draws upon other humanistic values about aesthetics and reciprocity, not in its strictly contractual sense but as it arises from emotions. Many of the influential writers outside Scandinavia began by revealing the hidden, asymmetric assumptions that underlie universalistic theories of liberal democracy and the welfare state and, particularly in France, deconstructing the images of women in the culture of capitalist society.[1] Deconstructionist and other 'postmodern' forms of analysis, in their rejection of the possibility of certainty and the very idea of searching for it, are often thought of as making meaningless the quest for political change (Bryson, 1992). But though feminist writers may sharply disagree in their identification of the fundamental causes of inequality, the totality of their works provides the beginnings of a reconstruction of a 'good society' that might also be a sexually just one.

The fact that only one of the Scandinavian countries – Denmark – belongs to the European Community does not mean that its influence on ideas about women and citizenship can be ignored now or even more in the light of the Danish referendum vote against the Maastricht Treaty.[2] It is true, as this chapter will show, that Community rights for women are more obviously about individual equity than about group justice (McCrudden, 1991, compares these two anti-discrimination approaches) or a new moral order. But non-Scandinavian women increasingly judge the Community not only by the standards of Scandinavian policy, but also by the flourishing transnational bodies of feminist ideas about citizenship in which Scandinavian feminists play an influential part.

The next section of this chapter expands on the problems identified in women's legal and political rights by introducing related arguments about the implications for them of social rights. The chapter then discusses ideas about the reconstruction of politics and welfare so as to make the idea of equal citizenship more meaningful for women. Thereafter it is argued that, in contrast to Member States (and the Commission in its role as employer which differs from its role as a policy initiator), the Court of Justice has been rigorous in establishing that sex equality is not equivalent to policies that might confer contingent privileges or serve economic objectives; rather, the right to sex equality is a fundamental right. Finally, however, the chapter sets this boldness in the light of criticisms about the narrowness of the conception of women's rights that stems from the Treaty of Rome. Nevertheless, the conclusion is that, drawing upon experience from Scandinavia and elsewhere, an assessment of the Community's potential need not be so pessimistic as some writers have begun to suggest.

Fictions of Universalism

With the exception of Scandinavia, and there only in recent decades, the granting of formal legal and political equality has not led to any significant growth in the presence of women in legislatures and governments. Modern feminists have attributed women's unequal participation in public life, despite formal equality, to their unequal situations in the economic and domestic spheres. Liberal feminists are often criticized for having espoused too simple a concept of equality; the same political rights as men in the 'first wave of feminism' and the same employment rights in the second, without giving due regard to the different situations of men and women. On the other hand, as Forbes (1991) and Mitchell

(1987) point out, appeals to equality, even in its simplest form, have had revolutionary potential for women as well as in general (see, for example, the reference in chapter 2 to Abigail Adams). In any case, it is inaccurate to suggest that liberal feminists have been unconcerned about the effect on public roles of sex differences in civil and private life (the latter, in this chapter, refers to the personal, domestic or family sphere; see notes 3 and 4 in chapter 1). Twentieth-century liberals have regularly campaigned for improvements in the taxation and welfare systems. But, while liberals may have placed their primary emphasis on political status, moving outward to financial independence, socialist feminists focus first of all on the connections between economic status and the domestic sphere. Despite 'equal rights' reforms of politics and employment, family life is organized around an assumption that women are responsible for domestic affairs. This provides a rationale for disadvantageous treatment at work and in public welfare policies. Despite their different foci, both liberal feminists and socialists in the social democratic or welfare tradition believe that it is possible to reform institutions and policies to enable women to play a fuller part in all spheres of life. But both strands have experienced disputes about how to reconcile the existence of sex differences with the goal of equal status.

For example, in the 1930s, there were disagreements among women in the British labour movement about whether a 'special' measure for women – family allowances paid to all mothers – institutionalized their status as inhabitants of the private sphere or gave them a modicum of independence from men (Land, 1990). Modern liberals, at the risk of confounding the basic principles of liberalism, often advocate policies that are interventionist and based on the recognition of difference (Forbes, 1991). That is, they may accept 'affirmative action' or 'special' measures to make childcare more available, and in education and training – to mitigate the effects of past discrimination, to engender confidence and to provide the material means of fuller participation in the labour market, in trade unions, professional associations, political parties and public life. As in the case of social rights in general, such measures are criticized by libertarians for reasons similar to those discussed in chapter 5.

The issue of the care of dependent relatives, mainly children but also the sick and elderly, is relevant not only to disputes about whether national policies should merely eliminate arbitrary distinctions or should retain the practice of treating men and women differently if the purpose is to promote equality. Both the practical problem and the competing conceptual criteria occur in the

European Community. Moreover, it is also possible to interpret Community rights for women in the light of other theories which indicate that women cannot be 'added-in' by amending our ideas and reforming our institutions accordingly.

More fundamental critiques of democracy reject the idea that women became citizens when it became impossible to suppress the contradiction between an idea that individuals were naturally equal, despite differences, and the denial of rights for women because they were 'naturally different' (a difference thought also to render them incapable of the citizen's duty to defend the state). Chapter 2 referred to the view that, since women were brought into civil society under the tutelage and sexual domination of men, the political contract was among brothers, not human beings (Pateman, 1988b). Pateman argues that sexual subordination was institutionalized in rules about marriage which, like the language of citizenship (see reference in chapter 2 to Vogel, 1991), also obfuscate the structured inequality of the sexes. Rules about marriage are called the marriage 'contract' – a word which, because it describes relations in the political fraternity which over-threw rule by status, apparently implies that marriage, too, is an arrangement entered into by free and equal individuals, whereas rules regulating the rights of married women continued, even into the twentieth century, to discriminate against them.

Social rights advocates, according to Pateman (1988a and 1989), wrongly take 'fraternity' to be a synonym for communality. While the new social contract of the welfare state may mean a more solidaristic order for men or enable them to exercise individual rights more universally, it continues to embody the assumptions about women of the old social contract – explicitly in the first welfare legislation, now disguised by gender-neutral terms such as 'head of household' and 'breadwinner'. In Pateman's view, it is not possible to realize women's citizenship in the context of contractual theories, even social rights versions, because of the fundamental asymmetry in the revolution against patriarchy. Similar considerations must apply – because employment is thought of as male – to ideas about participation in the workplace as a substitute for political instincts or as a 'training ground' for civic or republican virtues.

Pateman's analysis is essentially political but a concept of patriarchy also appears in analyses that are primarily economic – though as a contingent, not a necessary, condition of women's oppression. Whereas patriarchy and capitalism can be seen as antithetical to one another because of their respective status and contractual relations, socialist feminists in the Marxist tradition argue that patriarchy has been adapted to capitalism because it can be used to reduce the costs of labour. The culture of patriarchy means that the social needs of male workers are met by women in the home. Because women do the same kind of work in paid labour that they do at home for no pay, less investment in training them is necessary. Since women can be assumed, even if they are not in practice, to be dependent on a man, they can be paid less. And because of beliefs that employment is secondary to married women's family obligations, as well as the secondary labour-market status of the jobs to which women are often recruited, women can be treated as a 'reserve army' of labour, taken on and laid off with little protection. Both the assumption that women can depend on men and their being employed in the more casual, secondary labour market also make women's social security entitlements lower than they are for men.

Proposals have been made in the Community to protect women from conditions of employment that are associated with being a 'reserve army' of labour. But, as is shown in the conclusion to this chapter, there are criticisms of the Community's policies that could be used to suggest that it expresses on a grander scale the illusion of sex equality: excluding questions of sexuality and male sexual power from the realm of public policy; and, though incorporating social rights, describing those entitled to them in terms whose neutrality is more apparent than real – for example, 'migrant', 'worker' and now 'Citizen of the Union'. However, some ideas which 'reconstruct' a conception of citizenship that is hospitable to women's interests can temper such fundamental pessimism.

The Reconstruction of Citizenship

Many feminist theorists reject the contractarian idea as a basis for women's citizenship, not necessarily for the same reasons as Pateman, but because its theory of justice depends upon making an assumption that people are equally situated in relevant respects and encourages a sense that it is imperative to treat people alike – when women and men are seldom in similar practical situations and are usually thought of as different. Some try to find alternative traditions in modes of reasoning that could form the basis for quite different conceptions of justice. Others rework more familiar bodies of thought to show that they need not always entail the same treatment.

Sevenhuijsen (1991), among the former, provides a way of responding to Pateman's point that democracy cannot be properly so-called until it takes into account the politics of motherhood.

Chapter 2 noted Kymlicka's view (1991) that political theorists have conventionally regarded motherhood and power relations in the family as outside politics; and politicians have often regarded childbearing and rearing as women's duty to the nation, though a duty, unlike military service, without corresponding rights. Sevenhuijsen draws upon alternative conceptions of justice in other liberal traditions, mainly from David Hume and the Scottish Enlightenment. Similar to Jordan's account of Aristotle, this is a view that justice is not the same as equity but stems from moral reasoning about the nature of the social order. If recognized as such, Sevenhuijsen's polity could incorporate values about motherhood that did not at once extol it and yet treat it as a *disqualification* for citizenship. Jónasdóttir (1985, 1988), though she disagrees in general with Pateman, shares her call for politics to be seen in the language of promises not contracts. Halsaa (1988) finds alternative forms of reasoning about a moral order in the language of aesthetics.

Bussemaker (1991) re-examines John Stuart Mill's concept of autonomy in order to emphasize that liberalism can accommodate women's interests and the different treatment that would be necessary for women's freedom. Bacchi (1990, 1991) argues that, while liberals may think they are worried about the principle of treating people differently, the real worry at the heart of liberal principles is whether the purposes of differentiation are undemocratic; for example, in racial classifications and, as Hart (1993) discusses, in the exclusion of 'women's' work from the ambit of the American Fair Labor Standards Act. Bacchi points out that the confusion between differentiation *per se* and its purposes has made it difficult for liberal feminists to agree on how to deal with pregnancy. Biology was and is used by opponents of women's emancipation as a justification for lesser rights. Consequently some feminists argue that pregnancy should be treated in law as the same as disabilities which may be experienced by men or women. Conversely, others want it to be regarded as a normal event of life which public policy should take into account – which might involve what Georgina Ashworth (cited in Bacchi, 1991) calls 'specific', instead of 'special' treatment.

In Scandinavian countries it seems to have become more normal than elsewhere to look for an appropriate mix of the same and different treatment in public policy – though there have been disagreements about how to interpret this. For example, several writers have been concerned that solidarity, of the kind applauded by Jordan, and approval of state intervention to foster it, are male in conception (e.g., Parvikko, 1991). Women's interests or needs were not accommodated originally with 'women as women' in mind, though policies arising from the pursuit of class equality touched their lives. Thus, some writers fear that the growth of the welfare state does not reduce women's dependence but merely transfers it from the private to the public sphere. The state as employer and provider of services forms a public patriarchy – perhaps a parallel argument to the criticism of state capitalism touched upon in the last chapter. However, in her most recent work, Siim (1991), for example, has changed her mind about this, arguing that state intervention, even if originating in class politics, does contribute to a stronger material basis for women to be autonomous citizens – able to define their own interests and policy needs. Siim's empirical approach has a conceptual echo in Phillips (1991a, 1991b) and Dietz (1992).

Phillips and Dietz remind us that citizenship is essentially about participation in politics and that the question of political (in)equality has tended to be neglected by socialists and feminists in the socialist tradition. In this tradition, the primary source of injustice is located in the economic and social spheres and differences in these spheres between and among groups are said to render formal political equality meaningless (see also chapters 2 and 5). Both Phillips and Dietz suggest that feminist critiques of the public/private split in liberal political thought and practice and the feminist emphasis on the qualities (innate or social) of motherhood as a *special* qualification for citizenship are important. This is because they are a justifiable corrective, not only to the explicit exclusionists, but also to the liberal fallacy of slipping from the idea that differences should not count in the formal determination of who may participate, and have their interests on the public agenda, to the idea that differences between people do not matter at all. Since, Phillips argues, politics is an activity that is distinct from other things that we do, good mothers may be good citizens but are not necessarily so, even though, whether or not they engage in public activity, they are affected by public policy. Equal citizenship is likely to involve organizing around group identities but, echoing Tassin's (1992) point about the Community as a whole (see chapter 2), Phillips argues that being a citizen must involve interacting with others in the 'public space' to decide upon proper public policies. She concludes that this ought to mean a sphere of privacy for individual personal or sexual relations, and their renegotiation, but that general questions of the domestic division of labour or sexual politics must be regarded as legitimate topics for public discussion, collective participation and public policy-making. The possibility of seeing the European Community as open to some of the standards of Siim and Phillips is discussed in the conclusion to this chapter.

The Politics of Women's Rights in the European Community

As noted in chapter 4, sex equality once had pride of place in the Community's social policy. Even then – in 1980 – this position was not above criticism. The Commission itself did not have a good reputation as an equal opportunity employer and, indeed, has been taken to the Court of Justice in its capacity as a staff tribunal as many times as some Member States. Member States had been dilatory in implementing the Directives on pay and conditions of work. The United Kingdom and the Netherlands had just insisted on a longer than usual implementation period for the first social security Directive. Consent to the second was granted only after it was agreed to reject the Commission's proposal to introduce immediately the use of the same actuarial tables for both sexes and also to delay the enforcement of its provision for survivors' benefits. Until 1989, policy innovation in matters of employment declined. Proposals to deal with positive action, the burden of proof, part-time work, retirement and parental leave were weakened or vetoed. The European Social Fund stopped identifying women as a special category for vocational training and retraining (Whitting and Quinn, 1989). A network of information about women's training – IRIS – was set up which described its own existence modestly, as 'symbolic' of the Community's potential for women (*Social Europe*, Commission, 1989d: 49) and, though a new funding programme – NOW – has begun, it is under-resourced. Both the policy proposals and significant budgetary allocations would have been needed, as Mazey (1988) argues, for formal rights to have diminished the widespread sex-segregation of labour markets in Member States. Jackson (1990) argues that better training and childcare policies are crucial if women are not to be disadvantaged still further in the Single European Market (SEM).

The social dimension of the SEM is dealt with in the 'Social Charter' or Community Charter of Basic Social Rights for Workers (Commission, 1989c). Although it refers to the need for 'an intensification' of equality policies and that this 'shall imply' steps to reconcile the demands of occupational and family roles, the Action Programme includes few concrete proposals for doing so. The Social Charter has been condemned by the European Parliament (EP) for its failure to re-introduce the issues disputed in the past (EP Resolutions, *Official Journal* C323, 1989: 44–56).

Parliamentary Resolutions regret the rejection of a Directive on positive action in favour of a non-binding Recommendation (but see reference to new possibilities for Recommendations in note 2 in chapter 3), the vetoing of Directives on the other topics mentioned above (a Court ruling does something to mitigate the absence of one on the burden of proof – see next section), and the poor funding of the NOW programme. The only proposals in the chapter on women in the Charter's Action Programme are for a Recommendation on childcare and a Directive on the protection of pregnant women workers.[3] The latter builds upon concerns raised under the 1989 Health and Safety Framework – to which, unlike to the Charter, the UK is committed – such as dismissal, the maintenance of rights, exposure to dangerous substances and paid maternity leave. So far all that has been agreed, and the compromise is controversial, is the length of maternity leave and the amount of pay. Part-time work is included in the Charter's chapter on contracts – a chapter primarily designed to minimize the possibility of employers taking advantage of cheaper labour costs in less regulated Member States. Retirement is covered in the chapter on the elderly which is intended to deal with ageing populations. As noted in earlier chapters of this book, the final content of the Charter was diluted to appease the United Kingdom government which has now been allowed to exempt itself from the Social Chapter of the Maastricht Treaty. Sometimes the overt opposition of the UK government has been convenient for other governments with similar concerns which they may wish to conceal or which are less pressing. Open objections to full-hearted support of sex equality, and discreet reluctance, may stem from the implications of the more rigorous stance of the Court of Justice. Though its judgments are sometimes criticized, the Court has made it clear that sex equality is a fundamental right and its rulings often imply costs that governments may not have expected to bear. In the absence of any major measures that are designed with equality in mind, the enforcement of existing policies is important, as these augment existing provisions and may set standards for proposals intended for other purposes but which may impinge upon women's rights. The rulings that are discussed below focus mainly on the Directives for equality at work with some reference to the more recently enforceable social security Directives.

The Law and Women's Rights

Equal pay for equal, or the same, work is required by Article 119 of the Treaty of Rome. Other forms of sex equality are not mentioned in the Treaty but, drawing on powers to promote related Community objectives, the Commission and Council of Ministers have extended the application of equal treatment in Directives 75/117/EEC, 76/207/EEC, 79/7/EEC, 86/378/EEC and 86/613/EEC. (The new Directive on maternity leave is 92/85/EEC.)

The first, 75/117, redefines the principle of Article 119 by requiring equal pay for work of equal value. The second, 76/207, stipulates equal treatment in other conditions of employment such as recruitment, promotion and training. It rules out discrimination based on marital and family status and indirect, as well as direct, discrimination. Exceptions are possible where sex is a genuine occupational qualification for reasons of authenticity or because of the personal nature of work or the workplace. They are also possible in order to protect pregnant women and mothers. Both Directives exempt state pension schemes and matters relating to retirement set by national legislation.

The third, 79/7, covers risks similar to those in Regulation 1408/71 on the application of general social security schemes to migrant workers (see chapter 5); that is, it applies to employed, self-employed, retired and invalided workers who are covered by statutory schemes protecting against sickness, old age, redundancy, accidents at work and occupational diseases, and supplementary benefits intended to augment contributory ones. It exempts the statutory determination of pensionable ages, survivors' benefits and certain matters relating to dependent wives. The fourth, 86/378, differs from Regulation 1408/71 and Directive 79/7 by dealing with *private* occupational pension schemes that cover risks similar to those just mentioned and, in addition, introduces the possibility of equalizing survivors' benefits. Directive 86/613 covers self-employed women and women employed in family businesses, especially family farms.

Disputes about the meaning of Article 119 and the Directives come before the Court of Justice in direct actions and references for preliminary rulings (see chapter 3).

Equal Pay and Equal Treatment

The first three references to the Court of Justice for interpretation of Article 119 were considered in the 1970s. These were claims by Gabrielle Defrenne, an employee of the Belgian state airline, Sabena, and involved severance pay and retirement pensions (80/70 v Belgium [No. 1]), equal pay (43/75 v Sabena [No. 2]), and retirement age (149/77 v Sabena [No. 3]). Defrenne lost her cases about severance pay and pensions and retirement age. She won the equal pay case in 1976 and, though the Court drastically restricted her compensation rights, it stated that Article 119 was directly effective (see chapter 3) in national courts for public and private employees. Thus, though the Court was saying that there had been a right to equal pay since 1962 but with no tangible consequences between 1962 and 1976, its ruling made it possible for other women to claim their Community right without their cases being taken all the way to the European Court of Justice. And, in its third judgment, the Court made a robust statement about the importance of sex equality, saying that 'respect for personal human rights is one of the general principles of Community law', that there was 'no doubt that the elimination of discrimination based on sex forms part of those fundamental rights' and that the unity of Community law imposed a duty on all institutions, including national courts, to enforce such rights. In the following discussion of cases, I concentrate on issues that involve the assumptions, referred to earlier in this chapter, about women and family roles that disadvantage them in the labour market, both of which affect their social security entitlements. Most of the disputes arise from the United Kingdom, partly because the UK is one of the Member States with different statutory pensionable ages, which often leads to the need for clarification, and partly because the Equal Opportunities Commissions of Northern Ireland and of Great Britain have been active in using the Community to improve domestic law.

Though it is not a consistent European pattern that women work part-time and men full-time, it is common in some countries (Lewis, 1993); vertical and horizontal occupational segregation, parallel to the domestic division of labour, is general. By ruling that indirect discrimination in pay is unlawful, as well as under Directive 76/207 on equal treatment, the Court has ensured that part-time workers have rights. Different hourly rates (96/80 Jenkins v Kingsgate (Clothing Productions) Ltd),[4] no sick-pay (171/88 Rinner-Kühn v FWW Spezial Gebaüdereinigung GmbH) and exclusion from company pension schemes (170/84 Bilka-Kaufhaus GmbH v Weber von Hartz) have been ruled out unless they can be objectively justified. The Court has dealt firmly with unequal rights arising from segregation. Both Denmark and the United Kingdom have had to amend their national legislation to embody more clearly the right of equal pay in work that is different but of equal value (143/83 Commission v Denmark and 61/81 Commission v UK). A literal interpretation of equal value in Irish law has been brought into line with case law elsewhere by a ruling that, if work is of *higher* value, the fact that 'higher' does not mean the same as 'equal' cannot be allowed to justify *lower* pay; work of higher value must command at least equal pay (157/86 Murphy and Others v An Bord Telecom Eireann; a similar anomaly had been promulgated and rectified in the UK courts under the 'like work' provisions of the Equal Pay Act). The common practice (Mazey, 1988) of evading obligations by manipulating job evaluation schemes has been touched upon by the Court in its guidance about what factors ought to be present in a fair analysis (237/85 Rummler v Dato-Druck GmbH).

Different statutory pensionable ages (in Belgium, the Netherlands and the United Kingdom) are based upon assumptions about marriage and the 'normal' age difference between husband and wife. Statutory norms impinge upon pay from employment. The Court ruled that Defrenne's claim against her employers for equal pension rights was outside Community law because Sabena was a state airline whose pension scheme included a state subsidy; statutory retirement and pensionable matters were exempt from Article 119 and Directive 75/117. But it said that pensions, in principle, 'were not alien to the concept of pay'. Since then, it has ruled that contributions made by employers to occupational pension schemes (69/80 Worringham and Humphreys v Lloyds Bank) and retirement benefits in kind (12/81 Garland v British Rail Engineering Ltd) do constitute pay under Article 119 and Directive 75/117. In *Worringham* and in a case involving married civil servants (23/83 Liefting v Directie van het Academisch Ziekenhuis), higher gross pay, even if contributed immediately to a pension scheme, gave rise to differences in other benefits related to pay. However, the Court has made a distinction between gross and net salaries. In a case from the United Kingdom heard in 1987 about deductions from the pay of male civil servants, married or not, to fund a widows' pension scheme, the Court found that the scheme did not have adverse effects on the rights of women and, in this case, single men to other benefits which were calculated on the basis of gross salary (192/85 Newstead v Department of Transport and HM Treasury).[5] Moreover, since it was a 'contracted out' scheme, it was a substitute for the state pension scheme and could not be subject to Article 119 and Directive 75/117; even if it had been allowed to count as an occupational pension scheme, Mr Newstead could not have used the provision for survivors' benefits in Directive 86/613, as this part has not yet been activated. But, in 1990, the Court ruled that 'contracted out' schemes are not protected by the exemption of statutory pension schemes when it comes to *access* to benefits (C-262/88 Barber v Guardian Royal Exchange Assurance Group). It held that Article 119 covered any remuneration arising from the employment relationship. Pensions payable on redundancy were an element of remuneration. Thus, the practice of basing rules about the age of access to employment pensions on the norms of the state scheme led to unequal pay that was unlawful under Article 119.

Differences in statutory pensionable ages have also been deemed distinct from the ages at which employers may dismiss men and women or compel them to retire. The first of these cases (19/81 Burton v British Railways Board), like Barber but before it, involved different ages of access to severance pay. Here, the Court did not insist on a distinction between the state pension and pay arising from employment. With respect to the different ages, it emphasized that the severance pay should be seen in the context of the *voluntary* nature of the whole early retirement scheme. Four years later, in 1986, it ruled that *involuntary* early retirement was the same as redundancy or dismissal; here, it *was* lawful to use the same ages for men and women in the application of an early retirement scheme (151/84 Roberts v Tate and Lyle Industries Ltd). In the same week, the Court argued that normal retirement ages were also a condition of employment, like redundancy and dismissal, covered by Community law (152/84 Marshall v Southampton and South West Hampshire Area Health Authority (Teaching); 262/84 Beets-Proper v F. van Lanschott Bankiers NV); it was a matter of historical contingency not an analytic necessity that linked employers' rules about retirement ages with state pensionable ages.[6] In 1990, the Court ruled that, where women had been forced to retire at 60 while men could continue until 65, they must be entitled to effective compensation (C-188/89 Foster and Others v British Gas).

In general, then, there has been a move towards equal treatment in matters where men and women have been treated differently because of conventional assumptions about their domestic roles; that is, where jobs are different or done under different hourly conditions and in severance of employment. Community law allows specific treatment for the protection of mothers and where sex is a genuine occupational qualification. But it is not clear that the purposes to which such differentiations are put lead to a mix of the same and different treatment that would satisfy feminist standards of citizenship. For example, the Court's rulings on motherhood could be construed as reflecting traditional male attitudes, inhibiting more flexible boundaries between the public and private realms and discouraging choice for both sexes about inhabiting either or both of them; or, they could be seen as maintaining the significance of motherhood, argued by some feminists to be the only valued status that society grants to women.[7] The Court rejected a Commission claim that Italy was contravening Directive 76/207 by not allowing parental leave to adoptive fathers as well as mothers (163/82 Commission v Italy). And it upheld a German decision that an unmarried father who looked after his child was not entitled to leave and an allowance granted to mothers (184/83 Hofmann v Barmer Ersatzkasse). Both the Commission and Herr Hofmann argued that the arrangement existed, not or not only for the health of the mother, but for the care of the child. In both cases, the Court referred to the special need to ensure the protection of women and to the distinctive importance of bonding between mother and child. The Directive 'was not intended to deal with matters of family organisation or to "alter the division of responsibility between parents"' (Nielsen and Szyszczak, 1991: 106). In cases of discrimination against pregnant women workers, the Court has expressed its specific concern for women more forcefully than the English courts. In England, it has been held that, since a man cannot become pregnant, a pregnant woman has no point of comparison unless analogous treatment of a sick male can be brought in (which some feminists prefer for reasons mentioned earlier in the chapter). Other feminist approaches referred to above might find the European Court's rulings more congenial; that is, since pregnancy is unique to women, discrimination on grounds of pregnancy is direct sex discrimination; there is no need to bring in other factors (C-177/88 Dekker v Stichting Vormingscentrum voor Jonge Volwassenen (VJV-Centrum) Plus; C-179/88 Hertz v Aldi Marked A/S).

If the cases discussed above protect policies that are specific to women for benevolent purposes, the Court has been suspicious of the use of exemptions which have the effect of weakening women's rights. The use of stereotypes of 'womanly' skills and interpersonal relationships as the bases of defences under the genuine occupational qualification and public security derogation had been 'driving a coach and horses' through many national legislations (Vallance and Davies, 1986). For example, the Court has lowered the number of employees in what is to count as a small firm in the United Kingdom (165/82 Commission v UK), restricted the scope of French exemptions in the prison and police services (318/86 Commission v France) and, in the case of public safety, has called for strict scrutiny of the means of achieving safety, the choice of the least discriminatory method and proportionate treatment – if differentiation is unavoidable (222/84 Johnston v Chief Constable of the Royal Ulster Constabulary).

State Social Security

If, as we have seen, there is a complex relationship amongst pay
from employment, dismissal in its various forms, occupational
pension rights and the state pensionable age, experience in the
labour market and other state social security benefits are also
linked. This is particularly pertinent to married women treated in
most national social security legislation before Directive 79/7 as
dependent on husbands.

The Court of Justice has curtailed the freedom of Member States
to remove direct discrimination against married women in
unemployment benefits in ways that seek to minimize increases in
public expenditure (286/85 McDermott and Cotter v Minister for
Social Welfare and the Attorney General; 71/85 Netherlands v
Federatie Nederlandse Vakbeweging; 80/87 Dik and Menkutos-
Demicirci and Laar-Vreeman v College van Burgemeester en
Wethouders de Arnhem et Winterswijk). In so doing, the Court
has said that transitional measures to implement the Directive must
not perpetuate past discrimination and that it has direct effects in
national courts (Nielsen and Szyszczak, 1991: 111–13). The Court
was similarly strict in a case involving a British disability allowance
(384/85 Clarke v Chief Adjudication Officer). Here, transitional
measures introduced a sex-neutral test of eligibility in place of the
previous different treatment that required married women to show
that they could not do housework in order to qualify for an
allowance. Women eligible under the old test automatically became
entitled to the new allowance arising from the new test. Mrs Borrie
Clarke had been judged ineligible for the old allowance and,
therefore, ineligible for the new allowance. The Court held that she
must be treated as a man would be under the new rules and, if
eligible under the sex-neutral test, regardless of her disqualification
under the old test, she was entitled to the new allowance.

On the other hand, the payment of supplements to augment an
invalidity benefit, calculated on the basis of a previous law which
was discriminatory, was regarded as tolerable since the objective
was to prevent even more poverty among invalids with dependants
than among those without (30/85 Teuling v Bedrijfsvereniging voor
de Chemische Industrie). This case involves indirect discrimination
which will be taken up again in the conclusion. Steiner (1988: 245)
suggests that, since the reason for difference in treatment was the
'greater burden' borne by people with dependants, it was clearly
not based on sex. Nielsen and Szyszczak (1991: 114), however,
argue that it is a matter of policy priorities; despite the Court's
approach in the direct discrimination cases previously mentioned,

this case shows that 'budget constraints may elevate the need to alleviate poverty over the principle of eliminating sex discrimination'. But national budgetary constraints do not always inhibit the Court from making a wide interpretation of the scope of the Directive. In another case from the United Kingdom (150/85 Drake v Chief Adjudication Officer), an allowance for the care of dependent relatives was payable to all men and single women, assumed to need to earn their living, but not to married women. The United Kingdom argued that the allowance was not one that was in the categories covered by the Directive. But the Court ruled that the Directive should be construed as including a wide range of benefits, including social assistance. It also said that Mrs Drake should count as a worker, having been one and her work having been interrupted as a result of one of the risks, suffered albeit by her mother not herself, covered by the Directive.

Conclusion

Though the Court has been criticized, particularly for restricting compensation to the dates of significant judgments (for example, *Defrenne* No. 2 and *Barber*) and for sometimes making fumbling progress, it has developed rigorous standards in equal treatment at work and in matters arising from pregnancy. But it is possible to argue that neither it nor Member States can or want to make fundamental alterations to the material basis of women's citizenship. In addition to its comments about not altering family responsibilities under the Equal Treatment Directive, the Court has stated categorically that the two Social Security Directives are not intended to address the general condition of sex equality but only the situations of men and women as workers (Joined cases 48/88, 106/88, 107/88 Achterberg-te Riele, Bernsen-Gustin and Egbers-Reuvers v Sociale Verzekeringsbank). In addition to the budgetary effects of equalizing social security, the costs of equal rights at work increasingly fall upon governments (see chapter 7), with the result that it may be difficult to persuade them to carry out the stated intention of the Charter to take steps to reconcile work and family roles. There is much agreement among analysts of Community policy that neither the national means of implementing equal social security nor the Community concepts of work and worker do much to help women to be more autonomous.

On the face of it, changes in the patterns of industry and employment, already in train and likely to accelerate in the Single European Market, combined with demographic trends seem favourable to women (Hakim, 1990; Jackson, 1990; Morrissey,

1991). Traditional industries associated with male employment are declining while service industries are growing. But, as Jackson points out, new technologies in banking,' where there is a high density of female employment, may reduce opportunities unless there is appropriate training. Generally, work is being organized into 'atypical' forms with more 'flexible' contracts, more sophisticated types of home-working, more self-employment and more small enterprises. Although atypical work is still a small proportion of total Community employment, it is a much more significant dimension of women's employment analysed separately, and is becoming more so (Jackson, 1990: 44–9). Over a quarter of the Community's female workforce works part-time (more among married women) and many more do this involuntarily than had previously been estimated; in Spain and Greece, 10 per cent and 34 per cent, respectively, of working women are unpaid because they work in family businesses but in most countries women are more likely than men to be homeworkers or 'assisting relatives' as their paid employment. While pressures on women to accept atypical employment contracts are, according to Jackson, stronger in southern Europe, women are more likely than men throughout the Community to be on temporary contracts and the rate at which they are unwillingly in atypical contracts has been growing in the 1980s in half the Member States. Jackson predicts considerably more part-time, fixed-term or agency employment in the service sector.

Though such forms of employment appear to help women who have to be 'flexible' in managing two roles, home-working may continue to escape protection and success in transforming it into self-employment or a cooperative small business will require familiarity with new technologies and management planning. As indicated in chapter 4, investment in the remains of skilled manufacturing may be concentrated in the 'golden triangle' of Germany, France and the Benelux countries, thus requiring mobility. Low or semi-skilled manufacturing may increasingly be carried out in countries with poor levels of welfare, education and training. Without appropriate measures, labour markets segmented by sex may be reinforced – doubly so, within and across countries.

Yet, according to some writers, who are concerned primarily with Community sex equality rights and not with the expansive rulings discussed in chapter 5 on the needs of migrants and their families, work, not need, is an increasingly prominent criterion of entitlement to directly related benefits and to others that affect domestic welfare (Finch, 1990; Hakim, 1990; Luckhaus, 1990). Moreover, they argue, the idea of work in this connection is based on a model of male, full-time employment. As Jackson's research shows, this is significantly irrelevant to women and is beginning to be outdated for men. Most Member States are equalizing social security entitlements by eliminating direct discrimination but this does not always improve the situations of women and often increases indirect discrimination, which is also supposed to be unlawful. Individualizing rights by substituting benefits for husbands or fathers by ones with gender-neutral labels such as 'head of household' or 'breadwinner' does not tackle the problem that men and women are rarely similarly situated in the labour market from which access to and levels of benefit are derived (Hoskyns, 1988; Hoskyns and Luckhaus, 1989; Luckhaus, 1990; Millar, 1989; Sjerps, 1988). As Luckhaus (1990: 14) puts it, 'participation in the social security system remains entirely contingent on [women] being able to establish themselves, like men, as full-time paid workers'. Most writers suggest that women cannot enjoy equal social rights unless social security schemes are 'individualized' not in the labelling of rights but in how needs are calculated. Hakim (1990: 25) points out that where rights are individualized, women 'need to build up their own contributions instead of relying on husbands – having a special need for social insurance credits for the years they spend in unpaid work'.

Drawing on Hakim, Mangen (1990: 6–7) also argues for a more flexible definition of work that would enable socially important activity that was not subject to a formal labour contract to qualify for insurance credits. In a way that is reminiscent of the arguments in the 1930s about family allowances, Mangen points out that such a settlement might 'institutionalize sexism' since there are no serious moves afoot to encourage men to take up 'substantially more of the roles of housewife, child carer, care of the elderly and disabled'; but women would be guaranteed 'a certain level of protection that, in many countries, is still denied to them'.

The pessimism of these analyses appears to provide support for the idea, discussed earlier in this chapter, that the Community might be a fiction on a grander scale. But this can be countered in two ways. One is Siim's evidence from Scandinavia (1991), also referred to earlier, that measures devised for other reasons can provide the means through which women may be able to become political actors in Phillips's sense (1991a and 1991b) with the power to define their own needs, including the capacity to say where equal treatment is appropriate and when specific treatment would be better. The other is that, if political analysis must involve the revelation of meanings, then it must be that politics itself is a contest over meanings.

The concept of citizen-as-worker objected to by feminist critics of the Community derives from the 'four freedoms' of the Treaty of Rome, referred to in earlier chapters. But these leave a lot of scope for contests over meanings. In this and previous chapters it has been shown that economic instruments have been reformulated as rights. Cases in chapter 5, as well as the *Drake* case in this one, show that both the meaning of worker and categories of benefit covered by Community law have been extended well beyond what Member State governments intended. Edwards and McKie (1992) argue that the Community's approach to childcare is based on a meaning of equality that is not the narrow one of individual equal treatment but one which implies the promotion of group justice. Moss (1990) argues that, even in the absence of a Directive – which is so frequently regretted – the European Childcare Network has already brought about much greater awareness in each country of provisions in others and will continue to push Community policy into more concrete forms. It is, however, the case that it is difficult to construe the freedoms of the Treaty of Rome in such a way as to incorporate violence and male sexual power over women – the basic elements that would have to be in a radical feminist conception of citizenship. But such matters have not been ignored in the European Parliament. The networks through which women can try to inscribe their meanings in policy have been referred to already and are dealt with again in the final section of the next chapter on the equal protection of the laws.

Notes

1   I always find it curious that Inglehart, one of the most quoted writers about 'post-industrial' society, categorizes support for women's rights as a post-material value. Whether feminists mobilize around pay, taxation, social security or protection from male violence (symbolic or actual), all their preoccupations seem to me to be about the most material conditions of physical and economic security.

2   The groups that opposed the Treaty were odd bed-fellows, including both populists and the progressive or radical left. For some of the latter, the Treaty was seen as undermining the Danish concept of social citizenship in its sense of classlessness. The political scientist Drude Dahlerup was prominent among feminist opponents who understood the Community as patriarchal in the ways described in this chapter and as endangering the higher standards of women's liberation in Denmark. The idea that the Community undermined women's rights in Scandinavia, also an issue in the politics of Norway's reconsideration of membership, stems partly from the existence of more and less securely established normative standards in policy and partly from fear of the pressures on the domestic budgets of richer states that would result from proposals to reform and enlarge the Community's structural funds to assist its poor regions to cope with the advent of the Single European Market.

3   The final form of a measure to protect against hazards (draft directive 89/391) will be important. As Kenney (1992) has argued with reference to Britain and the United States, it is possible that, as with traditional protective legislation, women may be disproportionately excluded from particular occupations on grounds of incompletely articulated assumptions about women's 'natural' destiny and without rational analysis of the evidence of the effects on men as well as women. See note 5 for another kind of adverse impact on men arising from conventional assumptions about family life and sexuality.

4   The *Jenkins* case is often thought to be a bad one because it admits 'market forces' as a legitimate reason for different treatment and because it appears to say that different treatment is unlawful only if it can be shown that it was a way of depressing wages on the ground that a group of workers was mainly composed of women (Nielsen and Szyszczak, 1991). But, together with *Bilka-Kaufhaus GmbH*, the Court has outlawed discrimination where objective differences between part-time and full-time hours cannot be demonstrated and has given guidance on standards of proof. The burden of proof, not necessarily in connection with part-time work, was partly shifted on to employers in situations involving 'opaque payment structures' (see *Danfoss* case) (Nielsen and Szyszczak, 1991).

5   Mr Newstead's case reveals an assumption that all men are expected to become husbands responsible for dependent wives, even though they may be, as he was described, 'a confirmed bachelor'.

6   These two cases raise other issues which are taken up in the next chapter on the equal protection of the laws.

7   The Court has touched on abortion, saying that medical termination, performed in accordance with the laws of Member States, is a service within the meaning of Community law. But, if termination is forbidden within a Member State, it is not contrary to Community law to stop students, who are unconnected with clinics in other Member States, from distributing information about how to obtain terminations elsewhere (C-159/90, Society for the Protection of Unborn Children, Ireland v Grogan and Others).

7

The Equal Protection of Community Laws

Introduction

There are at least two strands of the theme of this book that lead to this chapter; the idea that rights, properly called, are universal and that universal rights entail impersonal application. Universalism and impersonalism distinguish a liberal system of civil rights 'governed by laws not men' from patriarchal systems of personal rule (Friedman, 1981). The same canons characterize liberal democracy in which legal equality is augmented by political equality. Arguments about whether welfare benefits and sex equality can be accommodated by the same regulatory principles are at the heart of the debate about whether citizenship entails social rights and, if so, what they look like. In liberalism and liberal democracy, equal legal and political status is accorded, in theory at least, to all individuals; status does not, or is not supposed to, depend upon the particularity of personal circumstances and relationships. In both the legal and political spheres, the extensions were at first class-based and then included women. The idea of universalism is expressed in the constitutional principle of the equal protection of the laws.

In the welfare democracy stage of political development, however, the status of economic, social or welfare benefits is controversial, not only because they require positive state intervention instead of the mere removal of arbitrary impediments, but also because they raise the difficulty of whether and how difference may be taken into account. This arises because the very nature of need means that personal circumstances cannot be left anonymous, yet what is required to be disclosed may be inappropriate or extracted without respect (see chapters 5 and 6). Or it may be because race and sex are immutable characteristics, the specifying of which in rules is sometimes considered dangerously fascist and sometimes thought necessary in order to eliminate particular forms of social deprivation which impinge upon political rights (see chapter 6).

Industrial rights, according to Barbalet's account (1988) of T.H. Marshall, are different in principle and practice from welfare rights, not only because of the problem of universalism and difference, but also because the former are the means of making claims against the state or powerful groups and the latter are claims for certain guarantees by the state, requiring, unlike civil rights, a major bureaucratic structure. Thus, industrial rights are a civil right because they are part of a unified set of rights to take certain forms of action (which some would classify as secondary political rights), while welfare rights are not. On the other hand, earlier chapters have shown that the provision of social benefits in cash or kind can also be argued to serve the same function that was once associated with the civil right to own property; that is, the means of fuller participation in the political community. Though Barbalet emphasizes contradictions between these forms of right and inconsistencies in Marshall's theory of social citizenship, as well as the susceptibility of social rights to being taken away, it can be argued, on the basis of Friedman's work, that at least some of the problems Barbalet identifies – particularly with respect to individual need, bureaucracy and the vulnerability of social rights – lie not in the idea of social rights as a form of citizenship or in differences that there may be between them and civil and political rights but in their imperfect entrenchment in the particular society (the United Kingdom) at the centre of the two analyses. As also noted earlier, the presence of deprivation can be said, just as much as a lack of legal protection and political participation, to indicate a breakdown in the entitlements of a modern (albeit with ancient roots) conception of citizenship. In other words, even if there are some differences among the three sets of rights, if one cannot be exercised properly without the other two, they have a crucial similarity and all of them can and ought to be judged by the same cardinal criterion. That is, like other rights, social rights, properly called, entail entrenchment and application according to the principle of the equal protection of the laws.

It was shown in chapters 5 and 6 that the Court of Justice defines Community law in these fields as conferring rights, not benefits that are dependent on political and economic expediency (except where it has invoked the principle of legal certainty for governments; see below). It is, then, incumbent that their application should follow the canons of the equal protection of the laws. This involves questions of procedural and material equality. But, since the existence of a developed legal federation is accompanied by a political system that has only the rudiments of federalism, this is difficult to practise and to analyse. The difficulty is manifold, to do with the nature of institutions and the nature of policies. Policies may be about common, abstract standards but require material equality *within* Member States through the same and different treatment (sex equality); they may be common requiring similar practice *across* Member States (workers' participation); or they may allow different material provisions in different Member States but require them to be coordinated so as not to disadvantage those who move (social security). There is a common rationality in the sense that shared Community objectives have been agreed and in the existence of a common system of the judicialization of rights in the legal federation; but the administrative adjudication of entitlements is not carried out by an overarching bureaucracy and, instead, is divided among twelve different national ones (hence the ETUC's concern – see chapter 4 – about the Social Charter). In examining the Court of Justice's capacities and incapacities to promote the equal protection of the laws, this chapter shows that in some instances the Court has appeared to demand a common material element, that is, the harmonization once rejected by politicians of Member States (chapter 4), and in other cases has left matters to piecemeal political resolution. The next part of this chapter relates controversies about national welfare rights to rule of law questions. It then examines the effect of the Court on material equal protection within and across states and in establishing common adjudicative standards. It also refers to the implications of some of these individual cases for harmonization. The section ends with a discussion of contradictory assessments of the impact of the Court's approach upon the development of a rational system of European entitlements and rights. It is noted here that some matters are outside its control. Finally, the chapter explores the experiments of the Commission, which does not have a service provision responsibility of its own, in developing a kind of informal equal protection of the laws through policy-networking. This is set in the context of similar processes in the United States.

The Rule of Law and National and Community Rights

The basic element of citizenship from which capacities for full participation arise is to live under the rule of law, under a system where laws and offences are known, where there is predictability and certainty that offences will be punished but that punishment for breaches can follow only from the application of the due processes of the law. The cardinal principles of equal access and equal protection express the Aristotelian distinction between the rule of law and the rule of men, remedy and punishment in the latter being liable to arbitrariness, personal favour or caprice on the part of rulers. Equal protection means that individuals in the same situation will be treated in the same way. There is a strong onus of proof on those who would wish to treat people differently in a way that is disadvantageous and a presumption that, if people are to be treated differently, the grounds for difference in treatment must be scrutinized strictly and the different treatment should be proportionate. In the United States, departures from the 14th Amendment – the equal protection clause of the Constitution – affecting racial groups can be justified only by demonstrating that a particular policy purpose is overriding and that there is no way of meeting it other than by making racial distinctions. For women, the standard of scrutiny is less strict but the policy purpose must be shown to be rationally related to the differentiation. In the European Community, the reasoning behind differentiation must be transparent (see below) and, if sustainable, the material consequences must not be unnecessarily harsh (from the German principle of proportionality – see Arnull, 1989).

These standards have come about generally as a result of situations in which groups have suffered from explicitly exclusionary legal and political arrangements, 'universalism' having been confined, say, to white males. The departure from universalism that worries commentators on social rights is different from concern about barriers. It is that governments pick out categories of people for the receipt of positive intervention. For some writers, the primary problem is that redistribution coerces those who are to be taxed in order to pay for the benefits (see chapter 5). From the point of view of this chapter, the main points are either that welfare cannot be provided according to the impersonal principles governing legal and political rights or that they are not so in particular systems. For the first kind of critic, the problem is inherent and cannot be resolved except either by abandoning the idea that the state has special responsibilities in this field or by maintaining that it does but that the relationship between state and citizen must be justified or explained by some means other than the language of rights. For the second, the problem is not inherent; systems of delivery can be made to approximate as far as possible to the canons of the rule of law, though difficulties are acknowledged (see discussion of Friedman and budgetary consequences below).

Among those who see an inherent problem in construing welfare benefits as social rights, most stress the difference between the capacity of governments to remove arbitrary civil and political inequalities without reference to particular people and the intrusiveness and heavy demands for information about persons that are necessary to bring about, say, a minimum income for all. It is even more dangerous when the information about persons and the consequent benefits are contingent upon innate characteristics such as race or sex. Their critics contend that the significance of universalism and impersonalism to a distinction between legal and welfare rights is more apparent than real (see chapter 5); moreover, they point out, those who defend the difference rarely object to the idea of the granting of legal aid to equalize access. If the right not to fall below an agreed poverty line can be claimed only through heavily bureaucratic and intrusive methods, this is a problem, not of the right itself, but of the system or culture of administration.

Neither of these examples solves the problem of objections based on rights being associated with innate characteristics; in principle, anyone may need a trial, fall ill or become very poor. In contrast, it is virtually impossible to change biological characteristics (though South African officials sometimes used to re-classify racial memberships and, conversely, men and women sometimes voluntarily change sex but are denied official recognition of new identities). The fact that genetic and ethnic classifications are considered illiberal has a lot to do with the malevolent purposes to which sometimes they have been put; Nazi Germany and South Africa are extreme examples but, in otherwise liberal democracies such as the United States and in Western Europe, they have been used to deny rights to women, blacks, immigrants and guest workers. However, as Bacchi (1990, 1991) argues (see chapters 2 and 6), the real problem is not the differentiation in itself but its intended effect. The picking out of groups in connection with welfare is usually intended to make a sense of community membership felt more strongly. While expectations about the nature of society have come to include protection against the insecurities of the market, fully universal provision of welfare is very expensive and, it seems, not always effective in reaching those most in need (e.g., Le Grand, 1991). Sen's (1977) 'informational constraints' (see chapter 5) relate to a combination of continuing poverty and resource constraints which compelled British governments to define entitlements to equality more precisely; for example, in terms of equal pay for different races and for men and women. Sen's argument is reinforced by the more recent evidence of the 'feminization of poverty' (e.g., Dex and Shaw, 1986; Land, 1987; Millar, 1990); that is, its concentration among women and the view that, if an attack is to be made on poverty in general, it might be more effective if it were more specifically aimed at women. Current legislation aimed at racial and sex equality is worded in ways which ought not to alarm the universalists; not as black or women's rights to housing but in terms of allocation being provided without racial or sex discrimination. And, indeed, it is not only blacks or women who use the legislation to seek remedy against discrimination in national systems or in the European Community.

One of the most sustained arguments that it is possible to justify social rights in the light of the civil and political standards of liberal democracy is that of Friedman (1981). She contrasts the personalism of pre-liberal systems of rule with the origins and further development of the rule of law, with particular reference to welfare in the United States and the United Kingdom. The aspect of her work that is relevant here is not that which is country-specific but her dual analysis of administrative and judicial developments. She starts from Weber's descriptions of administration and adjudication. The first is a system 'in which only the political authority has rights; the ruled do not' (1981: 26). Under adjudication, 'the right of political authority is limited, however rudimentarily, by the rights of the subjects' (1981: 26). In Weber's view, administration and adjudication were the antithesis of one another; under one, subjects had no choice but passivity while, under the other, they could be appellants. Friedman, however, argues that there can be a continuum between them. That form of administration which is antithetical to adjudication is the personalized type found in systems of rule that combine patriarchal households and paternalistic governments. Liberalism and liberal democracy are associated with impersonalized rule and bureaucracy. But, though rule-governed and characterized by decisions that are rationally related to one another, decisions in a liberal regime may not be open to challenge. This needs a system of 'judicialization' in which goals and intermediate policies are rationally related and administrative decisions are open to appeal to an external body (1981, chapter 7). The continuum exists because of features of the middle stage between personal rule and a 'judicialized regime'. Liberal bureaucratic administration derives its authority from the rule of law but, for many reasons, latitude is thought to be needed and is often granted by statute. Dicey's (1959 [1885]) suspicion of administrative adjudication and more modern criticisms of internal review procedures are similar to Friedman's worries about liberal democracy without judicialization. Even if decisions are not capricious, she argues, they are made in the light of some purpose useful to rulers. In such a situation, welfare benefits, even if impersonal, are contingent upon other policy purposes and principles; they are not yet rights but entitlements. They only become rights when there is a system of control over administrative discretion from outside the bureaucracy; that is, through 'judicialization'. Advocates of citizenship based on 'empowerment' such as Turner (1986, 1990, 1992), argue that there must be an element of discretion to take account of the differences that exist among people in need. On the face of it, this seems problematic since both Friedman and Turner are in favour of an idea of citizenship that includes welfare rights but the difference between them over discretion may be able to be resolved. Elements of discretion can be seen in traditional rights under the rule of law; for example, length of sentence may vary according to the circumstances of a crime or behaviour during imprisonment. So, matters of welfare need not fall foul of rule of law principles but, in order not to, the rationality of instances of discretion must be open to scrutiny.

Although Friedman writes of entitlements stemming from a rational bureaucracy and argues that they turn into rights only when they become justiciable, the Court of Justice sometimes appears to use the terms interchangeably. However, Friedman's distinction does have a relevance which will be referred to later. For the moment it is necessary to point out that it is difficult to test the existence of Community-wide social rights of citizenship in the light of her dual administrative and judicial analysis – because the European Community has only part of the functions of a national system.

In national systems, policy formation, the formulation of the regulatory framework and the practical provision of benefits in cash or services are all in the same hands – or, at least, in different sections of a relatively unified whole. Even in federal systems, there is a degree of integration, or, at least, rationalized rules for dealing with conflicts of laws between self-governing territorial units (Lasok and Stone, 1987: 1–7, 17–18). Friedman did not find the federalism of the United States too difficult to compare with the central–local system in the United Kingdom. Although Lasok and Stone (1987: 7) describe the legal relationship between Member States and the Community as analogous to the United States within the limits of the Treaties (national supremacy remaining in spheres outside the Treaties), the division of responsibilities, even within the spheres laid down by treaty, is more complex than in either the United States or the United Kingdom. This is because of the fragmentation of stages of a single policy. Though this does happen in the United States and England and Wales, in both systems the jurisprudence of the centre and periphery is more-or-less common. But, in the European Community, powers are divided between the centre and twelve different, otherwise sovereign systems and a lot hangs upon the legal federalism governing ceded areas of sovereignty and the role of the Court of Justice. For example, the Commission and Council of Ministers formulate and pass legislation expressing objectives in order to give effect to the Treaty of Rome or extend it in related ways (see chapter 3).

The Commission, with the approval of the Council, drafts and determines some of the regulatory framework. This is the situation *vis-à-vis* the Regulations governing the coordination of the social security and assistance systems of the different Member States; Regulation 1408/71, in particular, provides a vast set of rules for calculating the benefits of migrant workers and by whom they should be paid. But sometimes the two bodies do not even do this. In the case of Directives, objectives are stated but the regulatory framework is explicitly left to the different national legal and political traditions. In both cases, the actual provision of material protection is the business of twelve different national systems. National governments comply (some more conscientiously than others; for example the UK more than Italy with its more autonomous regions) because they have signed treaties that oblige them to do so and, so long as those treaties are thought to be in the national interest, compliance with their consequences is likely. Therefore, they accept the consequences of rulings in the Court that they may not have taken proper steps to ensure that individuals may claim rights granted to them by Community law.

Sometimes, self-imposed obedience to legal obligations is identified as a feature that distinguishes international law from domestic law (Holsti, 1974). But it can also be argued that all successful regulatory systems depend on voluntary compliance (Burch and Wood, 1989) and consensus about trade-offs between the regulator and regulatee (Langbein and Kerwin, 1985). Nevertheless, even if there is consensus between Member States and Community institutions, compliance with Community law in respect of disputes between private individuals or an individual and an arm of government has to be regulated by national, not Community, sanctions.

It might be argued, then, that to test the entrenchment of Community social rights according to Friedman's standard of analysis would require an account of whether all twelve countries had administratively rational systems of providing entitlements and justiciable decision-making procedures. This would require a book in itself, probably of several volumes. But, since we are dealing only with those entitlements that exist in a specific form because of Community law, we can say, because we know that they are justiciable, that they are rights, even though, as noted above, the Court uses both terms. Moreover, because disputes about rights are reviewed in the Court of Justice, we can ·see from its rulings something of the way that they are administered in the Member States and explore the potential of the review process for bringing about a common administrative regime of entitlements, lying behind the rights. It was noted in chapter 2 that the pattern of the acquisition of rights was not the same at the Community level as in national histories; that 'judicialization' spills over into administration instead of the other way round is another example.

The second difficulty in examining the European Community in the light of the rule of law principles employed by Friedman is less procedural or institutional and more to do with material outcomes. This is because of the nature of Community policies. In policies about social security and assistance, the common objective is not a common material standard. As noted in chapter 4, the idea of harmonized schemes was explicitly rejected by politicians. Instead, different schemes which may embody different levels of provision are coordinated to realize the twin principles of freedom of movement and no national discrimination. Impediments to the free movement of persons, such as direct discrimination in benefits or indirect discrimination, through, for example, residence conditions, are out of order. The material consequences of equality of nationality status will vary according to what actual entitlements exist in migrants' countries of origin and residence. Indirectly, this might encourage cross-Community material equality as more workers move from country to country but, as discussed later, this can lead to individual inequalities in the present. Workers' participation Directives are not wholly about material equality across the Community either, because they are about consultative rights and employment protection within each country, though there is a common, non-material objective. There is a material element in the idea of funds for redundancies but that level will vary from country to country. Conversely, sex equality Directives *do* have material objectives as they call for equal rewards and conditions for men and women within each country. This does not mean at present (but see comment below about how comparisons might be made) that, say, a Dutch woman will have the same substantive conditions as a French man. But both sets of Directives have an indirect common material element. Their exhortatory preambles explicitly state that they are about the development of common living standards. In a sense, this is rhetorical but behind this lies the idea that, without similar standards of workers' participation and sex equality, there will be impediments to the freedom of movement. As noted in earlier chapters, the Social Charter is motivated not only by the idea of rights, but also by concern that uneven standards of protection against market insecurities will encourage employers to relocate to cheaper labour markets and workers to migrate, in too large numbers, to countries with better protection.

The European Court of Justice and the Equal Protection of the Laws

From what has been said so far, it is obvious that there are several elements involved here. First, there is the question of adjudicative standards in the regulatory frameworks of both national implementation of Community policy and those of the EC itself. Here, the Court works on common principles of equality, certainty and proportionality as applied to individuals and institutions. The common application of abstract principles affects the equal protection of the laws in the sense of the legal and material rights of individuals within Member States and across Member States in terms of nationality and sex. Then there is the question of how well the Court has carried out its task under what constraints and with what effect on the political or administrative regime of social entitlements. It is argued, here, that while many individuals have benefited from the Court's rulings, the general nature of Community rights is constricted by the conception of the individual in Community policy, practices of national courts and the inconsistent viewpoints of the Commission and Council of Ministers. At various points in this section, it is pointed out that when limitations and contradictions appear in cases before it, the Court sometimes seems to demand harmonization – at least of a minimal kind – and sometimes leaves things to piecemeal political solution. It has been criticized for being too active so as to endanger its authority and, on the other hand, for being pusillanimous.

Equal Protection and Rights within Member States

Equality is the key principle in both social security and sex equality. Inequality may be the result of direct or indirect discrimination. Direct discrimination means treating two people in similar situations differently. The concept of indirect discrimination takes account of people's different circumstances. That is, indirect discrimination may occur when an apparently neutral rule is applied, without good reason, to all persons but one group is less likely to be able to comply with it and to be disadvantaged because of this. Articles 7, 48 and 52 of the Common Market Treaty of Rome clearly outlaw direct national discrimination and Regulation 1408/71 refers to 'all disguised forms of discrimination which . . . lead to the same result' (Arnull, 1989: 176). Directives about sex equality embody explicitly, if briefly, the concept of indirect as well as direct discrimination.

Migrants and National Discrimination   Indirect discrimination in social security has been developed by the Court to include decisions based upon the nationality of children (Arnull, 1989: 176–7) and, as shown in chapter 5, residence conditions attached to national benefits (notably, family allowances in France – see also 1989: 176–83). If these benefits derive from membership of a worker's family, denial of them on grounds of residence constitutes indirect discrimination against the worker (1989: 180). If the nature of the benefit is such that indirect discrimination against a worker cannot be said to have taken place, the Court has sometimes resolved the issue by identifying direct discrimination against family members under rules about social assistance or 'tax and social advantages'. In several cases discussed in chapter 5, plaintiffs were argued to have been directly discriminated against under Regulation 1612/68; for example, unemployment benefits for young persons, special old age allowances, allowances for the handicapped, residence permits (see also Arnull, 1989: 180–6).

Discrimination between nationals and resident migrants can also arise in the processes of claiming rights and the Court has tried to limit this through developing the principle of a right to hearing (Arnull, 1989: chapter 10). Those making social security claims are usually 'humble people' (Advocate General Warner, quoted by Arnull, 1989: 207), while their claims are likely to require travel to another country and legal advice, instructions and hearings in a foreign language. Moreover, legal aid may not be available. The Court has argued that a brief reference in Community rules to this problem must be read as meaning that no national court may reject documentation submitted in the language of another Member State, provided that claims being submitted are covered by Community social security rules, and, if they are not, care must still be taken to ensure that plaintiffs understand decisions reached. Hearings remain conducted in the language (or languages, see note 7 in chapter 5) of the Member State in which they are taking place but translations must be made available.

In developing the principle of legal certainty for plaintiffs, the Court has insisted that Community social security rules cannot deprive claimants of rights acquired in another country – as well as their having the right not to be discriminated against in a country of residence. On the other hand, Community policy was not intended to be more advantageous to those who move than to those who remain for all their lives in one country. One of the purposes of amending the first Regulation 3 to the current Regulation 1408/71 was precisely this. Even so, the Court still holds that, provided there is no duplication of benefits payable by more than one country, arising from the same period of insurance, rights acquired under the national rules of a single country cannot be diminished by applying, instead, the principles of aggregation and apportionment (overlapping benefits cases, see chapter 5). Conversely, if the rules about aggregation and apportionment lead to a higher amount than national legislation alone, then these must apply. As a result of a rigorous abstract standard of equality of nationality, there may be different material outcomes for migrants and non-migrants within one country ('reverse discrimination'; Arnull, 1989: 148–58, 197–9). Put more simply, this means that national laws in a host country must not discriminate between migrants and non-migrants but migrants must also suffer no loss as a result of moving from their countries of origin. Thus, Italian migrants, for example, may not be treated differently under French and German law from French and German workers but neither may they be made worse off than their co-nationals who remained in Italy, even if the result is that they are better off than the workers among whom they now live. Arnull (1989: 198) points out that the Court's view in the 1970s was that this did not amount to unequal treatment, since the persons concerned were not in comparable situations and that 'no discrimination could arise in legal situations that were incomparable'. Moreover, the freedom of movement of workers was *not* equivalent to freedom of trade. The criticism that an extra benefit arising from migration was similar to an export subsidy was rejected; workers were not inanimate objects and had to face a range of cultural and psychological barriers against movement (1989: 153). 'The migrant worker is not . . . a mere source of labour but . . . a human being' (Advocate General Trabucchi, quoted by Arnull, 1989: 153). The Advocate General could 'understand the view that it is unfair that a man who has worked in two Member States should receive more . . . than if he had worked all his life in either of them'. But, on the other hand, he found more tenable the view 'that a man who, finding no work in his own country . . . [and], instead of sitting there and drawing unemployment benefit [has] the enterprise to seek and find work in another country, ought not, when he becomes old or disabled, to be begrudged the extra advantage he has thereby earned'. Arnull argues that the reasoning employed in the 1970s was unsatisfactory, on the ground that the Court should have chosen interpretations that would have minimized the weakness of coordination instead of exacerbating it. Nevertheless, in 1982, the Court was still holding that individual material differences existed because of the Community's failure to harmonize social security provisions. For example, in that year, the Advocate General pointed out that 'the coordination of the various [social security]

schemes is an operation which does not always run smoothly and
may in practice lead to paradoxical results' (274/81 Besem v
Bestuur van de Nieuwe Alegemene Bedrijfsvereniging). It seems,
then, that the Court regards inequality as a consequence of the
political decision to go for coordination and unavoidable until
politicians reconsider harmonization – which would mean steps
towards the equal protection of the laws across the Community.

Sex Discrimination Ambiguity in how far Community Directives
are binding can be another source of legal and material inequality
within states. Although the Court held in 1976 that the principle of
equal pay in Article 119 of the Treaty of Rome could be relied upon
directly by plaintiffs in national courts in claims against governments or other private persons, and although there was case law
that straightforward aspects of Directives were directly effective, the
question remained as to whether the direct effect of Directives
applied to governments alone or private persons as well. In 1986,
the Court finally touched upon this matter but not quickly or clearly
enough to meet the approval of legal specialists in the field (Lester,
1987). The main pronouncements involved the age of retirement
cases discussed in chapter 6. The key issue here was whether
Community Directives were directly effective only on 'states qua
states', in view of the fact that they direct governments to take
satisfactory general measures to implement them, or also in respect
of 'states qua employers'. The United Kingdom and other governments maintained that they were directly effective on states, not on
employers, and only on states in their capacity as states not as
employers. In the Marshall and Beets-Proper cases on retirement
ages (see chapter 6), one public the other private, the Court
accepted the submissions of governments that Directives were
directly effective only on states but denied that the 'state qua state'
could be distinguished from the 'state qua employer'. Moreover, the
state was the state in all its institutional emanations, including
health authorities and (see also the *Foster* case in chapter 5)
nationalized industries. In the absence of satisfactory general
measures, public employees, able to rely on the principle of 'direct
effects', have more entrenched rights than private sector employees.
Documentation in Beets-Proper, Marshall and Roberts referred to
earlier jurisprudence (14/83 von Colson and Kammann v Land
Nordrhein-Westfalen and 79/83 Harz v Deutsch Tradax GmbH)
case, that the unity of public institutions was a principle of
Community law. This meant that all institutions, including national
courts, were obliged to implement Community law.[1] If national
rules were such that public employees had more enforceable rights

than private employees, this could be only because Directives had not been implemented properly and courts had a duty to consider this. Thus private employees have to rely on more tenuous reasonings to ensure that their rights will be protected in the national courts.

Employing the principles of legal certainty and proportionality, the Court has reduced some differences between different types of employee within Member States in ways that were touched upon in chapter 6; that is, it has held that exceptions based on reasons of authenticity, inter-personal relationships and national security must be drawn narrowly and that the reasons for exceptions must be rigorous and transparent. Blanket stereotypes cannot be allowed to debar equal treatment in any but the smallest units of employment and exceptions in, for example, the police and probation services must be open to scrutiny. Proportionate different treatment in legitimate instances might include the imposition of some specific condition, short of blanket exclusion.

Limitations to Both on Ground of Legal Certainty   The principle of legal certainty applied under Regulations and Directives also protects governments as well as individuals. For example, although the Court ruled that national discrimination in fees for education might contravene Regulation 1612/68 and vocational training provisions, it also argued that inefficiencies on the part of the Commission and the long-standing system of university funding in Belgium meant that repayment of fees improperly charged by universities was obligatory only to those who had claims lodged at the time of the controlling judgment (see *Gravier*, *Blaizot* and other cases in chapter 5); the right to equality for those who had not was, therefore, a nominal one. Similarly, though the Court said that there was a universal right to equal pay dating back to 1962, it limited actual compensation for unequal pay to 1976, the date of the operative judgment (see *Defrenne* No. 2 in chapter 6).

Equal Protection across Member States

Cases about individual rights as between migrants and non-migrants and men and women *within* countries can contribute to common norms about how rights are to be administered and adjudicated *across* countries. These rules may affect both Community and national provisions. For example, the family allowance cases ruled out differences permitted by Community rules themselves. Arnull (1989: 178–9) argues that the Pinna case (see chapter 5) might have been resolved simply by saying that, for the purposes in hand, his children must be regarded as residing in

France. Instead, the exception allowed in the Regulation in respect of France, which had been intended as temporary, was overturned, the Court 'overcoming the legislative inertia of the Council of Ministers' in responding to overtures by the Commission to remove this disparity between the provisions of different Member States. In a case arising not from the Directives on workers' participation but their rights in situations of insolvency, the Court criticized Community documentation for being inconsistent in different languages, arguing that specific language versions of common provisions cannot be relied upon alone in assessing the scope of EC law throughout the Member States (135/83 H.B.M. Abels v Bedrijfsvereniging voor de Metaalindustrie en de Electrotechnische Industrie). Semantic consistency in national implementation measures has also been touched upon, a Danish argument that the Danish word *'samje'* included the idea of 'equal value' being rejected as not clearly the same as intended by the common provision (143/83 Commission v Denmark).

Convergence in National Definitions, Procedures and Consequences The rulings of the Court in sex equality cases are argued by Landau (1985: chapter VI) to have brought about significant convergence in Community-wide law and practice; for example, in definitions of pay and permitted exceptions. But she also points out that there is at least one important area of divergent standards. This is over how a plaintiff may choose a comparator: in some countries, it is restricted to other workers within the same, immediate place of employment; in others, the comparison may be made with another national establishment involving the same employer; and, in yet others, comparisons can be made in undertakings run by different employers but in similar industries in the same locality. Though Steiner (1988; 1990: 231) suggests that the absence of national systems of evaluation would inhibit comparisons made on an industry-wide basis, there is nothing in Community law to stop comparisons being made between employment conditions in undertakings that operate across Member States. This would contribute to common material standards – but has still to be tested.

Developing common norms may be relatively easy under directly applicable Regulations, notwithstanding the individual material 'paradoxes' within states (see above), and those provisions of Directives which, embodying clear policy objectives, can be relied upon in national courts. But the Court has also ventured into the more difficult territory of discretionary elements of Regulations and those parts of Directives which allow for different national conventions and procedures in the realization of common objectives. This has taken place mainly in its use of the principle of proportionality in rulings about the consequences for those who try to claim rights. Arnull (1989: chapter 9) illustrates this in connection with Regulation 1408 by reference to the situations of unemployed migrants who leave one country (Germany in the cases in question) to seek employment in another and, failing to find it, return to the first country to claim unemployment benefit. Part of the social security rules permits eligibility to depend upon return within three months. The Court held that the rules also allowed some discretion and that Germany had been too draconian in suspending all benefits without taking into account the circumstances of a late return. In making its judgments in such cases, the Court also said that the particular articles of the Regulation were 'not simply a measure to coordinate national law' but also established 'an independent body of rules in favour of workers claiming the benefit thereof which constitute an exception to national legal rules and which must be interpreted uniformly in all the Member States irrespective of the rules laid down in national law regarding the continuance and loss of entitlement to benefits' (quoted in Arnull, 1989: 156).

The Court's intervention into such parts of Directives has been objected to by the United Kingdom and Denmark (*von Colson* and Harz v Deutsch Tradax GmbH mentioned previously). The objections and the rulings occurred over national differences in remedies for unlawful discrimination; in Germany, compensation for all unlawful recruitment was limited to the costs of application (for example, notepaper and train fares) whereas in Italy a contract of employment had to be offered, with other states having various intermediate possibilities. The Court held that the consequences of unlawful practices must not be so slight that they undermined Community objectives and, as a result, Germany amended its laws. The Court agreed with Denmark and the United Kingdom that non-specific provisions in Directives could have no direct common application, while effectively calling for some greater uniformity across the Community.

Material Implications   As in cases about discrimination between migrants and non-migrants within a country, the 'judicialization' of rules about whether benefits can be 'exported' when migrants move away appears to imply the harmonization of material provisions. From 1967, the Court has maintained that 'the aim of Article 51 of the Treaty of Rome was not in the first instance intended to equalize social security provision across Europe' (2/67 de Moor v Caisse de Pension des Emploies Privés). But its judgments about the 'exportability' of insurance-based benefits, supplemented sometimes by need-based benefits, seem to compel some steps towards equalization. In 1975, the Court agreed with the Advocate General that 'there was no question of the general application of exportation to all cases of supplementary benefits' and that exportability was possible only when the plaintiff was a worker (24/74 Biason v Caisse Régionale d'Assurance Maladie de Paris). In 1983, however, the Court decided that a pension paid to a woman who was *not* a retired worker was assimilable to benefits that could be exported (*Piscitello*, see chapter 5). In discussing these two cases and others, Steiner argued in 1985 that the extent of assimilation may mean that very few benefits are not 'exportable' and that even the Commission thought 'shocking results' would follow from general exportation. As noted in chapter 5, she has pointed out since (Steiner, 1988) that the Court has tended to switch to extending what counts as a 'social advantage' under Regulation 1612/68, benefits which are not exportable under that Regulation. But this approach, too, has financial implications and might, if less directly, reinforce the Court's calls (in *Piscitello*, supported by the Commission in 279/82 Jerzak v Bundesknappschaft-Verwaltungsstelle Aachen) for common measures for assessing income and need – a form of harmonization – by its impact on the process of social budgeting, informed by collaborative investigations of poverty in general (see chapter 4) and among women (see chapter 6).

Assessments of the Work of the Court

Although the Court has benefited many individuals, it has been criticized over its impact upon the development of a common regime of procedural and material rights, not only for the specific reasons suggested by Arnull and Steiner, referred to above, but by observers with political interests and by other legal scholars. Unfortunately, these criticisms are not consistent! On the one hand, the Court has been said to be too cautious and inconsistent (e.g. Lester, 1987) and, on the other, too bold (Rasmussen, 1987). Some of the faults may indeed lie within the the Court itself but others are, to some extent, outside its control or that of the Commission.

In contrast to the views of politicians who oppose social regulation, most of all by supranational political and legal authorities, and of some legal specialists, it is often said by claimants or advocates of Community rights that the Court too readily defers to the submissions of Member States about their economic interests (e.g. in *Defrenne* No. 2 and the Belgian education cases, see above and chapters 5 and 6). But its rulings do reveal that it tries to maintain some independence from governmental interests in order to protect the rights of 'Citizens of the Union'. For example, it refuses to accept defences of non-compliance based on appeals to busy legislative time-tables, partisan difficulties and budgetary constraints (e.g. 215/83 Commission v Belgium, 131/84 Commission v Italy, and *Pinna*, see chapter 5; 58/81 Commission v Luxembourg; 29/84 Commission v Germany, see chapter 5). Nor has it allowed pleas based on national conventions and traditions to override the need for clarity and transparency for plaintiffs (e.g. 248/83 Commission v Germany, 165/82 Commission v UK, *Johnston*, and *Barber*, see chapter 6; 143/83 Commission v Denmark, see above).

Lester (1987) is also critical, for reasons of a different order, of a lack of activism in the Court's approach. He draws attention to considerable defects in its handling of Article 177 references (requests for preliminary rulings, see chapter 3). Substantial costs are incurred in making such references and, in his view, the Court has not provided a clear and rational set of answers to questions of principle put before it. He quotes the view of one of its judges that Article 177, involving individual disputes, is not a suitable means for resolving problems that usually stem from conflicts between national and Community law. Infringement proceedings brought by the Commission under Article 169 would be better. Be that as it may, in Lester's view, it is Article 177 references that are virtually the only effective means for the Commission to compel the disclosure of the kind of information that would be necessary for proceedings under Article 169 to be brought. He argues that interventions by UK governments in Article 177 references have been so vigorous that 'the Court has limited the scope and effect of its judgments more narrowly than would have been possible under infringement proceedings' (1987: 193). It does so by redefining carefully constructed questions of principle put by British and other national courts so as to avoid the systematic rationalization of inconsistencies.

Other problems stem from the different habits of national legal systems in whether plaintiffs' representatives or judges formulate the questions and from which level of court they emanate. Whatever their origins, the length of time disputes take to be resolved, Lester also argues, is a serious impediment to the protection of both individual entitlements and a rational system of rights. Since he wrote, the Court of the First Instance has begun its work which may reduce the time for individuals but, since matters of common interest are still to be dealt with by the main Court and since most individual cases appear to involve the common interest, it remains to be seen whether this innovation will do much to solve the general problems.

Rasmussen (1987: 379–80) suggests that 'the role of the Community judiciary is of paramount importance for the survival of the Community, the political processes having often failed to provide the momentum required' for integration in breadth and depth. 'Communitarizing' activism can be 'a public good' but, like Arnull, who would have preferred the Court not to have exacerbated the weakness of coordination, Rasmussen also suggests that the Court has been over-zealous in intervening in political processes (while following a time-honoured habit of denying this). As a result, it has created political antagonisms. He criticizes the Court's use of legal techniques, which Steiner (1985) also does in making a point that coincides with Friedman's (1981) discussion of the budgetary consequences of 'judicializing' rights in national systems. This was touched upon in chapter 5, that the creative technique of combining the standards of different instruments throws unexpected costs on to governments.

As Friedman argues in connection with the United States, the financial implications of court judgments impinge on the political authority to set budgets and, thus, upon the separation of powers. The financial implications of the Court's use of 'a formidable array of techniques and arguments' are so great, in Steiner's view, that responsibilities for migrant workers and their families have far outgrown the limits of obligations originally agreed upon by Member States (1985: 40–1). At the height of their use, these techniques included the 'filling of lacunae' in one Regulation by applying the tests and standards of the other. At the time of her argument, the main effect of this was to extend the benefits covered by 1408/71 and, therefore, the range of 'exportable' benefits. Hence, she recommended that ways of sharing burdens should be found. About the same time, the Court began to change its approach from extending social security to expanding 'non-exportable' social assistance. Although this places limits in the immediate future on unanticipated expenditure by one country for migrants who have moved to another, it still increases the financial responsibilities of states for migrants and, as noted above, may have a longer-term impact on harmonization. As noted in earlier chapters, it was the fear that harmonization of social security would lead to higher public expenditure, and loss of sovereignty over its control, that was the context in which national politicians accepted the idea of Community sex equality policies – whose costs might have been thought to fall upon consumers or employers.

Partly as a direct result of Court rulings and partly because of the greater public awareness engendered by them, the costs of sex equality policies increasingly fall upon governments themselves; for example, in the ability of public employees, a large proportion of whom are women, to rely on the direct effects of Directives and the vulnerability of governments, as large employers of women, to expensive equal value claims. It is governments as employers who are caught by the transparency required in defences based upon exceptions on the grounds of national security and public policy. Moreover, the whittling away of exemptions of state pension (and/or retirement) schemes means that statutory differentiation is increasingly irrational and kindles grass-roots demands for equalization – an outcome which, depending on how it might be implemented, could increase public expenditure. As noted in chapter 2, further measures towards sex·equality (and workers' rights) have been opposed, notably by UK governments, but with some support on some issues from other Member States.

By making social policy more expensive, then, the Court may or may not have 'politicized' itself but it has 'politicized' the policy field; or at least, moved it from the realm of 'low politics' where, according to all but the most recent analyses (see chapter 4), agreements are easy to reach, to the realm of 'high politics' where they are not. Opportunities for debating future political priorities are dealt with in the concluding section of this chapter. But it should be noted here that, if social policy has not gone far enough in the eyes of some to protect rights within and across states, part of the reason lies in complications and gaps in existing Community policies.

Present Policy Limitations

As a result of inconsistencies between different sets of rules relating to lawful residence, insured status and eligible membership of an eligible family, not all individuals are protected in the same way. Part of this stems from what Friedman (1981) would probably see as an incomplete rationalization of administrative entitlements and, partly, the problem is more fundamental. From the first point of view, for example, the rights of students to equal treatment in grants and fees vary according to the migratory and/or work histories of themselves or their parents and whether they are in general education or vocational training.[2] The hope of the Commission that, in the interest of simplicity, fees will be the same for all nationals depends on voluntary national action, which will not be an example of the rationalization of Community regulation. Type of work affects protection (see chapter 5) and residence rights are stronger for those employed or made unemployed after moving than for those travelling in search of work (see above and note 5 in chapter 5). The position for foreigners and Community nationals whose origins lie outside EC countries is very complicated and, depending on their circumstances, their rights vary greatly. In addition to the situations of the foreign families of Community workers, whether or not they have migrated within the Community and whether or not they come from a country with an association agreement (notes 17 and 18 in chapter 5), other differences exist among workers and families who reside in or come from former colonial dependencies – because of differences in forms of past imperial relationships. Sometimes, these reach the Court. For example, citizens of Algeria and the former Congo count as French for the purposes of social security, if they paid contributions as French citizens before their nationality was administratively changed as the result of the granting of independence. The situations of people whose origins are in former British dependent territories tend not to have to be tested in Community law: either because they have remained citizens of their independent countries and, therefore, have no claim on Community law, or because they have migrated to the United Kingdom, have acquired UK citizenship and, as a result, are indisputably Community nationals.[3] But residents of Crown possessions, such as the Channel Islands and the Isle of Man, do not count as Community nationals. The ability of descendants of Community nationals who no longer have the same nationality as their ancestors, such as those who have migrated to the Commonwealth, to reclaim their association with Europe varies according to whether a Member State has patrilineal rules or matrilineal ones as well.[4]

There are several fundamental difficulties in the extent of a modern concept of citizenship on a Community-wide basis. Three of these are more-or-less common to most of the Member States. One has been discussed in chapter 6; that is, that though the concept of worker has been extended (chapter 5), its essential meaning (and that of related concepts such as 'head of household' or 'breadwinner) remains male and based on a traditionally male model of full-time employment that lasts throughout working life (though some Danes would deny that this described their system, see chapters 5 and 6). Secondly, gender stereotypes compound the absence of policies banning discrimination based on sexuality or sexual preference.[5] Thirdly, black Community nationals, especially women, are vulnerable to marginalization from the idea of a common European citizenship. In theory, black women may be protected twice, if their countries have laws outlawing racial discrimination, by both national laws of that sort and Community sex equality rights. In practice, they are likely to experience double discrimination (Prondzynski, 1989). Proposals to bring race discrimination within the ambit of Community regulation of economic and social rights have been controversial[6] and, as noted in the final chapter, all black Community nationals and would-be nationals may be unfairly treated in connection with residence and free movement (see note 3 again). Fourthly, the existence of fundamentally different systems of industrial rights, their statuses in constitutions and the powers between the 'social partners', reflected in both, seriously hinder the ability of the Community to enter into a common regime of workers' participation (Nielsen and Szyszczak, 1991; Rhodes, 1991a and b). For these problems, it is necessary to turn to the informal means of inscribing new meanings into the concepts on which Community policies are based.

The Commission and the Informal Equal Protection of the Laws

In accounts of public policy and civil rights in the United States, it has been argued that benefits or entitlements may be symbolic. Governments *may* pass laws designed to protect 'victims' without any tangible distributive or redistributive consequences. In his seminal work, Edelman (1964) argued that this happened because agencies were 'captured' by the groups whose behaviour was supposed to be regulated in the interest of the intended beneficiaries; for example, railway magnates 'captured' the interstate Commerce Commission which was supposed to have protected the interests of travellers and the sellers of agricultural products in having fair prices. Sometimes, symbolic laws may satisfy the 'victims' and sometimes they may create expectations for further action. For expectations to be transformed into tangible consequences, it is necessary for the 'victims' to enter into a bargaining relationship with public administrators (Edelman, 1964; Freeman, 1975). If such a policy network is to succeed, administrators must play an interventionist part in respect of the 'victims'. What Blumrosen (1977) calls 'bland neutrality' by administrators as between, say, large corporations and racial minorities cannot lead to improvements for racial minority employees. Administrators need to counterbalance the pre-existing inequality of power by providing the supposed beneficiaries of legislation with special help and information on the use of the law to secure their rights. Heclo (1977, 1978) argues that in the last days of the New Deal ascendancy, Democrat Presidents tried to ensure that civil rights and anti-poverty agencies were headed and staffed by people who were sympathetic to the then prevailing version of the liberal public philosophy.

There is some evidence that the European Commission has tried to fulfil a role that is similar to that of American public administrators in the 1960s and 1970s. Earlier chapters referred to links between the Commission and national and cross-national trade unions and women's organizations and to the significance of sympathetic 'insiders'. In chapter 4, it was noted that these contacts once tended to be used to improve domestic situations more than serving as an acknowledgement of common values and the promotion of common rights. Even though governments restricted contacts with trade unions (see chapter 4) and 'communautaire' attitudes in the Commission may have weakened (see chapter 2), efforts to maintain networks continue (Streeck and Schmitter, 1991) – especially with *trans-Community* specialists and representatives of organized labour and women, for the sake of efficiency and the promotion of common policies. Visits to the Commission are encouraged, there may be financial support, much written information is disseminated (for example, in newsletters like *Women of Europe*) and information offices have been set up in the Member States to deal specifically with rights (in addition to the general presence of the Commission in national capitals and major cities). A vast number of committees exist, composed of Commission staff and national nominees, to monitor policy implementation, a process which reveals defects and can lead to reforms. Committees have not always been wholly successful. The employment committees have extensive contacts with national trade unions but these contacts may be better at revealing the problems (such as the divergence of systems of workers' rights) rather than the possibilities of devising common policies. The equality committees have reported difficulty in establishing links with national groups. On the other hand, there are two Brussels-based non-governmental organizations, with contacts with groups in the Member States. These, the Centre for Research on Women and the European Network of Women, are consulted, like UNICE and ETUC, in order to encourage convergent social standards – with some, if limited, success (Hoskyns, 1986). Since some of the activists are also on Commission committees, grass-roots links could improve. Moreover, the new officially sponsored European lobby is made up of representatives of national grass-roots organizations. In general, the more complicated identities and public opinions about Community social policies and its Parliament, noted in chapters 2 and 8, suggest that the networking, as well as publicity given to social policy cases in the ECJ, is having some impact on the cross-fertilization of ideas and expectations.

The existence of channels through which to influence Community policies means that Community nationals have some of the secondary political rights associated with metics in a hospitable country (see chapter 2). That such channels or networks can be used by ordinary people for political interaction with the purpose of defining for themselves their own policy needs, or at least influencing meanings – instead of being passive recipients of policies defined by other people – is corroborated by Hart's (1993) focused comparison between the American Fair Labor Standards Act and the Social Charter. She points out that in 1936 there was a similar criticism of the concept of worker in the United States – that it was assumed to imply a model of male employment in manufacturing. This meant that agriculture and domestic service were not accepted as 'work' and were deemed to be governed not by contracts of employment, but by the conventions of familial relationships. Thus, black farm workers (mainly male) and all domestic workers (black and white females) were not protected by the American 'charter'. But she also points out that, inspired by a political culture of constitutionalism and rights, the unprotected were able to use the pluralistic and permeable institutions of the United States to get their situations redefined and, thereby, regulated by the Act. It took a long time but it is their success that encourages her to be more optimistic than many of the critics referred to in chapter 6. Siim's account (1991) of citizenship and feminism in Scandinavia, also referred to in that chapter, suggests that Hart may be right. It is the case that, though the Commission has been criticized for diluting the Social Charter from something for citizens to something for workers (Nielsen and Szyszczak, 1990: 34), the Maastricht Treaty of Union finally talks about the rights of 'Citizens of the Union'. It is with them and their primary political rights that this book concludes.

Notes

1 Not that they always do; see note 3 below.
2 General education is not covered systematically by Community law but is touched upon in various ways, not all of which have been discussed in this book. Vocational training is covered by Community law (see chapter 5).
3 But Mr Sandhu, the Indian spouse of a German migrant in the United Kingdom,

was not allowed by the Court of Appeal or the House of Lords to remain in the UK after his estrangement from his wife and her return to Germany (Steiner, 1990: 168).

4 As a result of a previous publication which touched upon this, the author has received a distressing account from a victim of this problem. See also Baldwin-Edwards, 1991, 1992a; Brubaker, 1989; Loescher, 1989.

5 As well as the absence, except in parliamentary debates (see chapter 6), of matters of sexuality pertaining to culture and male violence, the absence of a policy against discrimination on grounds of sexual preference can disadvantage men as well as women. The description of Mr Newstead quoted in note 5 of chapter 6 is commonly taken to mean a discreet reference to his homosexuality. See also note 3 in that chapter on the possibility that male rights to be protected from reproductive hazards at work may not be treated as seriously as those of women.

6 That is, in distinction to the rules that have been discussed in this book about national discrimination between Community citizens of one Member State and another. In note 18 of chapter 5, it was noted that Member States have been recommended to treat 'third country migrants' in the same way that they treat Community migrants.

8

Political Rights and Political Union

Introduction

It has been argued in this book that citizenship can be thought of as residing in the European Community (EC) as well as in national polities because of links among social and other rights. There are several aspects to this; philosophical, historical and political. First, earlier chapters have discussed substantial bodies of political ideas that propose there is a theoretical and practical interdependence amongst political, legal and social rights. Secondly, the book has also drawn attention to histories of the citizenship ideal which show that, in its various meanings to real people across time and territories, social rights have also been thought of as a necessary condition of equal citizenship – and practised, if imperfectly (chapters 1 and 2). Thus, it would not be in order to rule out the European Community as one of the guarantors of the rights of citizenship on the ground that it is responsible for social, not political, rights – unless it could be shown that the meaning of citizenship for most of its participants was similar to that of Aron (1974) and that almost none of them thought of the concept in the broader way proposed by Heater (1990). Thirdly, it has been argued that it has proved impossible in the formulation and enforcement of Community policies to maintain a distinction as strictly as Aron does between the social rights of Community nationals and their legal status, the latter associated by Aron with membership of a national political community. It has been shown that the enforcement of social rights has 'spilled-over' into previously exclusive national competences and that, in many ways, Community individual legal and social rights are virtually the same thing (chapters 3–7). In this final chapter, it is necessary to explain the ways in which those legal and social rights are imping- ing in logic and practice on the possibility of common political rights. This throws into sharp focus, however, the logical and sociological links between citizenship and nationality discussed by Aron and Leca (1990). Thus, the chapter also discusses the ques- tion of identities and argues that, since legal nationality is not the defining determinant of all that we do in the civil and political spheres of national life, there is no reason why the various other identities that we all hold, as well as our national identities, should not come into play in our interactions in the European 'public space' (Tassin, 1992). These other identities are not only social but also regional. The book ends, then, not with certainties about the future shape of the European Community, but with questions about the further reconstitution of societies and associations in which nation-states might be, as Dennis Kennedy puts it, 'useful, traditional units, not fierce guardians of some imagined historic identity or spurious racial distinctiveness' (The Sunday Times, 26 April 1992).

Proposed Political Rights in the European Community

In earlier chapters, it has been noted that, notwithstanding expanded definitions in Court rulings, the EC concept of citizen is defective and cannot be otherwise because legal nationality remains a matter for Member States (Evans and Jessurin d'Oliveira, 1989) and because, in so far as citizenship has a Community dimension, citizens are citizens-as-workers, not citizens-as-human-beings. The first of these is dealt with below. The second has been identified as a cause of the existence of social policies that cannot deal coherently with needs arising from conditions that may be unconnected with work (for example, the needs of AIDS victims; Spicker, 1991) or effectively with the needs of citizens whose social roles and work histories give them unequal entitlements (see chapters 4 and 6). The preference of Member States for retaining the idea of citizen-as-worker in the social field has not prevailed in the political sphere, in the face of analogies drawn throughout Community institutions in the rationales for social and political rights; that is, if the denial of all sorts of 'social advantages' constitutes barriers to free movement, and these must be eliminated, it is inconceivable not to think the same way about the loss of political rights, generally denied to migrants except in countries with bilateral agreements on reciprocal rights.

The resuscitation of the idea of citizen-as-human-being, familiar among the early federalists, coincides with movements towards political union. The first major innovations in this field were the Solemn Declaration on European Union by the European Council (at Stuttgart in 1983) and the Draft Treaty Establishing the European Union, adopted by the European Parliament in 1984. In the same year, the European Council set up an *ad hoc* committee, chaired by Pietro Adonnino, which reported in 1985 (Commission of the European Communities, 1985). The committee is remembered mostly for its recommendations on the cultural and social aspects of the People's Europe and on the symbols of politics, such as the Community emblem, anthem, flag and passport cover; another of its consequences was the Citizen's Europe Advisory Service, with offices throughout the Member States, where nationals can go to inquire about their legal and social rights (Commission of the European Communities, 1990b). But the committee also dealt with political rights, asking the Council to invite Community institutions to introduce measures to bring into existence 'the citizen as a participant in the political process in the Community' and in the Member States. The Committee made specific recommendations that were similar to some of those which, after negotiations and controversy during the late 1980s, now appear in the Maastricht Treaty of Union. In the meantime, the word 'person' had been used in the Single European Act in 1987, partly as a result of the Court's expansive rulings (which impinge upon the capacity of states to exercise exclusive control over specific aspects of the legal status of citizens) as well as the new ideas of union. The European Commission and Parliament took a close interest in how 'persons' and 'political participants' were to be inscribed in the final agreement. Between 1989 and 1991, both made reports, and the latter passed Resolutions, to try to ensure that rights of 'Union Citizenship' would have substance (European Parliament, 1992). Although the Parliament criticized the eventual Treaty in many important respects, it broadly welcomed the introduction of a number of proposals that include the two dimensions of democratic political citizenship (discussed in chapter 2), the control of public powers and individual rights.

If the Maastricht Treaty, or something like it, is ratified, the Parliament will have some new powers *vis-à-vis* the Commission and Council of Ministers, and the Court of Justice *vis-à-vis* the Member States. The Court will be able to impose penalties on Member States that do not comply with Community law. The cooperation procedure in law-making by the Parliament and the Council of Ministers, described in chapter 2, will be augmented by a conciliation procedure in situations where there is disagreement between the two institutions over those issues that are subject to majority voting in the Council. The procedure will operate in policy fields that cover the free movement of workers, training and education, culture, health, consumer affairs, the environment, research and development and new trans-European networks in energy, telecommunications and transport. If no agreement can be reached even then, the Parliament will have the right to reject proposals. However, neither European nor national parliaments are to have any serious influence on the workings of European

Monetary Union and the proposed European Central Bank will be accountable only to the Council of Ministers.

The Commission is to be appointed for a period of five years to coincide with the Parliamentary term so that Commissioners can be presented to the Parliament for approval. Members of the European Parliament see this as potentially similar to the influential American process of Senate ratification of presidential appointments (as guests were told at a seminar in the European Parliament in 1992). The Maastricht Treaty also introduces some legislative powers of initiative, extends or confirms certain budgetary and financial controls and the right of petition through which citizens, using a new Parliamentary Ombudsman, may pursue allegations of maladministration in the Commission.

Proposed individual rights, in addition to the use of the Ombudsman, are to be brought about by specific arrangements instead of being enshrined in a constitutional charter – to the regret of the Parliament. They are: the right of any Community national, resident in another Member State, to vote in local elections and to stand for local office; the right of all Community nationals, wherever they are, to vote in European elections and stand as a candidate for the European Parliament; the right to participate in Community politics under a uniform electoral system; the right to be protected outside the Community by the consular and diplomatic services of any Member State; and the right to more transparent information from Community institutions.

The last of these rights is seriously attenuated by the continued ability of the Council of Ministers to meet in private and, perhaps, by secrecy rules proposed recently by the Commission, 'bearing the hallmarks of British government pressure' (*The Independent*, 23 June 1992). These seek to classify documents connected with policy areas expanded in the Maastricht Treaty; defence, foreign affairs, asylum and immigration. The Parliament is hoping to use a debate to persuade the Commission to modify or drop its proposals. The rights to vote and to stand for office have been argued to be fundamentally flawed for three reasons (Moxon-Browne, 1992). They can be derogated when governments think they have overriding, specific national problems or judge the public interest to be at stake. Secondly, they are not granted to people who are 'real' Citizens of the Union by the authority of that Union, because Community nationals are defined as the nationals of Member States and have rights only if Member States have already accorded them the legal status of being national citizens (see chapter 7). Thirdly, these rights confer a second-class order of citizenship because they do not include the right to vote and to stand for office in general elections throughout the Member States. Another critique has been launched recently by the European Lobby (see below) which, with some controversy as to whether the underlying motivation is that women are 'essentially' different, is calling for half of all public offices to be reserved for women.

The research for this book suggests that derogations are possible in theory in all Community policies but, though defences on the basis of them are frequently put forward, the Court employs a strict standard of scrutiny, which means that the defences usually fall entirely or in part. The second and third of Moxon-Browne's points are made too soon, if the histories of states and national citizenship rights are anything to go by. The formation and democratization of nation-states was not straightforward. Movements for universal political rights, and their extension into social rights, have struggled, even in situations of legal rights, usually for at least a century – perhaps 300 years, if the first, relatively isolated calls are taken into account. This is not to say that political rights in the European Community will take so long; the fact that Moxon-Browne's criticism is made, not only by analysts, but also by activists in the trans-European networks, indicates that the absence of a core part of political rights will be increasingly protested about. Indeed, it seems to be the case that nationalistic opposition in the referendums of 1992 was at least matched by views that the Maastricht Treaty does not do enough to promote democratic rights for European citizens – rights for all at the common level and for migrants living outside their own countries. There is, in any case, another way of considering the status of different kinds of elections as first- or second-class forms of citizenship. The topics with which I end this book may imply a significance for local and EC elections at least as strong as that which today inheres in national elections. Before reaching the end, it is necessary to revert to the topics of nationality and identities.

Legal Nationality, Political Representation and National and Social Identities

It has been noted several times that, under current conventions, legal nationality is conferred by nation-states, which also determine political status and rights within national political communities. The existence of Community institutions can create problems for political representation in the Member States. Not only the supremacy of Community law but also 'like-mindedness' between unelected national and Community civil servants, the volume and timing of innovations, can inhibit, even more than in domestic

developments, the capacity of national parliamentarians to represent the interests of citizens in questions of common policy.
Spencer (1990) makes this point in connection with the protection
of civil liberties. The Maastricht Treaty would introduce improvements in this general area and in the relationship between the European and national parliaments. This has been welcomed by the
European Parliament but the proposed steps are unlikely to be
enough to meet Spencer's criticisms. But, in a way, the criticisms
are misplaced because they do not recognize that some of the
interests of national citizens may have the potential of being better
served by common institutions. This is especially true of systems
where domestic institutions are themselves inadequate because, for
example, of electoral and executive systems that facilitate powerful
governments without majority popular support. Grahl and Teague
(1990) draw attention to the fact that in a number of the social
policy controversies, discussed in chapter 4, the United Kingdom
government opposed innovations which there are good reasons to
suspect would have been welcomed by substantial blocs of voters
among the oppositional majority. This raises the question of the
sources of our identities and reinforces the need for democratic
institutions at the common level.

This book has referred several times to Leca's point (1990) that
there is a powerful overlap in people's thinking amongst citizenship, legal nationality and national identity. The xenophobia that
is being expressed by the various nationalities once united in the
former communist countries exemplifies this in a terrible way. But
neither the power of the construct and the example nor the current
legal basis of Community citizenship need compel us to conclude
that a neo-national conception of citizenship with a European
dimension 'added-in' must be a more likely outcome than the neo-
imperial version (see chapter 1 and Leca, 1990). If, as Grahl and
Teague (1990) indicate, people's interests do not always coincide
with dominant conceptions of the national interest, their identities
must also either conflict with or transcend their legal nationality to
start with, or they may become like this as they interact with those
who do share their interests – in some respects, at any rate.

There is, indeed, evidence that people recognize that some of
their interests transcend national sovereignties. For decades,
citizens of Member States in the European Community have been
saying that they approve of the idea of integration, even if it means
some sharing of sovereignty. However, it is emphasized by Richard
Sinnott and others (in research for the European University
Institute which is still continuing and not yet published) that
support has to be measured by more specific means. In 1989,

David Usborne reported in *The Independent* (15 June 1989) that there were high levels of general support for 'European Government' answerable only to a European Parliament and for a range of specific actual and proposed EC policies. With the exception of Denmark, these attitudes were present in all Member States – even the UK. Richard Sinnott's research is revealing that significant majorities of citizens in Member States simultaneously regard problems related to the social rights discussed in this book – unemployment and poverty – as having high priority and as issues for which it is legitimate for Community institutions to act upon. Highest support for a Community competence lies in environmental matters and, perhaps surprisingly (see chapter 3), foreign policy. Such findings mean that opposition to the Maastricht Treaty should not be equated with opposition to integration. Indeed, during the week of the 'paving' bill in the UK House of Commons (see chapter 3), it was reported that, while one survey showed a drop in support for Maastricht, especially in the UK, another showed that a large majority of UK citizens *wanted* the UK government to be taken by the Commission to the Court of Justice for non-compliance with Community regulations on water pollution.

There is also evidence that the experience of integration is making senses of identity more fluid. That this should be so seems intuitively correct when we remember that many people, migrants or not, think of themselves as having two nationalities and link them when describing themselves; for example, Scottish and British, sometimes Irish and British, Black American, French Canadian, Bavarian German and, to use an example heard in a broadcast about migrant Welsh farmers, Welsh-British-French. That the idea of citizenship might be associated more with the nature of society and the state than with their 'nationalness' is suggested by accounts of the outlooks of both migrants and people who remain mainly at home. Writing in *The Independent on Sunday* (17 February 1991), Geraldine Bedell reported that there is a growing band of middle-class British migrants in Western Europe who enjoy a sense of 'Europeanness' because infrastructures, amenities and education are treated more seriously on the continent as components of citizenship. At a meeting held in 1991 under the auspices of the European Consortium for Political Research, it was pointed out by members of metalworkers' organizations that, though metalworkers in Emilia–Romagna had some interests which were best articulated nationally, they also had other important ones, such as health and safety, where there was common cause with similar workers in Germany and other steel producing regions.

It is already the case that such workers look across borders and to the framework of the Community to develop these interests. Anthropologists, it is claimed (Wilson and Smith, 1992), pay more attention to, or take more seriously, people's awareness of their multiple identities, including social identities, than do political scientists. Feminist political theory, however, *does* treat identities seriously.

In chapter 6, it was noted that theories of equal citizenship for women show that it is possible for us to identify with our group and to recognize that, if we are to be political, we must interact with other groups in the public space. If citizenship is to be equal, there must be a place in the public sphere of discourse and decision-making for the policy interests of our group, a place that is as secure as in the case of other groups. Similar arguments for democratic citizenship in general have been made recently by Mouffe (1992) and Walzer (1992). Walzer (1992) was quoted by Leca (1990) in his argument that the inherited membership of communities can lead more easily than contractual association to 'closures' of citizenship (see chapter 2). Here, Walzer argues that civil society gives rise to various roles and associations; we are acting as citizens when, through those associations with which we choose to identify, we interact with other communities or associations of interest. In comparing and contrasting her approach with communitarianism, civic republicanism and liberalism, Mouffe points out that democratic participation, freely entered into, needs not a neutral state but a political authority that takes positive steps to ensure that there is equal liberty for all in a pluralist public space. (See also Blumrosen, 1977, on the problem of neutral authority in administration, discussed in chapter 7.)

Leca (1992) points out that the fact that so many of us live in multi-cultural and multi-ethnic, though so-called 'national', societies means that it is imperative to have within our polities the kind of democratic citizenship outlined by Mouffe and her contributors. This is an imperative that is urgent because of ethnic conflicts inside liberal democracies and seems the more so in the face of what is happening in countries that are making a transition from communism to something else. Tassin (1992: 188) argues that the European Community cannot be the precondition for a public space in a communitarian sense because, like multi-ethnic states, it does not embody a cohesive common original identity. But, as noted earlier in this book, he argues that it can be the result of 'a politically constituted public space in which the plurality' of political interests, feelings, wills, initiatives, judgements, decisions and actions come 'face to face'. Mouffe's argument about the nature of the state is central to the ideas of all those on whom I have drawn in this section. The actions of the political authority are critical in determining whether or not the public space is democratic. In this respect, the European Community is defective in ways that are not always thought of as part of the so-called 'democratic deficit' and which are aggravated, as its Parliament has pointed out, in the Maastricht Treaty.

Chapter 3 referred to the tendency to reach multilateral, intergovernmental decisions instead of common ones, especially since the recognition of the European Council. This means that policies are formulated without proceeding in the same way that common policies do. As a result, the usual consultations with non-governmental organizations, both 'official' and those outside the executive machinery, are unlikely to happen. Though the Parliament may be told about what is going on, it has no formal input. And when multilateral agreements come into force, they are not reviewable – because they are not common policies – by the Community's administrative and legal machinery. Most of the policies that alarm civil liberties and human rights organizations and anti-racism movements (Spencer, 1990) have come about in this way. These policies, in which Citizens of the Union have virtually no influence, except – if they know about them – through their national governments, could have a profound impact upon the freedoms and 'closures' of citizenship at the common level. The Schengen Agreement of 1985, about the elimination of internal borders amongst the territories of its five signatories, is a case in point. It and later provisions stemming from the Single European Act, which *is*, of course, a common policy, appear to increase the freedom of Citizens of the Union. But, in order to counteract claims by some governments that opening borders would make it more difficult to control the international drugs trade, terrorism and illegal immigration, this freedom is expected to bring about more extensive police cooperation, more frequent random checks within borders, more covert surveillance of Community citizens and national immigration rules that bring the level of the most open Member States up to that of the most restrictive. This last consequence is analogous to questions of state security and national citizenship (see chapter 2). In the new context it 'closes' Community citizenship to 'outsiders' and might undermine Community rights for refugees and stateless persons. And, on the basis of the experience of black UK citizens travelling on the continent with UK Visitors Passes instead of passports, some organizations expect black and Asian Europeans to be more harassed than white citizens by random checks inside borders. Such matters are usually agreed upon in the intergovernmental Terrorism, Radicalism,

Extremism and International Violence (TREVI) group, outside Community scrutiny (Baldwin-Edwards, 1991, 1992a). The agreements on foreign policy and defence and security in the Maastricht Treaty extend the scope within which governments can act multilaterally and, as we have seen, are already causing the common institution of the Commission, which has acquired a recognized role in European Political Cooperation (EPC), to act in a way that would not satisfy the citizenship theorists referred to above.

Another way in which some Member States are sometimes said to be trying to minimize the place of citizens in the European public space lies in their attitude towards enlargement. Moxon-Browne (1992) suggests that it will be so difficult to cope with the large numbers of poor, new Community citizens who might be admitted from east central Europe, and perhaps Turkey, that the material content of national entitlements, regulated by Community standards of rights, would have to be so slight that they would be vacuous. Similarly, the inclusion of unstable political communities could be used as a public interest justification for postponing indefinitely the entrenchment of primary political rights. Thus it is that, as Roy Jenkins argued in his lecture, referred to at the beginning of this book, we have to choose between 'widening' the Community and 'deepening' it, multilateralist governments, obviously, preferring the option to widen.

Nevertheless, it seems to me that the Community can still be regarded as a potential arena for the realization of democratic citizenship. This is because it already offers us the opportunity to act on the fact that we have more identities than our nationality; the framework of the Community makes it possible to recognize people who share such identities, but who are of other nationalities; and it means that we can understand that our interests are best articulated by an appropriate combination of vertical channels through governments and of horizontal routes through common institutions. The cases in this book have shown that we have a range of identities and interests of this sort which have been furthered as a result of Community membership; for example, not only as male and female workers and employers or 'women as women', but also as artists, as unemployed, buyers of houses and cars, carers of dependent relatives, invalids, pensioners, protectors of the environment, sports men and women, members of a variety of professions, and victims of crime – to name but a few. As such, we have acquired some secondary rights of political participation in transnational associations (see chapter 7) and it is precisely the experience of those avenues that encourages people to think that primary, as well as secondary, political rights are needed. As

Walzer and Mouffe both argue, civil society is and must be a challenge to the political authority that delineates the areas in which its associations may be active. If they are right, the participants in European civil society cannot but continue to challenge the way in which the European public space is being shaped by national and common political authorities. An additional factor is the opportunity the Community provides for the reassertion, or assertion in new ways, of local and regional identities. It is to this that I turn in conclusion.

Regional Identities, New Frameworks and New Claims for the Right of Self-determination, within the Community

There are two basic origins to the possibility that there might be new frameworks for the exercise of citizenship, in which states become but one of several territorial components. Both began as economic and, inevitably, both have acquired administrative and political aspects. First, the well-being of the regions of the Community has always been seen as necessary to economic cohesion. From the standpoint of common policy-making (if not always from the national viewpoint), uneven economic and social development is an even greater hindrance than before to equal conditions of competition in the Single European Market (see references in chapter 4 to production relocations and 'social dumping'). The significance of the regions has been acknowledged in the Maastricht Treaty, which proposes new and larger structural funds and a Committee of the Regions to advise the Commission and Council, similar to the Economic and Social Committee – a kind of 'Committee of the Social Partners'. As in all Community policies, the funding of regional projects is often conditional on 'partnerships' in cross-border areas or with other regions elsewhere. During recent discussion of reforms to English local government, newspapers reported fears among local authorities that they would be made too small to be able to participate in projects funded by the Regional Fund or to be otherwise assisted by the Community. But, the second development could be an alternative entreé for local authorities.

This relates to the provision of services, which, as a result of changing ideas about the role of the state, is increasingly carried out in Member States in 'a mixed economy of welfare' (Baine et al., 1992: 41); that is, not directly by local authorities but through contracts with the voluntary organizations and in joint ventures. Community institutions take an interest in this by funding cross-national networks of voluntary service provision and charitable associations, for reasons that are unclear but with motivations (1992: 41–2) that might be similar to those suggested in chapter 4 in respect of organized labour and women. Because of the now blurred distinction between local government and the voluntary sector, this may provide a channel for horizontal ties between local official, as well as civil, service-providers in different countries who, acting together, have access to common institutions.

Although the bureaucracy is cumbersome and success in securing funds is uncertain (complicated in the United Kingdom by the problem that additional amounts gained from elsewhere are taken into account in Treasury funding decisions; the 'additionality' controversy), subnational authorities and voluntary agencies have found informational advantages in belonging to networks. Horizontal contacts are often more rapid and comprehensive sources of information than the vertical channels that run from the localities and regions up through national bureaucracies and, through them and ministers, to Community institutions (Interviews). Many regional public agencies or public/private alliances have established a presence in the vicinity of Community institutions; for example, the German Länder, Strathclyde Regional Council and Northern Ireland all have offices in Brussels. Constitutionally speaking, these have no representative function and are there to facilitate the flow of information. But it seems unlikely that proximity and routine familiarity between their staff and those of the Commission would have no informal influence on policy ideas. That, after all, is the explicit function of the pressure groups and trade associations which also have such offices in Brussels.

The political dimension is apparent in that the Länder and Strathclyde Regional Council are forms of government as well as administrative agencies. This is specially clear in the case of the Länder because of protests by them that their constitutional responsibility for social affairs is usurped when the Federal government negotiates in Community institutions about such issues. As noted in chapter 3, the status of the Länder has been institutionalized in the condition attached to support of Chancellor Kohl and the ratification of the Maastricht Treaty; that is, that, through the Bundesrat, they should be fully involved in future Community developments. The case of Strathclyde may be a symptom of elections which produce different party majorities in England and Scotland.

Though for the time being the interests of regional administrators and nationalist political movements may coincide, the former are using new opportunities in order to be more effective policy-makers within what is basically the existing state system while the latter see the Community as a contributory factor in the reconstruction of that system. Contrary to Aron's supposition (1974), nationalist political parties, with few exceptions, have not been slow to recognize the potential for their territories to free themselves from current constitutional arrangements and to become autonomous, though interdependent, units in the European public space. The Scottish Nationalists have adopted a policy of 'Independence in Europe'. It has been alleged the UK government's efforts to convince the Scottish electorate that admission to the EC as an independent state would be arduous and uncertain stemmed from pressure by the Spanish government, worried that Scottish Nationalist success would fan the flames of a similar strategy in Catalonia. The two Tyrols, one in the EC by virtue of its Italian legal identity, the other not, have said that they would like to be a united member of the EC. In Northern Ireland, the Social and Democratic Labour Party has proposed – controversially – that an EC Commissioner might play a part in the governance of the Province. It has also been suggested that the Community could play a part in at least moderating the complicated pattern of Irish, Northern Irish and British economic conditions, constitutional positions and identity claims; for example, by reviving the Council of Ireland, which involves both governments, and giving it the task of administering for the whole of the island, both parts of which are economically similar, the Community structural funds (O'Leary, 1991). These funds are very unevenly distributed at present by virtue of the constitutional position which includes the North in a Member State that is less eligible than the Republic for assistance.

It has been noted in chapters 3 and 4 that the idea of 'subsidiarity' has varied meanings. In the context of the politics of the Council of Ministers and European Council, it is a means of protecting the sovereign rights of nation-states against powers accruing unnecessarily to common institutions. But, if it means that powers should be exercised at no higher a level than where they can be effective, there is no reason why subsidiarity should not mean more autonomy for organizations, including civil society associations, below the level of the nation-state. Indeed, this is already happening in the Commission's dealings with regions, cities and localities, voluntary bodies, sectoral representatives and pressure groups. And the Parliament has applauded the proposed Committee of the Regions – while regretting that its members do not have to be democratically elected representatives – as a recognition that subsidiarity must defend regional, as well as national, powers.

The long-term outcome of these developments cannot be predicted with any certainty, though it has been proposed recently that candidates for membership could bring the Community to forty-two members in the next twenty years (*Observer*, 10 May 1992). These include territories that have already broken out of their old 'nation'-states into units that are similar in size to regions in existing Member States. It may not be unreasonable to suggest that membership of a common public space of territories with similar aspirations but different constitutional statuses would fuel existing discontents inside current Member States. Widening the Community, then, might not be such a comforting prospect for those who wish to see a minimal reconstitution of the present state system in the Community. But we cannot tell whether the Europe of the future will reflect the visions of Proudhon, Saint Simon or modern nationalists. What seems plausible to say for the time being is that there is a new framework – a complex, multi-dimensional configuration that is both difficult to cope with and provides opportunities. Our political actions are now having to be carried out through a web of common institutions, states, regional and local authorities and voluntary associations on the domestic front and simultaneously, in national and/or transnational alliances, at the common level. Sometimes, alliances will be vertical, bringing together domestic interests that may be antagonistic at other times, such as unions and employers, in collaboration with subnational political authorities. Such an alliance might find its interests best articulated through national governments, and thence, to the common institutions to confront a countervailing interest from another state – for example, in situations of threat to a national industry. Sometimes, issues may provoke alliances made within regions to cooperate with similar or complementary subnational groupings in other regions – for example, to promote urban or rural regeneration. Sometimes, alliances will be entirely horizontal, including sympathetic common institutions – when there is a shared interest among civil associations in promoting a common policy against the wishes of their respective governments. Such alliances have been seen, for example, over common interests among the metalworkers referred to above, and among women in securing the inclusion of the costs of childcare in training and re-training programmes.

While the complexity of this framework is intimidating in the demands it makes in finding our way around the European public space, it can provide many openings for challenging authority, for expressing our various loyalties associated with our various identities, and for exercising our rights and duties in more than one arena. It therefore meets the criteria found by Heater (1990) in the history of the citizenship ideal and embodies the pluralism that would need to be present for modern radical democrats. But it also has features that undermine equal citizenship if people do not use its opportunities – to make authorities accountable and to claim a place for their interests in the public sphere.

Bibliography

Andrews, Geof (ed.) (1991) *Citizenship*. London: Lawrence and Wishart.

Arnull, Anthony (1989) *The General Principles of EEC Law and the Individual*. Leicester: Leicester University Press/Pinter Press.

Aron, Raymond (1974) 'Is multinational citizenship possible?', *Social Research*, 41(4): 638–56.

Ashford, Douglas (ed.) (1978) *Comparing Public Policies*. Beverly Hills, CA: Sage.

Ashton, Frankie and Whitting, Gill (eds) (1987) *Feminist Theories and Practical Policies*. Bristol: School for Advanced Urban Studies.

Bacchi, Carol (1990) *Same Difference. Feminism and Sexual Difference*. Sydney: Allen and Unwin.

Bacchi, Carol (1991) 'Pregnancy, the law and the meaning of equality', in Elizabeth Meehan and Selma Sevenhuijsen (eds), *Equality Politics and Gender*. London: Sage.

Baine, Sean, Benington, John, and Russell, Jill (1992) *Changing Europe. Challenges Facing the Voluntary and Community Sectors in the 1990s*. London: NCVO Publications and Community Development Foundation.

Baldwin-Edwards, Martin (1991) 'Immigration after 1992', *Policy and Politics*, 19(3): 199–211.

Baldwin-Edwards, Martin (1992a) 'Migration policy', in Simon Bulmer, Stephen George and Andrew Scott (eds), *The United Kingdom and EC Membership Evaluated*. London: Pinter.

Baldwin-Edwards, Martin (1992b) 'Vocational training and manpower', in Simon Bulmer, Stephen George and Andrew Scott (eds), *The United Kingdom and EC Membership Evaluated*. London: Pinter.

Barbalet, J.M. (1988) *Citizenship*. Milton Keynes: Open University Press.

Barker, Ernest (1947) *Social Contract*. London: Oxford University Press.

Bendix, Reinhard (1964) *Nation Building and Citizenship*. New York: John Wiley.

Berlin, Isaiah (1958) 'Two concepts of liberty' (Inaugural Lecture), Oxford: Clarendon Press. Reprinted in shorter form in Anthony Quinton (ed.) (1967) *Political Philosophy*. Oxford: Oxford University Press.

Bluestone, Natalie Harris (1987) *Women and the Ideal Society: Plato's Republic and Modern Myths of Gender*. Amherst, MA: University of Amherst Press.

Blumrosen, Alfred W. (1977) 'Toward effective administration of new regulatory statutes, Parts I and II', *Administrative Law Review*, Winter and Spring: 90–120, 209–37.

Bosanquet, Bernard (1925) *The Philosophical Theory of the State*. London: Macmillan.

Brewster, Chris and Teague, Paul (1989) *European Community Social Policy. Its Impact on the UK*. London: Institute of Personnel Management.

Brubaker, William Rogers (1989) 'Immigration and the politics of citizenship', *Transatlantic Perspectives*, 20(August): 7–10.

Bryson, Valerie (1992) *Feminist Political Theory. An Introduction*. Basingstoke: Macmillan.

Buckley, Mary and Anderson, Malcolm (eds) (1988) *Women, Equality and Europe*. Basingstoke: Macmillan.

Bulmer, Martin, Lewis, Jane and Piachaud, David (eds) (1989) *The Goals of Social Policy*. London: Unwin Hyman.

Bulmer, Simon, George, Stephen and Scott, Andrew (eds) (1992) *The United Kingdom and EC Membership Evaluated*. London: Pinter.

Burch, Martin and Wood, Bruce (1989) *Public Policy in Britain*, 2nd edn. Oxford: Basil Blackwell.

Burnham, James (1941) *The Managerial Revolution*. Harmondsworth: Penguin.

Bussemaker, Jet (1991) 'Equality, autonomy and feminist politics', in Elizabeth Meehan and Selma Sevenhuijsen (eds), *Equality Politics and Gender*. London: Sage.

Butler, Fiona (1991) 'Social policy and the European Community: Proposals for worker participation legislation', *Public Policy and Administration*, 6(1): 72–9.

Byre, Angela (1989) *Leading Cases and Materials on the Social Policy of the EEC*. Deventer and Boston: Kluwer Law and Taxation Publishers.

Carroll, Christine A. (1992) 'The European anti-poverty network', in Linda Hantrais, Steen Mangen and Margaret O'Brien (eds), *7. Dualistic Europe: Marginalisation in the EC of the 1990s*. Loughborough University: Cross-National Research Group, Cross-National Research Papers. New Series: The Implications of 1992 for Social Policy.

Cary, Eve and Peratis, Kathleen Willert (1977) *Women and the Law*. Skokie, Ill.: National Textbook Company.

Cassese, A., Clapham, A., Weiler, J. (no date) *1992. Quels sont nos Droits? Un Programme d'Action en Matière de Droits de l'Homme*. Doc Fr\DV\76160. Fr3 DH 15. Florence: European University Institute.

Centre for Research on Women (regularly published) *Reports* [on women and the EC]. Brussels: Centre for Research on Women.

Chirkin, Veniamin (1985) *Constitutional Law and Political Institutions*. Moscow: Progress Publishers.

Coates, Ken and Topham, Tony (1974) *The New Unionism. The Case for Workers' Control*. Harmondsworth: Penguin.

Collins, Doreen (1975) *The European Communities: The Social Policy of the First Phase*, vol. 1. Oxford: Martin Robertson.

Collins, Evelyn and Meehan, Elizabeth (1993) 'Women's rights in employment and related areas', in Gerry Chambers and Christopher McCrudden (eds), *Human Rights in the UK since 1945* (provisional title). Oxford, London: Oxford University Press/Law Society.

Commission of the European Communities (1983a) *Compendium of Community Provisions on Social Security*. Luxembourg: Office for Official Publications of the European Communities.

Commission of the European Communities (1983b) *The Court of Justice of the European Communities*. European Documentation, Periodical 3/83. Luxembourg: Office for Official Publications of the European Communities.

Commission of the European Communities (1983c) 'Employee information and consultation procedures', *Bulletin of the European Communities, Supplement 2/83*. Luxembourg: Office for Official Publications of the European Communities.

Commission of the European Communities (1985) 'A People's Europe' (Adonnino Report), *Bulletin of the European Communities, Supplement 7/85*. Luxembourg: Office for Official Publications of the European Communities.

Commission of the European Communities (1988) 'Europeans: a universal right to vote in local elections', *European File 19/88*. Luxembourg: Office for Official Publications of the European Communities.

Commission of the European Communities (1989a) 'Proposal for a Council Decision proposing the adoption of a Community action programme for the development of continuing vocational training', COM(89) 567 Final. Brussels: Directorate General for Employment, Industrial Relations and Social Affairs.

Commission of the European Communities (1989b) 'The Commission proposes a Community charter of fundamental social rights', *Background Report* ISEC/B25/89, 11.10.89. London: Jean Monnet House.

Commission of the European Communities (1989c) *Communication from the Commission concerning its Action Programme relating to the Implementation of the Community Charter of Basic Social Rights for Workers*. COM(89) 568 Final. 11.10.89. Brussels: Commission of the European Communities.

Commission of the European Communities (1989d) 'IRIS, the Community network of demonstration projects on vocational training for women', *Social Europe*, 2/89: 49–51. Luxembourg: Office for Official Publications of the European Communities.

Commission of the European Communities (1990a) see Jackson (1990).

Commission of the European Communities (1990b) 'The Citizen's Europe Advisory Service', *Background Report* ISEC/B5/90, 25.1.92. London: Jean Monnet House.

Commission of the European Communities (1991a) *Euro-Labour Markets: The Prospects for Integration*. Proceedings of a conference organized by European System of Documentation on Employment. Brussels: Directorate General for Employment, Industrial Relations and Social Affairs.

Commission of the European Communities (1991b) *Premières Contributions de la Commission à la Conférence Intergouvernementale: 'Union Politique'*. Working document SEC9610 500. Brussels: Commission of the European Communities.

Commission of the European Communities (1991c) 'Public opinion in the European Community: Results of Eurobarometer no. 35'. Brussels: Directorate General for Information, Communication, Culture and Survey Research.

Commission of the European Communities (1991d) *Background Report and Briefing Note on the Maastricht Agreement*. ISEC/B33/91, 18.12.91. London: Jean Monnet House.

Commission of the European Communities (1991e) *Treaty on Political Union*. Version consulted, 'Final draft by the Dutch Presidency as modified by the Maastricht Summit'. Brussels: Agence Europe.

Commission of the European Communities (1992) 'Proposal for a Council Regulation on the security measures applicable to classified information produced or transmitted in connection with EEC or Euratom activities'. COM(92) 56 Final. Brussels: Commission of the European Communities.

Commission of the European Communities (regularly published) *Employment Observatory Trends*. Brussels: Directorate General for Employment, Industrial Relations and Social Affairs.

Commission of the European Communities (regularly published) *Social Europe*. Brussels: Directorate General for Employment, Industrial Relations and Social Affairs.

Commission of the European Communities (regularly published) *Women of Europe*. Brussels: Directorate General for Information, Communication, Culture, Women's Information Service.

Coombes, David (1970) *Politics and Bureaucracy in the European Community*. London: Allen and Unwin.

Coombes, David (1986) 'Britain and the European Community', in Jack Hayward and Philip Norton (eds), *The Political Science of British Politics*. Brighton: Wheatsheaf Books.

Council of Ministers of the European Communities, President's Office (1991) *Projet d'Articles de Traité, en vue de la Mise en Place d'une Union Politique*. Luxembourg: Office of the President of the Council of Ministers.

Court of Justice of the European Communities (regularly published) *Synopsis of the Work of the Court of Justice of the European Communities*. Luxembourg: Information Service of the Court of Justice.

Court of Justice of the European Communities (regularly published) *Weekly Proceedings*. Luxembourg: Information Service of the Court of Justice.

Cranston, Maurice (1973) *What are Human Rights?* London: The Bodley Head.

Crosland, C.A.R. (1964 [1956]) *The Future of Socialism*. London: Jonathan Cape.

Crozier, Mourna (1991) *Cultural Traditions in Northern Ireland. All Europeans Now?* Belfast: Institute of Irish Studies.

Cunningham, Sue (1992) 'The development of equal opportunities theory and practice in the European Community', *Policy and Politics* 20(3): 177–90.

Dahlerup, Drude (1988) 'From a small to a large minority; women in Scandinavian politics', *Scandinavian Political Studies*, 11(4): 275–98.

Dahrendorf, Ralf (1988) *The Modern Social Contract. An Essay on the Politics of Liberty*. London: Weidenfeld and Nicolson.

Dearlove, John (1989) 'Bringing the constitution back in: political science and the state', *Political Studies*, XXXVII(4): 521–39.

Dex, Shirley and Shaw, Lois B. (1986) *British and American Women at Work. Do Equal Opportunities Policies Matter?* Basingstoke: Macmillan.

Dicey, Alfred Ven (1959 [1885]) *Introduction to the Study of the Law of the Constitution*. London and Basingstoke: Macmillan.

Dietz, Mary (1992) 'Context is all: feminism and theories of citizenship', in Chantal Mouffe (ed.), *Dimensions of Radical Democracy. Pluralism, Citizenship, Community*. London: Verso.

Djilas, Milovan (1957) *The New Class, an Analysis of the Communist System*. New York: Praeger.

Dutheil de la Rochère, Jacqueline and Vandamme, Jacques (1988) *Intervention Publique et Droit Communitaire*. Paris: Edition Pedone.

Dye, Thomas R. (1975) *Understanding Public Policy*, 2nd edn. London: Prentice-Hall.

Dyson, Kenneth (1980) *The State Tradition in Western Europe*. Oxford: Martin Robertson.

Edelman, Murray (1964) *The Symbolic Uses of Politics*. Urbana, Ill.: University of Illinois Press.

Edwards, Julia and McKie, Linda (1992) 'The European Community: a vehicle for promoting equal opportunities in Britain?', Paper presented to the annual conference of the British Sociological Association, Kent.

European Industrial Relations Review (1990) *Commentary on the Social Charter*, No. 192, January.

European Network of Women (regularly published) *Newsletter*. London and Brussels: European Network of Women.

European Parliament (1992) *Documents on Political Union*. Dublin: European Parliament Office.

European Parliament (regularly published) *EP News*. Brussels: EP Directorate General for Information and Public Relations.

European Parliament (various dates) Reports:

From the Committee on Institutional Affairs on Union Citizenship, A3-0139/91, 23.5.91.

From the Committee on Women's Rights on activities of the committee, DOC-EN\ACT\105380, 27.2.91.

From the EP Directorate General for Research; Report on 1993 and the employment of women, Citizens' Europe Series No. 1, March 1990.

Report on resolutions proposed by the Committee on Women's Rights and adopted by the Parliament, PE 148.139, 1.3.91.

European Parliament (various dates) Resolutions:

22.11.89 on the Community Charter of Fundamental Social Rights, and related matters. *Official Journal of the European Communities*. C323, 27.12.89, 44–57.

13.6.90 on rights of residence, and related matters. *Official Journal of the European Communities*. C175, 16.7.90, 89–101.

11.7.90 on a draft constitution for the European Union and the Intergovernmental Conference in the context of the Parliament's strategy for European Union. *Official Journal of the European Communities*. C231, 17.9.90, 91–105.

21.11.90 on the principle of subsidiarity. *Official Journal of the European Communities*. C324, 24.11.90, 167–8.

12.12.90 on the constitutional basis of European Union. *Official Journal of the European Communities*. C19, 28.1.91, 65–74; and on the enhancement of democratic legitimacy in the context of the Intergovernmental Conference on Political Union. B3-0551/91: 18–20.

14.6.91 on Union Citizenship, *Official Journal of the European Communities*. A3-0139/91.

European Unification Research Committee of the International Political Science Association (regularly published) *Newsletter*. Loughborough: Centre for European Studies, Loughborough University.

Evans, A.C. and Jessurin d'Oliveira, H.U. (1989) *Nationality and Citizenship*. Florence: European University Institute.

Finch, Janet (1990) 'Women, equal opportunities and welfare in the European Community: some questions and issues', in Margaret O'Brien, Linda Hantrais and Steen Mangen (eds), *3. Women, Equal Opportunities and Welfare*. Aston University: Cross-National Research Group, Cross-National Research Papers. New Series: The Implications of 1992 for Social Policy.

Forbes, Ian (1991), 'Equal opportunity: radical, liberal and conservative critiques', in Elizabeth Meehan and Selma Sevenhuijsen (eds), *Equality Politics and Gender*. London: Sage.

Foster, Deborah (1991) 'Privatisation policy in local government: the response of public sector trade unions'. PhD thesis, Bath University.

Freeman, Jo (1975) *The Politics of Women's Liberation*. New York: David McKay and Co.

Friedman, Kathi V. (1981) *Legitimation of Social Rights and the Western Welfare State*. Chapel Hill: University of North Carolina Press.

Gamble, Andrew (1974) *The Conservative Nation*. London: Routledge and Kegan Paul.

George, Peter (1977) 'Citizenship and welfare'. Paper presented to annual conference of sociologists in polytechnics.

George, Peter (1981) 'The ideology of the British Welfare State'. Paper presented to the annual conference of the Social Administration Association, Leeds.

George, Stephen (1985) *Politics and Policy in the European Community*. Oxford: Clarendon Press.

George, Stephen (1991) *Politics and Policy in the European Community*, 2nd edn. Oxford: Clarendon Press.

Gough, Ian and Baldwin-Edwards, Martin (1990) 'The impact of EC membership on social security and health in the UK', in Steen Mangen, Linda Hantrais and Margaret O'Brien (eds), *1. The Implications of 1992 for Social Insurance*. Aston University: Cross-National Research Group, Cross-National Research Papers. New Series: The Implications of 1992 for Social Policy.

Gough, Ian and Baldwin-Edwards, Martin (1991) 'European Community social policy and the UK', in N.P. Manning (ed.), *Social Policy Review 1990/91*. London: Longman.

Gough, J.W. (1956 [1936]) *The Social Contract. A Critical Study of its Development*. Oxford: Clarendon Press.

Gorz, Andre (1967) *A Strategy for Labour*. Boston: Beacon Press.

Grahl, John and Teague, Paul (1990) *1992 The Big Market. The Future of the European Community*. London: Lawrence and Wishart.

van Gunsteren, H. (1978) 'Notes on a theory of citizenship', in P. Birnbaum, J. Lively and G. Parry (eds), *Democracy, Consensus and Social Contract*. London and Beverly Hills, CA: Sage/ECPR.

Habermas, Jürgen (1976) *Legitimation Crisis*. London: Heinemann.

Hakim, Catherine (1989), 'Workforce restructuring, social insurance coverage and the black economy', *Journal of Social Policy*, 18(4): 471–503.

Hakim, Catherine (1990) 'On the margins of Europe? The social policy implications of women's marginal work', in Margaret O'Brien, Linda Hantrais and Steen Mangen (eds), *3. Women, Equal Opportunities and Welfare*. Aston University: Cross-National Research Group, Cross-National Research Papers. New Series: The Implications of 1992 for Social Policy.

Hall, J. and Ikenberry, G. (1989) *The State*. Milton Keynes: Open University Press.

Halsaa, Beatrice (1988) 'A feminist utopia', *Scandinavian Political Studies*, 11(4): 323–36.

Hantrais, Linda (ed.) (1990) *Franco-British Comparisons of Family and Employment Careers*. Aston University: Cross-National Research Papers, Special Issue.

Harden, Ian (1991a) 'The Community budget, national budgets and EMU: a constitutional perspective' in John Driffill and Massimo Babor (eds), *A Currency for Europe*. London: Lothian Foundation Press.

Harden, Ian (1991b) 'The constitution and its discontents', *British Journal of Political Science* 21(4): 489–510.

Harden, Ian and Lewis, Norman (1986) *The Noble Lie. The British Constitution and the Rule of Law*. London: Hutchinson.

Harris, Jose (1989) 'The Webbs, The Charity Organisation Society and the Ratan Tata Foundation: social policy from the perspective of 1912', in Martin Bulmer, Jane Lewis and David Piachaud (eds), *The Goals of Social Policy*. London: Unwin Hyman.

Hart, Vivien (1993) 'The right to a fair wage: American experience and the European Community Charter of the fundamental social rights of workers', in Vivien Hart and Shannon Stimpson (eds), *Writing a National Identity: Political,*

Economic and Cultural Perspectives on the Written Constitution. Manchester: Manchester University Press.

Hartwig, Richard (1978) 'Rationality and the problems of administrative theory', *Public Administration*, 56: 159–79.

von Hayek, Friedrich (1960) *The Constitution of Liberty*. London: Routledge and Kegan Paul.

Hayward, Jack and Narkiewicz, Olga A. (eds) (1978) *Planning in Europe*. London: Croom Helm.

Hayward, Jack and Norton, Philip (eds) (1986) *The Political Science of British Politics*. Brighton: Wheatsheaf Books.

Heater, Derek (1990) *Citizenship. The Civic Ideal in World History, Politics and Education*. London, New York: Longman.

Heclo, Hugh (1977) *A Government of Strangers*. Washington, DC: The Brookings Institution.

Heclo, Hugh (1978) 'Issue networks and the executive establishment', in Anthony King (ed.), *The New American System*. Washington, DC: American Enterprise Institute.

Holloway, John (1981) *Social Policy Harmonisation in the European Community*. Farnborough: Gower.

Holsti, K.J. (1974) *International Politics: A Framework for Analysis*, 2nd edn. London: Prentice-Hall.

Hoskyns, Catherine (1985) 'Women's equality and the European Community', *Feminist Review*, 20: 71–88.

Hoskyns, Catherine (1986) 'Women, European law and transnational politics', *International Journal of the Sociology of the Law*, 14: 299–315.

Hoskyns, Catherine (1988) ' "Give Us Equal Pay and We'll Open Our Own Doors" – a study of the impact in the Federal Republic of Germany and the Republic of Ireland of the European Community's policy on women's rights', in Mary Buckley and Malcolm Anderson (eds), *Women, Equality and of the Law*. Basingstoke: Macmillan.

Hoskyns, Catherine and Luckhaus, Linda (1989) 'The European Community Directive on equal treatment in social security', *Policy and Politics*, 17(4): 321–36.

Incomes Data Services (1990) *Briefs 414* and *415*, February. London: Incomes Data Services.

Jackson, Pauline Conroy (1990) *1992. The Impact of the Completion of the Internal Market on Women in the European Community*. Working Paper prepared for the Equal Opportunities Unit of Directorate General V of the European Commission, V/506/90-EN. Brussels.

Jamieson, Anne (1990) 'Care of older people in the European Community', in Linda Hantrais, Steen Mangen and Margaret O'Brien (eds), *2. Caring and the Welfare State in the 1990s*. Aston University: Cross-National Research Group, Cross-National Research Papers. New Series: The Implications of 1992 for Social Policy.

Jessop, Bob (1992) 'The Schumpeterian Workfare State: or: "On Japanism and Post-Fordism" '. Paper presented to Eighth Conference of Europeanists, Chicago.

Jobert, Bruno (1978) 'Aspects of social planning in France', in Jack Hayward and Olga A. Narkiewicz (eds), *Planning in Europe*. London: Croom Helm.

Johnson, Nevil (1977) *In Search of the Constitution*. Oxford: Pergamon Press.

Jónasdóttir, Anna (1985) 'On the concept of interest, women's interests, and the limitations of interest theory', in Kathleen Jones and Anna Jónasdóttir (eds), *The Political Interests of Gender*. London: Sage.

Jónasdóttir, Anna (1988) 'Does sex matter to democracy?', *Scandinavian Political Studies*, 11(4): 299–321.

Jordan, Bill (1989) *The Common Good. Citizenship, Morality and Self-Interest*. Oxford: Basil Blackwell.

Keane, John (1989) *Democracy and Civil Society*, London: Verso.

Keatinge, Patrick (ed.) (1991) *Ireland and EC Membership Evaluated*. London: Pinter.

Kelsen, Hans (1989 [1929]) *La Démocratie, Sa Nature, Sa Valeur*, 2nd edn. Paris: Economica.

Kenney, Sally (1992) *For Whose Protection? Reproductive Hazards and Exclusionary Policies in the United States and Britain*. Ann Arbor, Mich.: University of Michigan Press.

King, Desmond S. (1987a) 'The state and the social structures of welfare in advanced industrial democracies', *Theory and Society*, 16: 841–68.

King, Desmond S. (1987b) *The New Right, Politics, Markets and Citizenship*. Basingstoke: Macmillan.

King, Desmond S. (1991) 'Citizenship as obligation in the United States: Title II of the Family Support Act of 1988', in Ursula Vogel and Michael Moran (eds), *The Frontiers of Citizenship*. Basingstoke: Macmillan.

King, Desmond S. and Waldron, Jeremy (1988) 'Citizenship, social citizenship and the defence of welfare provision', *British Journal of Political Science*, 18: 415–43.

King, Desmond and Ward, Hugh (1991) 'Working for benefits: rational choice and the rise of work–welfare programmes', *Political Studies*, XL(3): 479–95.

Kirchner, Emil and Schwaiger, Konrad (1981) *The Role of Interest Groups in the European Community*. London: Gower.

Körner, Stephan (1991) 'On the relation between commonsense, science and metaphysics', in A. Phillips Griffiths (ed.), *A.J. Ayer: Memorial Essays*. Cambridge: Cambridge University Press.

Kymlicka, Will (1991) *Contemporary Political Philosophy. An Introduction*. Oxford: Clarendon.

Land, Hilary (1987) 'Social policies and women in the labour market', in Frankie Ashton and Gill Whitting (eds), *Feminist Theories and Practical Policies*. Bristol: School for Advanced Urban Studies.

Land, Hilary (1990) 'Eleanor Rathbone and the economy of the family', in Harold L. Smith (ed.), *British Feminism in the Twentieth Century*. Aldershot: Edward Elgar.

Landau, Eve (1985) *The Rights of Working Women in the European Community*. Luxembourg: Office for Official Publications of the European Communities.

Langbein, Laura and Kerwin, Cornelius M. (1985) 'Implementation, negotiation and compliance in environmental and safety regulation', *Journal of Politics*, 47(3): 854–60.

Lasok, D. and Stone, P.A. (1987) *Conflict of Laws in the European Community*. Abingdon: Professional Books Ltd.

Le Grand, Julian (1991) *Equity and Choice, An Essay in Economics and Applied Philosophy*. London: Harper Collins.

Leca, Jean (1990) 'Nazionalità e cittadinanza nell'Europa delle immigrazioni', in WAA (Italian for various editors/authors), *Italia, Europa e Nuove Immigrazioni*. Turin: Edizione della Fondazione Giovanni Agnelli. (Translated for Leca, 1991).

Leca, Jean (1991) 'Immigration, nationality and citizenship in Western Europe'. Paper presented to conference on Social Justice, Democratic Citizenship and Public Policy in the New Europe, ECPR/Erasmus University, Rotterdam.

Leca, Jean (1992) 'Questions of citizenship', in Chantal Mouffe (ed.), *Dimensions of Radical Democracy. Pluralism, Citizenship, Community*. London: Verso.

Leruez, Jacques (1978) 'Macro-economic planning in mixed economies: the French and British experience', in Jack Hayward and Olga A. Narkiewicz (eds), *Planning in Europe*. London: Croom Helm.

Lessnoff, Michael (1986) *Social Contract*. Basingstoke and London: Macmillan.

Lester, Antony (1984) 'Fundamental Rights: The United Kingdom Isolated?', *Public Law*, Spring: 46–72.

Lester, Antony (1987) 'Article 177. EEC. Experiences and problems', in Henry Schermers, C.W.A. Timmermans, Alfred E. Kellermann and J.S. Watson (eds), *Proceedings of T.M.C. Asser Institute Conference, 1985*. Amsterdam: North Holland Press.

Lewis, Jane (ed.) (1993) *Women and Social Policies in Europe: Work, Family and the State*. Cheltenham: Edward Elgar.

Lloyd, Genevieve (1984) *The Man of Reason. 'Male' and 'Female' in Western Philosophy*. London: Methuen.

Lock, Geoffrey (1989) 'The 1689 Bill of Rights', *Political Studies*, XXXVII(4): 540–61.

Lodge, Juliet (1989) 'Social Europe: fostering a People's Europe', in Juliet Lodge (ed.), *The European Community and the Challenge of the Future*. London: Pinter.

Lodge, Juliet (1990) 'EC institutions', *Contemporary Record*, 3(3): 1–10.

Loescher, Gill (1989) 'The European Community and refugees', *International Affairs*, 65(4): 619–36.

Lovenduski, Joni and Outshoorn, Joyce (1986) (eds), *The New Politics of Abortion*. London: Sage.

Luckhaus, Linda (1990), 'The Social Security Directive: its impact on part-time work', in Margaret O'Brien, Linda Hantrais and Steen Mangen (eds), *3. Women, Equal Opportunities and Welfare*. Aston University: Cross-National Research Group, Cross-National Research Papers. New Series: The Implications of 1992 for Social Policy.

McCrudden, Christopher (ed.) (1991) *Anti-Discrimination Law*. Dartmouth: International Library of Essays in Law and Legal Theory.

Mackie, J.D. (1978) *A History of Scotland*, 2nd edn. Harmondsworth: Penguin.

Macpherson, C.B. (1962) *The Political Theory of Possessive Individualism*. Oxford: Oxford University Press.

Mangen, Steen (1990), 'The implications of 1992 for social policy: social insurance', in Steen Mangen, Linda Hantrais and Margaret O'Brien (eds), *1. The Implications of 1992 for Social Insurance*. Aston University: Cross-National Research Group, Cross-National Research Papers. New Series: The Implications of 1992 for Social Policy.

Marshall, T.H. (1973 [1964]) *Class, Citizenship and Social Development*. Westport, Conn.: Greenwood Press.

Mayne, Richard and Pinder, John (1990) *Federal Union: The Pioneers. A History of Federal Union*. Basingstoke: Macmillan.

Mazey, Sonia P. (1988) 'European Community action on behalf of women: the limits of legislation', *Journal of Common Market Studies*, XXVII(1): 63–83.

Mazey, Sonia P. and Richardson, Jeremy J. (1992) 'British pressure groups in the European Community: the challenge of Brussels', *Parliamentary Affairs*, 45(1): 92–107.

Mazur, Amy (1991) 'Agendas and Egalité Professionelle: symbolic policy at work in France', in Elizabeth Meehan and Selma Sevenhuijsen (eds), *Equality Politics and Gender*. London: Sage.

Meehan, Elizabeth (1985) *Women's Rights at Work. Campaigns and Policy in Britain and the United States*. Basingstoke: Macmillan.

Meehan, Elizabeth and Sevenhuijsen, Selma (eds) (1991) *Equality Politics and Gender*. London: Sage.

Michon, François (1990) 'The "European Social Community", a common model and its national variations? Segmentation effects, societal effects', *Labour and Society*, 15(2): 215–36.

Millar, Jane (1989) 'Social security, equality and women in the UK', *Policy and Politics*, 17(4): 295–300.

Millar, Jane (1990) 'The socio-economic situation of single women in Europe', in Margaret O'Brien, Linda Hantrais and Steen Mangen (eds), *3. Women, Equal Opportunities and Welfare*. Aston University: Cross-National Research Group, Cross-National Research Papers. New Series: The Implications of 1992 for Social Policy.

Mitchell, Juliet (1987) 'Women and equality', in Anne Phillips (ed.), *Feminism and Equality*. Oxford: Basil Blackwell.

Morrissey, Hazel (1991) 'Women and the impact of 1992', in Paul Hainsworth (ed.), *Towards 1992. Europe at the Crossroads*. Jordanstown: University of Ulster Press.

Moss, Peter (1990) 'Childcare and equality of opportunity', in Linda Hantrais, Steen Mangen and Margaret O'Brien (eds), *2. Caring and the Welfare State in the 1990s*. Aston University: Cross-National Research Group, Cross-National Research Papers. New Series: The Implications of 1992 for Social Policy.

Mouffe, Chantal (1992) 'Democratic citizenship and the political community', in Chantal Mouffe (ed.), *Dimensions of Radical Democracy. Pluralism, Citizenship, Community*. London: Verso.

Moxon-Browne, Edward (1992) 'The concept of European Community citizenship and the development of political union'. Paper presented at ECPR Joint Sessions, Limerick.

Nielsen, Ruth and Szyszczak, Erika (1991) *The Social Dimension of the European Community*. Copenhagen: Handelshojskolens Forlag.

Norris, Pippa (1987) *Politics and Sexual Equality. The Comparative Position of Women in Western Democracies*. Boulder, CO: Reinner.

Nozick, Robert (1974) *Anarchy, State and Utopia*. Oxford: Basil Blackwell.

Nugent, Neill (1989) *The Government and Politics of the European Community*. Basingstoke: Macmillan.

Nugent, Neill (1991) *The Government and Politics of the European Community*, 2nd edn. Basingstoke: Macmillan.

O'Leary, Cornelius (1991) 'Anglo-Irish relations, the Northern Ireland problem and the possible mediatory role of the European Community', in Preston King and Andrew Bosco (eds), *A Constitution for Europe. A Comparative Study of Federal Constitutions and Plans for the United States of Europe*. London: Lothian Foundation Press.

Page, Edward C. (1990) 'The political origins of self-government and bureaucracy: Otto Hinze's conceptual map of Europe', *Political Studies*, XXXVIII(1): 39–55.

Parker, Julia (1975) *Social Policy and Citizenship*. London: Macmillan.

Parry, Geraint (1978) 'Citizenship and knowledge', in P. Birnbaum, J. Lively and G. Parry (eds), *Democracy, Consensus and Social Contract*. London and Beverly Hills, CA: Sage/ECPR.

Parry, Geraint (1991) 'Conclusion: paths to citizenship', in Ursula Vogel and Michael Moran (eds), *The Frontiers of Citizenship*. Basingstoke: Macmillan.

Parry, Geraint, Moyser, George and Day, Neil (1992) *Political Participation and Democracy in Britain*. Cambridge: Cambridge University Press.

Parvikko, Tuija (1991) 'Conceptions of gender equality: similarity and difference', in Elizabeth Meehan and Selma Sevenhuijsen (eds), *Equality Politics and Gender*. London: Sage.

Pateman, Carole (1970) *Participation and Democratic Theory*. Cambridge: Cambridge University Press.

Pateman, Carole (1985) *The Problem of Political Obligation. A Critical Analysis of Liberal Theory*, 2nd edn. Cambridge: Polity Press.

Pateman, Carole (1988a) 'The patriarchal welfare state', in A. Gutmann (ed.), *Democracy and the Welfare State*. Princeton, NJ: Princeton University Press (reprinted in Pateman, 1989).

Pateman, Carole (1988b) *The Sexual Contract*. Oxford: Basil Blackwell/Polity Press.

Pateman, Carole (1989) *The Disorder of Women*. Oxford: Basil Blackwell/Polity Press.

Pateman, Carole (1990) ' "Does sex matter to democracy?" – Comment', *Scandinavian Political Studies*, 13(1): 57–63.

Phillips, Anne (ed.) (1987) *Feminism and Equality*. Oxford: Basil Blackwell.

Phillips, Anne (1991a) 'Citizenship and feminist politics', in Geof Andrews (ed.), *Citizenship*. London: Lawrence and Wishart.

Phillips, Anne (1991b) *Engendering Democracy*. Oxford and Cambridge: Polity Press.

Plant, Raymond (1988) 'Ideology', in Henry Drucker, Patrick Dunleavy, Andrew Gamble and Gillian Peele (eds), *Developments in British Politics 2*, rev. edn. Basingstoke: Macmillan.

Plant, Raymond (1991) 'Social rights and the reconstruction of welfare', in Geof Andrews (ed.), *Citizenship*. London: Lawrence and Wishart.

Polanyi, Karl (1944) *The Great Transformation*. New York: Reinhart.

Prechal, Sacha and Burrows, Noreen (1990) *Gender Discrimination Law of the European Community*. Aldershot: Dartmouth.

Prondzynski, Isabelle (1989) 'The social situation and employment of migrant women in the European Community', *Policy and Politics*, 17(4): 347–54.

Rasmussen, Jürgen (1987) 'The Court of Justice of the European Communities', in Henry Schermers, C.W.A. Timmermans, Alfred E. Kellermann and J.S. Watson (eds), *Proceedings of T.M.C. Asser Institute Conference, 1985*. Amsterdam: North Holland Press.

Rawls, John (1971) *A Theory of Justice*. London: Oxford University Press.

Rhodes, Martin (1991a) 'The social dimension of the Single European Market: national versus transnational regulation', *European Journal of Political Research*, 19: 245–80.

Rhodes, Martin (1991b) 'The politics of the social dimension: national versus transnational regulation in the Single European Market', *Working Papers 1/91*. Manchester University: European Policy Research Unit, Department of Government.

Rimlinger, Gaston (1971) *Welfare Policy and Industrialization in Europe, America and Russia*. New York: Wiley.

Roberts, Geoffrey and Lovecy, Jill (1984) *West European Politics Today*. Manchester: Manchester University Press.

Rutherford, Françoise (1989) 'The proposal for a European Directive on parental leave: some reasons why it failed', *Policy and Politics*, 17(4): 301–10.

Sachs, Albie and Hoff Wilson, Joan (1978) *Sexism and the Law. A Study of Male Beliefs and Judicial Bias*. Oxford: Martin Robertson.

Sainsbury, Diana (1988) 'The Scandinavian model and women's interests: the issues of universalism and corporatism', *Scandinavian Political Studies*, 11(4): 337–46.

Scarman, Leslie (1979) 'Public administration and the courts', *Public Administration*, 57(Spring): 1–5.

Schulz, Fritz (1936 [1934]) *Principles of Roman Law*, trans. M. Wolff. Oxford: Clarendon Press.

Schulz, Fritz (1951) *Classical Roman Law*. Oxford: Clarendon Press.

Schumpeter, Joseph (1952 [1943]) *Capitalism, Socialism and Democracy*. London: Unwin.

Scottish Constitutional Convention (1990) *Towards Scotland's Parliament. A Report to the Scottish People*. Edinburgh: Scottish Constitutional Convention.

Sen, Amartya (1977) 'On weights and measures; informational constraints in social welfare analyses', *Econometrica*, 45(7): 1539–72.

Sen, Amartya (1990) Interview with Peter Aspden. *The Times Higher Education Supplement*, 1 June 1990.

Sevenhuijsen, Selma (1991) 'Justice, moral reasoning and the politics of child custody', in Elizabeth Meehan and Selma Sevenhuijsen (eds), *Equality Politics and Gender*. London: Sage.

Showstack Sassoon, Anne (1991) 'Equality and difference: the emergence of a new concept of citizenship', in David McLellan and Sean Sayers (eds), *Socialism and Democracy*. Basingstoke: Macmillan.

Siim, Birte (1991) 'Welfare state, gender politics and equality policies: women's citizenship in the Scandinavian welfare states', in Elizabeth Meehan and Selma Sevenhuijsen (eds), *Equality Politics and Gender*. London: Sage.

Sjerps, Ina (1988), 'Indirect discrimination in social security in the Netherlands: demands of the Dutch Women's Movement', in Mary Buckley and Malcolm Anderson (eds), *Women, Equality and of the Law*. Basingstoke: Macmillan.

Skocpol, Theda (1988) 'Comparing national systems of social provision; a policy-centred approach'. Paper presented to the International Political Science Association, Washington, DC.

Smith, Harold L. (ed.) (1990) *British Feminism in the Twentieth Century*. Aldershot: Edward Elgar.

Smith, Trevor (1986) 'The British Constitution; unwritten and unravelled', in Jack Hayward and Philip Norton (eds), *The Political Science of British Politics*. Brighton: Wheatsheaf Books.

Smith, Trevor (1991) 'Citizenship and the constitution', *Parliamentary Affairs*, 44(4): 429–41.

Spencer, Michael (1990) *1992 and All That. Civil Liberties in the Balance*. London: Civil Liberties Trust.

Spicker, Paul (1991) 'The principle of subsidiarity and the social policy of the European Community', *Journal of European Social Policy*, 1(1): 3–14.

Springer, Beverley and Riddle, Dorothy (1988) 'Women in services industries:

European Communities–United States comparisons', in Rita Mae Kelly and Jane Bayes (eds), *Comparable Worth, Pay Equity, Public Policy*. New York: Greenwood.

Steiner, Josephine (1985) 'The right to welfare: equality and equity under Community law', *European Law Review*, 10: 21–41.

Steiner, Josephine (1988) *Textbook on EEC Law*. London: Blackstone Press.

Steiner, Josephine (1990) *Textbook on EEC Law*, 2nd edn. London: Blackstone Press.

Steinmo, Sven, Thelen, Kathleen and Longstreth, Frank (eds) (1992) *Structuring Politics: Historical Institutionalism in Comparative Analysis*. Cambridge: Cambridge University Press.

Streeck, Wolfgang and Schmitter, Philippe C. (1991) 'From national corporatism to transnational pluralism: organized interests in the Single European Market', *Politics and Society* 19(2): 133–64.

de Swaan, Abram (1988) *In Care of the State: Health Care, Education and Welfare in Europe and the USA in the Modern Era*. Oxford: Oxford University Press.

Tassin, Etienne (1992) 'Europe; a political community?', in Chantal Mouffe (ed.), *Dimensions of Radical Democracy. Pluralism, Citizenship, Community*. London: Verso.

Taylor, P. (1983) *The Limits of European Integration*. London, Canberra: Croom Helm.

Taylor-Gooby, Peter (1982) 'Two cheers for the welfare state: public opinion and private welfare', *Journal of Public Policy*, 2(4): 319–46.

Taylor-Gooby, Peter (1983a) 'The distributional compulsion and the moral order of the welfare state', in A. Ellis and K. Kumar (eds), *Dilemmas of Liberal Democracies*. London: Tavistock Publications.

Taylor-Gooby, Peter (1983b) 'Moralism, self-interest and attitudes to welfare', *Policy and Politics*, 11(2): 145–60.

Thompson, Joel A. (1981) 'Outputs and outcomes of state workmen's compensation laws', *Journal of Politics*, 43(4): 1129–52.

Trotsky, Leon (1973 [1936]) *The Revolution Betrayed. What is the Soviet Union and Where is it Going?* London: New Park Publications.

Turner, Bryan (1986) *Citizenship and Capitalism. The Debate over Reformism*. London: Allen and Unwin.

Turner, Bryan (1990) 'Outline of a theory of citizenship', *Sociology*, 24(2): 189–217.

Turner, Bryan (1992) 'Prolegomena to a general theory of the social order'. Paper presented at seminars on citizenship organized by the Economic and Social Research Council, 1991. Proceedings edited by Bryan Turner. Swindon: ESRC.

Usher, John (1981) *European Community Law and National Law. The Irreversible Transfer?* London: University Association for Contemporary European Studies/George Allen and Unwin.

Vallance, Elizabeth and Davies, Elizabeth (1986), *Women of Europe. Women MEPs and Equality Policy*. Cambridge: Cambridge University Press.

Vincent, Andrew and Plant, Raymond (1984) *Philosophy, Politics and Citizenship*. Oxford: Basil Blackwell.

Vogel, Ursula (1991) 'Is citizenship gender-specific?', in Ursula Vogel and Michael Moran (eds), *The Frontiers of Citizenship*. Basingstoke: Macmillan.

Walzer, Michael (1983) *Spheres of Justice*. New York: Basic Books.

Walzer, Michael (1992) 'The civil society argument', in Chantal Mouffe (ed.),

Dimensions of Radical Democracy. Pluralism, Citizenship, Community. London: Verso.

Warner, Harriet (now Jones) (1984) 'EC social policy in practice', *Journal of Common Market Studies*, XXIII(2): 141–67.

Watson, D. (1977) 'Welfare rights and human rights', *Journal of Social Policy*, 5(1): 31–46.

Watson, Phillippa (1980) *Social Security of the European Communities*. London: Mansell.

Watson, Phillippa (1981) 'Harmonization of social security and labor law in the European Community', *Comparative Labor Law*, 4(4): 227–55.

Whitting, Gill and Quinn, Jane (1989) 'Women and work: preparing for an independent future', *Politics and Policy*, 17(4): 337–46.

Wight, Martin (1991) edited posthumously by Wight, Gabriele and Porter, Brian, *International Theory. The Three Traditions*. Leicester and London: Leicester University Press/Royal Institute for International Affairs.

Wilkeley, N.J. (1988) 'Migrant workers and unemployment benefit in the European Community', *Journal of Social Welfare Law*, No. 5: 300–15.

Wilson, Thomas M. and Smith, M. Estellie (1992) *Cultural Change and the New Europe: Perspectives on the European Community*. Boulder, CO, and London: Westview Press.

Women's Studies International Forum (1992) Special Issue edited by Claire Duchen, 15(1).

Young, Iris (1989) 'Polity and group difference: a critique of the ideal of universal citizenship', *Ethics* 99(2): 250–74.

Zellick, Graham (1985) 'Government beyond the law', *Public Law*, Summer: 283–308.

Zolberg, Aristide (1991) 'Ethical dilemmas of immigration policy in the New Europe'. Paper presented to conference on Social Justice, Democratic Citizenship and Public Policy in the New Europe. ECPR/Erasmus University, Rotterdam.

Zweigert, Konrad and Kotz, H. (1987) *Introduction to Comparative Law*, vol. 1: *The Framework*. Oxford: Clarendon Press.

Index of European Court of Justice Cases Cited in the Text

Index

Index compiled by Meg Davies